PASSION & PURPOSE

Stories from the
Best and Brightest
Young Business Leaders

PASSION&
PURPOSE

JOHN COLEMAN

DANIEL GULATI

W. OLIVER SEGOVIA

HARVARD BUSINESS REVIEW PRESS

Boston, Massachusetts

Library of Congress Cataloging-in-Publication Data

Coleman, John, 1981-

    Passion & purpose : stories from the best and brightest young business leaders / John Coleman, Daniel Gulati, W. Oliver Segovia.

      p. cm.

  ISBN 978-1-4221-6266-8 (alk. paper)

  1. Leadership.   2. Executives.   3. Success in business.   4. Organizational effectiveness.   I. Gulati, Daniel.   II. Segovia, W. Oliver.   III. Title.   IV. Title: Passion and purpose.

  HD57.7.C644 2012

  658'.049--dc23

2011025148

Contents

Foreword

Many baby boomers like to characterize the Facebook generation as entitled slackers. In reading the amazing stories of the leaders in *Passion and Purpose*, you quickly realize that nothing could be further from the truth. The reality is that this new generation of leaders is committed to making a difference and is ready to lead—not tomorrow, but now.

The authors of this remarkable collection of twenty-six stories, all written by exceptional young leaders, were deeply impacted by the leadership failures of 2008 that led to the Great Recession. The three authors conclude, "We have faith in the young generations of leaders who have witnessed the lessons of the crisis and are now seeking to learn from the mistakes that were made and offer a new vision for the future."

Georgian John Coleman believes that "business offers solutions to some of the most pressing problems we face." Filipino Oliver Segovia quotes the local saying, "He who doesn't appreciate his roots shall never succeed." Australian Daniel Gulati saw firsthand examples of how organizations can meet their financial goals and simultaneously make positive contributions to society.

Unwilling to wait their turn in line, these leaders are already having enormous impact. Look at the global citizens being developed by Abby Falik, the transformation of leadership that Jon Doochin is leading at Harvard College, Marine Captain Rye Barcott's initiative to help the slums of Kenya's Kibera become a safe community that works for everyone, and Katie Laidlaw's efforts to make agriculture in Tanzania profitable for all. Theirs are just a few of the initiatives that vividly illustrate how this generation of leaders really is different from mine.

Anthropologist Margaret Mead once said, "Never doubt the power of a small group of people to change the world. Indeed, it is the only thing that ever has." Through their initiatives, young leaders are confirming Mead's wisdom.

My generation started out just as idealistically as these young leaders. We were kids of the Kennedy era who flocked to Washington, D.C., Selma, and Watts to try to change the world. Somewhere along the way we lost sight of that idealism. Was it the futility of the Vietnam war and the assassinations of the Kennedy brothers and Martin Luther King, Jr., or were we seduced by flawed economic theories into believing that self-interest should take precedence over the common good? Whatever the answers, the leadership failures of the last decade—from the fall of Enron through the economic meltdown of 2008—have vividly demonstrated the flaws in twentieth-century leadership and the need for a new generation of leaders to take charge.

The response of this new generation, as these stories vividly illustrate, is to use their talents now to make a positive impact in helping others. As a professor of management practice at Harvard Business School the past eight years, I have had the privilege of working closely with several of these leaders and many more like them.

After completing my tenure as CEO of Medtronic in 2001 and board chair in 2002, I took a working sabbatical in Switzerland to teach at two leading Swiss institutions. It was there that I decided to devote myself for the next decade to helping develop the next generation of leaders, from MBA students to the new generation of corporate CEOs. In early 2004 I returned to my alma mater, Harvard Business School, to help launch a new course, Leadership and Corporate Accountability, and later created Authentic Leadership Development, a course based on leading from within and built around six-person Leadership Development Groups.

During these years I have spent hundreds of hours in the classroom and many more in private discussions with students in my office.

Through these open, thoughtful, often poignant talks, I have learned just how committed these young leaders are about using their talents to have an impact. They are willing to work countless hours to realize their dreams, yet they also want to lead integrated lives. I have seen them follow their hearts to unite people around common causes, and the impact has often been stunning.

Their approach to leadership differs sharply from that of the baby boomer generation. Command-and-control is out. So is exerting power over others. They eschew bureaucracy, hierarchical organizations, and internal politics. That's why many are opting to start their own organizations rather than joining established institutions.

The focus of their leadership is to build on their roots and align people around a common purpose and shared values. They recognize that they cannot accomplish their goals by using power to control others, as so many in my generation did. Instead, they amplify their limited power by empowering others to take on shared challenges.

Their leadership style is collaborative, not autocratic. Nor are they competitive with their peers. They seek to surround themselves with the most talented people representing a wide range of skills that can be helpful in achieving their aims. They care little who gets the credit, so long as their mutual goals are achieved. Most of all, these young leaders seek to serve, using their gifts and their leadership abilities.

One of the characteristics of this new generation of leaders is their ability to move easily between the for-profit, nonprofit, and government sectors. In fact, that's because many of them have worked in all three sectors. They have firsthand knowledge of how people in each of these sectors think, how they measure success, and how they get things done. A number of the contributors to this book have joint master's degrees in government and business, with a substantial dose of social enterprise courses and projects.

This broad perspective is increasingly important because developing workable solutions to the world's intractable problems—global health, energy and the environment, education, poverty and jobs, and global peace—requires multisector approaches. For example, take the challenges of AIDS in Africa. It isn't sufficient for pharmaceutical makers like Glaxo-SmithKline to give their AIDS drugs away. It takes support from local governments to get the drugs to the people who need them most, NGOs like Doctors Without Borders to administer the drugs to HIV patients, and funds from global organizations like the World Health Organization and the Bill & Melinda Gates Foundation. These emerging leaders, with the diversity of experiences they have accumulated before the age of thirty, understand how to bring people together from these organizations and get them to collaborate to solve major problems.

That's what former Marine Captain Rye Barcott is doing to address the problem of poverty in Kibera, Nairobi's largest slum. While still a student at the University of North Carolina, Barcott formed Carolina for Kibera, investing $26 and combining it with the sweat equity of nurse Tabitha Festo and a local youth named Salim Mohamed. Incredibly, he was able to build this new organization while serving for five years as a counterintelligence officer in Bosnia, Iraq, and the Horn of Africa.

Barcott sees similarities between the tactics he used in building the Kibera community and the Marines' task in community building in war-torn towns like Fallujah, Iraq. He writes, "I feel fortunate to have been able to work across the public, private, and nonprofit sectors at a young age, and I aspire to continue to incorporate such a balance throughout my life. The solutions to our world's toughest problems, such as the growth of megaslums, require full engagement and collaboration from each sector, and we have no time to waste."

These leaders of the future are global in their outlook and comfortable working across diverse cultures. By the time they reach graduate school, they have lived and worked all over the world. In sharp contrast, I never traveled outside North America until my honeymoon at twenty-six, and first moved overseas at age thirty-seven.

Abigail Falik is typical of this new generation. Completing her MBA in 2008, Falik didn't follow her classmates into financial services or consulting. Instead, she took a big risk and founded Global Citizen Year. Its purpose is to enable talented high school graduates to do a gap year of service before entering college by immersing themselves in a developing country.

In a sense, Falik is trying to replicate for others the experience she had as a sixteen-year-old in a rural village in Nicaragua. She believes these formative experiences will enable young people to learn the empathy and gain the insights they need to address twenty-first-century challenges. Falik concludes, "Not until we walk in another's shoes can we truly feel others' hopes and fears, and have the wisdom to know what it would mean to work together toward a common cause."

Katie Laidlaw had a similar experience in Tanzania during a summer internship with TechnoServe, studying how to make fruit and vegetable markets run profitably. She concludes, "This experience confirmed my own hypothesis that future leaders will be better equipped to tackle the problems of tomorrow by being successful in operating across geographies and sectors today."

The Facebook generation may be the first that is genuinely color-blind, gender-blind, and sexual preference–blind. Writes former HBS LGBT president Josh Bronstein, "My call to action for our generation is simple: be authentic. That means bringing your *whole* self to work, not just those characteristics that you think your employer wants to see . . . A defining characteristic of our generation is that we want to be recognized as individuals—not anonymous cogs forced to think, act, and dress in the same way."

These new leaders are changing the way leaders are educated as well. Jonathan Doochin, who struggled with dyslexia throughout his school years, couldn't wait to graduate from Harvard College to transform the school's education of future leaders. During his senior year Doochin founded the Leadership Institute on the premise that developing leaders requires practical experiences that cause individuals to reexamine their perspective of the world, learn to empathize with others, and develop their unique leadership style.

Doochin organizes students into Leadership Development Groups that enable them to understand their authentic selves by sharing their life stories, how they have coped with their failures, and what brings them genuine happiness. Doochin writes, "Each of us has the capacity to lead . . . all of the mysterious qualities that once defined 'leadership' are not inherent, but eminently teachable . . . The model for leadership is not one-size-fits-all, but should be individualized as we play to our own strengths and personalities."

In 1966 Robert F. Kennedy, Jr., said prophetically, "Few will have the greatness to bend history itself, but each of us can work to change a small portion of events. It is from numberless diverse acts of courage and belief that human history is shaped." The acts of these young leaders will write the history of this generation as they focus their talents on making the world a better place for everyone.

If these emerging leaders stay on course through the inevitable pitfalls, setbacks, and disappointments, I have confidence their accomplishments will exceed their greatest expectations. The time is ripe for the baby boomers to provide emerging leaders the opportunities to take charge. Their passion and dedication to their purpose gives all of us hope that our future is very bright indeed.

—Bill George

Bill George is professor of management practice at Harvard Business School and former chair and CEO of Medtronic, Inc. He is the author of four national best-sellers: Authentic Leadership *(2003),* True North *(2007),* Finding Your True North: A Personal Guide *(2008), and* 7 Lessons for Leading in Crisis *(2009). His newest book,* True North Groups *(2011), was released in September 2011.*

Introduction

It's been an interesting time to come of age in business.

Arguably, the past decade has been one of the most intriguing and terrifying in history. Technological innovation has led us from the infancy of the Internet to the nearly ubiquitous online connectedness, social networking, and location-based technology we enjoy today. The world order has shifted dramatically—billions of people in developing economies have joined the ranks of the middle class, and business has become ever more global, with goods and services moving more freely over national boundaries and corporations seeking greater growth in transnational commerce. And, of course, the global economy crashed, falling from a period of unmatched prosperity into one of frightening destruction and uncertainty.

It's an era that cries out for new leadership and new thinking. And it's an era that has left a generation of young leaders wondering how they can contribute even as they seek a life of meaning, passion, and purpose in the private sector. Whether in the world's biggest corporations, local small and medium business, or nimble start-ups, they aren't entering business solely for financial gain, but as a way to find meaningful work and make a positive difference in the world.

Yet few forums have provided these young leaders an outlet to voice their visions for the future, to highlight the trends they've seen emerge from the chaos of the last decade, or to offer both practical advice and hopeful inspiration to their friends and colleagues as they embark on their careers.

We hope this book helps fill that void. Our purpose? To share the stories of young business leaders and thereby give a glimpse into the future of business and leadership—offering both practical learning and inspiration. To do this, we "crowd-sourced" much of the content—asking more than twenty young business leaders to tell their stories, conducting an exclusive MBA Student Survey of more than five hundred current and recent MBAs from top U.S. business schools, and interviewing seven business luminaries who offer a seasoned perspective on the themes analyzed.

We "crowd-sourced" in this way because we wanted to present a broader set of views than the three of us could provide alone; we've been constantly impressed with and encouraged by the vision, entrepreneurship, and passion of our classmates and colleagues, and we wanted to give readers a better sense of that diversity. We also wanted to capture their views on several key themes we saw among the young leaders in our cohort. We organized those themes into six chapters and put out a call for submissions, from which the book's stories were drawn. We derived these six chapter themes from our own experiences in school and in the workplace; from conversations with friends, professors, and colleagues; and from the input we got from more than a hundred initial essay proposals. We read through these proposals in depth, looking for the most interesting, compelling, and inspirational stories, then worked over the course of three years to refine them—evolving our six themes in the process.

For young leaders today we believe these are the core issues—sector convergence, globalization, people leadership and diversity, educational evolution, technology, and sustainability. The chapters built around them illuminate the topics from the point of view of young leaders who are finding passion and purpose in their profession and reimagining the future of business leadership. The stories that follow, however, aren't frameworks, nor do they follow a single narrative with one point of view. Rather, they are powerful, candid accounts of successes and setbacks, personal dilemmas, and reflections on the future. From launching start-ups in Boston to taking on the family business in India; from teaching debate in the Arabian Gulf to helping rebuild war-torn Rwanda; from striving for gender equality in the workplace to helping people bring their "whole selves" to work, these stories reveal that leadership is a deeply personal journey unique to every individual.

The structure of the book is simple.

First, each chapter begins with a short introduction that frames the context of the chapter.

Second, the chapter illustrates and elaborates on these trends through several stories from current and recent MBAs who are trying to make a difference in a fast-changing world.

Third, these stories are supported by outside research and our own MBA Student Survey. Between September and October of 2010, we conducted a survey of more than five hundred current and recent MBA students from Harvard Business School (HBS), Stanford, Darden, Tuck, Wharton, MIT Sloan, and other business schools. We've collected and analyzed those results here.

Finally, each section is capped by an interview with a senior leader—distinguished men and women such as Dominic Barton (global managing director of McKinsey & Company), David Gergen (adviser to four presidents, Director of Harvard's Center for Public Leadership, and senior political analyst for CNN), Rich Lyons (dean of Haas Business School, former chief learning officer of Goldman Sachs), Deborah Henretta (president of P&G Asia), Joe Kennedy (president and CEO of Pandora), and Carter Roberts (CEO of World Wildlife Fund). These leaders possess a rich array of experiences that make them uniquely positioned to comment on the generational changes taking place in business.

HBS professor and former Medtronic CEO Bill George introduces the book with a foreword on his views of the challenges and opportunities that will confront young leaders, and HBS Dean Nitin Nohria ties these themes together with a concluding interview. We then cap the discussion with a detailed appendix of the results of our MBA Student Survey.

The result is a holistic picture—quantitative and qualitative, empirical and anecdotal—about the trends we see shaping the passions of young leaders and the future of business.

Why Passion and Purpose

So who are we, and why is finding passion, purpose, and a new vision for the future important to us?

For John, business has been an experiment. A product of Georgia and Florida, he grew up with an appreciation for the power of private enterprise. His dad, a former rodeo cowboy turned financial advisor, had used business to build opportunities for his family; but for most of high school and college, John thought he'd more likely be a journalist or professor than a marketer or investment banker. Then, after an itinerant year following his college graduation, John found an organization in business that still allowed him to think about hard problems, write a little on the side, and take his ideas from the printed page to organizations where he could put them into action. He met colleagues he genuinely enjoyed and found mentors willing to take chances on him and invest in his future.

And the more businesspeople he met, the more he realized his private sector colleagues were some of the most passionate people he'd encountered— many pursuing their careers not out of necessity but because it was through those careers they'd found purpose, a way to channel their talent and creative energy. He saw businesses creating opportunities for millions of people, and while he's never abandoned his other passions, he truly believes that business offers solutions to some of the most pressing problems we face. *Passion and Purpose* was a way for him to think more deeply about those solutions and meet some of the young people creating them.

Every day of his first year at HBS, meanwhile, Oliver would see the Philippine flag displayed across his section's classroom. In HBS, first-year classrooms are adorned by the flags of each student's country of origin. For Oliver, this was a powerful reminder of the importance of the past, and how the past helps leaders form their self-identity through their personal stories. In Filipino, there's a saying: *"Ang hindi marunong lumingon sa pinanggalingan ay hindi makakarating sa paruruonan"* ("He who doesn't appreciate his roots shall never succeed").

The Philippines has a turbulent past. One of the most prosperous Asian economies after World War II, decades of institutional corruption and political upheaval since the Marcos era in the 1970s have stagnated growth. It's the resiliency of private businesses and overseas remittances that have kept the country afloat. Oliver's story reflects those of millions of Filipinos living around the world. In his twenties, he too worked abroad and also became part of the Filipino diaspora. His interest in business and leadership was sparked by growing up with entrepreneurial parents. Witnessing everyday the immense poverty and inequality that persists in his homeland and in other parts of Asia, he came to believe in the power business can have to make a difference in the world. Oliver believes that the stories of young leaders featured in *Passion and Purpose* can help catalyze similar reflections in young people throughout the developing world.

Daniel came to HBS with a sense of optimism about the role of business in the world. Like Oliver, Daniel spent his childhood outside the United States—in Wollongong, a seaside Australian city. Over the course of his young adult life, Daniel witnessed firsthand the power of business to change lives. Whether observing a start-up, a large investment bank, a management consulting firm, or a mature industrial company, Daniel saw examples of how organizations could simultaneously meet their financial objectives and contribute enormously to modern society.

It is this raw conviction that motivated Daniel to write *Passion and Purpose*. At the time of the financial crisis, journalists accused "businesspeople"—particularly alumni of top business schools who had reached executive-level positions—of arrogance and greed. At a time when the world desperately needed glimmers of hope, this negative stereotyping hid from public view the individual stories of young people using business as a lever to positively impact their communities. The stories of these young business leaders—the best and brightest—had to be told.

In the spring of 2009, Oliver ran an article in the HBS campus newspaper looking for someone to help coauthor a book on our generation's ability to "reimagine leadership" in the midst of crisis. John responded almost right away. Then he and Oliver spent the next few months working with former Random House CEO and HBS senior lecturer Peter Olson to think through a book manuscript that could help voice the aspirations of the friends and colleagues with whom they interacted every day while offering a fresh and compelling view of the future. In the fall of 2009, Dan joined the team, and gradually we came up with an idea—a crowd-sourced book on leadership, targeted toward the younger generation, that could help give voice to new visions of leadership.

Today's Young Leaders: Passionate and Purposeful

Young businesspeople want to find purpose in their profession and have a passion for what they do. As they come of age, they are growing up with the belief that business can provide us with a way of translating a meaningful, personal purpose into work that impacts the world in a positive way. In our own 2010 survey of more than five hundred current or recent MBAs, "intellectual challenge" came up as the most important reason for choosing one's work, significantly more important than compensation or a firm's prestige.

We hear a lot about generations—millennials, Gen-X'ers, boomers—but whatever you call them, today's young leaders have a fresh perspective about what it will take to lead moving forward. They're twenty-somethings in the early years of their careers, but they're in jobs that require tremendous amounts of responsibility, whether it's managing a brand, starting a new venture, or transitioning in the family business. Most have a few years of work experience and are readying themselves for the next step in their careers, such as getting promoted, moving abroad, or joining another company. They are current MBA students and recent graduates embarking on new paths after business school. Regardless of what stage they're in, these young leaders share several characteristics.

According to the Pew Center, they are the most educated generation in history—in the United States, 54 percent of millennials have college degrees, compared to 36 percent of boomers.[1] In our own survey, fully 80 percent agreed or strongly agreed with the statement, "My generation views business leadership differently than previous generations." Moreover, they see the *world* differently compared to previous generations. According to the IBM Future Leaders Survey, 77 percent of current MBAs see rising complexity in the current environment, compared to 60 percent of current

CEOs.[2] And 65 percent of students believe that the scarcity of resources—water, food, land, and talent—will significantly impact businesses in the next few decades, compared to 29 percent of CEOs.

These emerging business leaders represent a shift in thinking. They have exciting visions for the future. They are the first generation raised in a truly global and networked world. They're thinking about careers that integrate the public, private, and nonprofit sectors; and they're learning from the current crisis in ways that we hope will lay the foundation for an ethical and economic recovery and long-term innovation.

As previously mentioned, our chapters are organized around six core themes we see as prominent in the lives of rising young business leaders:

- Convergence: Creating Opportunities Across Sectors. More than anything else, we hear from our colleagues about the convergence of the public, private, and nonprofit sectors. In the nonprofit world, the term *social enterprise* has recently gained prominence to describe organizations with a social purpose but a self-sustaining business model. More students, even early in their careers, are switching between the sectors almost frenetically—cross-applying lessons from government and nonprofit to business and vice versa. In this chapter, contributors reflect on their cross-sector experiences, and CNN analyst and presidential advisor David Gergen talks about generational changes in cross-sector careers.

- Globalization: Embracing the Global Generation. As globalization has leveled the walls between countries, the first decade of the twenty-first century has led to an unprecedented opportunity for collaboration, cooperation, and learning. Young leaders are gaining international experience earlier in their careers, shaping the first truly global generation of young leaders. Here, several young businesspeople talk about learning to lead in a global world, and McKinsey & Company global managing director Dominic Barton talks about his own global career and what it will take to survive in an environment in which national boundaries are lower than ever.

- **People: Leading in a Diverse World.** As labor force participation increases and old racial, class-based, religious, and gender barriers are gradually lowered, the workplace will benefit from the multiplicity of perspectives that these newly integrated groups can bring. Our contributors look at ways that unprecedented diversity is impacting the workplace and how rising business leaders can embrace that diversity as a way to generate greater happiness and more "wholeness" at work. They also look at how leading diverse people requires diverse leadership experience. P&G Asia president Deborah Henretta talks about P&G's efforts to use diversity to create greater people leadership and how the next generation can shape these trends.

- **Sustainability: Integrating Preservation and Profits.** One of the biggest trends in global business has been the push for sustainability. Many businesses are attempting to become more environmentally friendly and, in the process, more cost effective and energy efficient. The young people in these firms are now focused clearly on "green" business and alternative energy—and think of sustainability as a way to build a career. They're also emphasizing a culture of environmental intelligence that emphasizes eliminating the trade-offs that have made sustainability movements so unsustainable in the past. Contributors discuss their own passion for sustainability, and World Wildlife Fund CEO Carter Roberts talks about building a sustainable world through sustainability-focused careers.

- **Technology: Competing by Connecting.** No discussion of the future of business would be complete without thoughtfulness about the way technology—social media, mobile connectivity, and transportation—is revolutionizing business. Today's young leaders are the first to have truly come of age in a connected society, and our contributors—including founders of innovative new technology companies like thredUP and RelayRides—talk about the ways in which technology has influenced their lives and will change the way organizations do business. Pandora president and CEO Joe

Kennedy talks about life, career, and innovation in the fast-changing world of online technology.

- **Learning: Educating Tomorrow's Leaders.** By many conventional measures, the next generation is one of the most educated in history, and young businesspeople are looking increasingly to educational experiences, within or beyond their everyday jobs, to make them better managers and leaders. Yet there's a growing feeling among young business leaders that current learning models are not enough. Amid increasing complexity and uncertainty, how are young people learning to lead? Our contributors discuss learning in business school, through entrepreneurship, and in corporations; Haas Business School Dean and former Goldman Sachs chief learning officer Rich Lyons talks about what business learning has looked like and what it will look like in the years ahead.

Within each of these topics, we seek to explore the subtrends that make them meaningful, and we support these trends in a few distinct ways.

We should note that we don't consider ours the only perspective on these issues. We developed our views based on conversations with professors and colleagues, independent and external research, and reflections on our own experiences. But our writers come from one school (HBS) among many. More than anything, this focus resulted from our own understanding of how difficult it would be to capture the impossible diversity of all young leaders in fewer than thirty stories. And so, we focused on a subsegment of classmates and friends we know well, hoping that this effort becomes part of a wider discussion. We want this to be an invitation to other schools, businesses, and institutions to join the conversation about how passion and purpose shape one's path to leadership. To that end, you can find more material—from blog posts, new stories, videos, and more—at www.hbr.org/passion-purpose, where we'll continue to post stories from young leaders at HBS and around the world.

These are trying times—but with every challenge, there is also opportunity. We—the authors of this book—have faith in the rising generation of leaders who have witnessed the lessons of the crisis and are now seeking to learn from the mistakes that were made and offer a new vision for the future. As a global community, our goal should be to come out of these most recent challenges stronger, more united, and more dedicated than before to gaining purpose from our work and living with a passion for the future.

—John, Daniel, and Oliver

CHAPTER 1

Convergence

Creating Opportunities Across Sectors

I believe that in the years ahead, the organization and expansion of public-goods markets will become one of the most important areas of philanthropy, and will be an area where philanthropy sometimes blurs into strict private enterprise.

—Bill Clinton, 2007[1]

What do a Pakistani dreamer, a Swahili-speaking ex-marine, and an investment banker have in common? In many ways, not much. Their careers have been as messy and, at times, unfocused. But they share a common desire prevalent among many of today's young business-people to work across sectors—managing careers in the for-profit, non-profit, and government arenas—often building both financial well-being and a legacy of social good.

Fortunately for them, the world seems to be moving in the same direction. In the United States, GDP grew 36.6 percent between 1994 and 2004, but, according to the Urban Institute, nonprofit revenues grew an astounding 61.5 percent over the same period; and in 2005, more than 61 million Americans volunteered.[2] While private sector employment collapsed in the most recent economic crisis, public employment in the United States remained relatively stable—with high-profile public sector agencies like the U.S. Treasury attracting top talent from private industry, and public sector salaries surpassing those of employees in the private sector.[3] Simultaneously, the past several decades have seen the privatization of many previously government-operated activities—in transportation, utilities, and warfare—even as sovereign wealth funds, public-private partnerships, and other hybrid organizations have begun to gain prominence on the international stage. The approaching reality is that, in many cases, meaningful distinctions between these sectors and their activities are disappearing even as talented young professionals seek to chart careers that cross traditional boundaries.

This is certainly not a novel concept. Business schools have produced a number of notable participants in the public and nonprofit spheres, including Hank Paulson, Robert McNamara, Mitt Romney, Michael Bloomberg, George W. Bush, Elaine Chao, P. Chidambaram, and Antony Leung, to name a few. But the prevalence with which graduates actively seek cross-sector careers seems to be growing.

HBS's Social Enterprise Initiative, founded in 1993, now has nearly a hundred involved faculty and more than four hundred cases and notes for use in classroom environments; the student-run Social Enterprise Club is one of the school's largest, with more than four hundred members.[4] The mission of the Yale School of Management—"to educate leaders for business and society"—explicitly outlines this cross-sector focus. And many of today's top social entrepreneurs are business school grads, like Stanford's Jessica Jackley, cofounder of Kiva.[5] HBS saw a 106 percent increase in the number of students finding employment in the government and nonprofit sectors between 2008 and 2009.[6] And many business and law schools support this transition with various loan forgiveness and fellowship programs that encourage work in the government and social enterprise sectors.

In our own survey, we found an astonishing amount of interest and experience in cross-sector careers (see figure 1-1). Despite the fact that all of our respondents were students of self-described *business* schools, 30 percent had worked in the public sector prior to school and 30 percent in the nonprofit sector. Thirty-nine percent believe they will have worked in the nonprofit sector within ten years of graduation, with 33 percent predicting work in the public sector.

FIGURE 1-1

Employment experiences and expectations

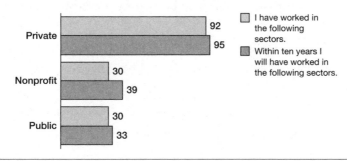

Further, 11 percent of those surveyed had worked in all three sectors, and of those who worked in the private sector prior to school, 24 percent had also worked in the public sector and 30 percent in the nonprofit sector.

When asked about the nature of this overlap, the response was even more astonishing (see figure 1-2). Fully 88 percent of respondents answered "agree" or "strongly agree" when prompted with the statement, "Most business principles can be transferred to the public or nonprofit sectors," with rates not differing appreciably depending on whether the respondent had worked in the public, private, or nonprofit sector. And 84 percent answered

FIGURE 1-2

MBA views on cross-sector interaction

Percent who agree or strongly agree with the following statements

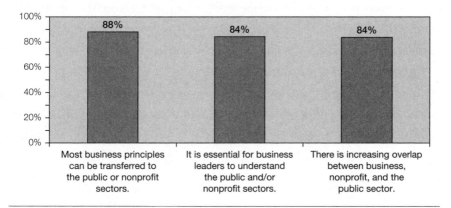

"agree" or "strongly agree" to the statement, "It is essential for business leaders to understand the public and/or nonprofit sectors." Further, 84 percent of respondents saw "increasing overlap between business, nonprofit, and the public sector."

This shouldn't surprise us. Our generation has been raised in an era of global privatization of public utilities and in an America where banks and even automakers have been "bailed out" by the federal government. We've seen arguably the greatest businessperson of recent decades, Bill Gates, become the world's most prominent philanthropist; and we've seen next-generation businesses, like Google, frame their mission statement in social terms: "Don't be evil." Democratic revolutions are now facilitated by social networking sites like Facebook and Twitter. And while not all of this convergence is necessarily good, it's happening. What should you do about it?

Managing the Next-Generation Career for Convergence

For young professionals, this convergence alters the landscape of career opportunities and changes the ways in which we seek training, education, and mentorship.

First, successful young businesspeople will need knowledge of how the nonprofit and public sectors work, and employees in those sectors will need a better understanding of business. Some graduate school programs, like Harvard's, offer joint master's degree programs from their business and public policy schools. Stanford offers a similar joint program with its school of education, and many young professionals are seeking such cross-sector work early in their careers to cement their credibility across sectors.[7] Young professionals can scarcely hope to operate effectively in private sector enterprises like finance, health care, or even agriculture without an extensive knowledge of the public sector, and the increasing relevance of models like microfinance make nonprofits relevant to those businesses as well. For the next generation, cross-sector training and understanding will be essential to effective leadership—particularly because best practices can and should be shared between sectors.

Second, the "boxes" into which professionals once conveniently confined their careers are not as relevant or constraining as they may have been for previous generations. Businesspeople don't have to either relegate their non-profit and public sector work to nights and weekends or to later in their careers. Private sector organizations themselves increasingly incorporate positions that intersect closely with social and public sector work—in government relations, social initiatives, sustainability, and other areas. For instance, TOMS shoes promises that for every pair of shoes bought by a consumer, it will give away one pair to a needy child.[8] The structure of the firm allows it to increase its brand recognition through its social initiatives and free media, while doing good and attracting employees who are looking for purpose-driven careers. Many professionals are also finding value transitioning between public and private organizations early in their careers. For those seeking to chart careers, these options should gain increasing consideration.

Managing the Modern Organization for Convergence

Similarly, managers will have to acknowledge these trends and work to position their organizations for an environment that reflects them and a labor force that desires them.

From the perspective of current executives, those tasked with managing the next generation should seek to use these young professionals' interest and experience in cross-sector initiatives to their advantage. For generations, business has recognized the valuable leadership experience provided by the U.S. military, but understanding more broadly the role that those who have worked in emerging markets, public organizations, FOPSEs (for-profit social enterprises), political campaigns, think tanks, and academic organizations can have in private sector organizations will be essential to managers who wish to navigate a new environment where the sectors are more closely intertwined. Similarly, managers in nonprofit and government should continue awakening to the increasing usefulness of private sector experience, models, and best practices in their organizations. In a 2007 *Atlantic Monthly* article, journalist Jonathan Rauch noted the ways in which Bill Clinton was incorporating private sector practices, employees, and models into his own nonprofits; and organizations like the Gates Foundation and governments like Singapore have followed similar paths. Multinational organizations in particular—which must often interact with hybrid government/private sector industries in a multiplicity of countries, from China to Great Britain—must be keenly sensitive to this transition.

These managers should also seek not only to hire talent that understands the cross-sector perspective, but also to train their workforce to value these experiences and offer opportunities to young professionals to pursue jobs—temporarily or permanently—that suit their passions. The consulting firm McKinsey & Company, for example, offers professionals an opportunity to do private, public, and nonprofit work simultaneously (as law firms have done for many years); and organizations like Bain & Company offer opportunities through partner or sister organizations that allow professionals to work on social problems about which they are passionate while gaining valuable experience they can later transmit back to the firms for which they work. Public organizations and political bodies—in Singapore, Brazil, and even the United States—seem to be placing a higher premium on business experience, with many policy makers moonlighting in the private sector between appointments and administrations. The result is a different way of thinking about value creation in businesses. Senior managers create value not simply by defining an opportunity, crafting a strategy, and allocating economic and human capital. More and more, the real challenge of leadership lies in creating roles, organizations, structures, and belief systems that allow disparate individuals to work together in pursuit of a common vision.

Organizations in every sector would be better served by acclimating to a new environment in which all three sectors are gradually and in certain ways, converging—and organizations can use the talents and passions of a new generation of cross-sector professionals to help them chart their courses. And young leaders should feel empowered to find their passion and purpose in cross-sector careers.

Floating Above the Boxes

Business, Nonprofit, and the Age of Falling Boundaries

Born in Pakistan and raised in Saudi Arabia, **UMAIMAH MENDHRO** was the first woman in her family to leave the country for higher education. She studied human development at Cornell University and completed her MBA from Harvard Business School as a Baker Scholar. Umaimah is currently a senior manager at Microsoft Corporation, where she leads corporate entrepreneurship and incubation efforts. She is also the cofounder of thedreamfly.org, a global initiative that strives to create human connections across communities in conflict around common causes.

Nothing but the bleak darkness of a starless night. Deafening thumps of what felt like a thousand elephants marching into our living room. Shrieks of panic. My first reconstructed memory of life. "What did my father do? Why are all the soldiers after him?" In 1980, when Zia Ul Haq proclaimed a military coup, my parents, young aspiring revolutionaries-cum-physicians, escaped Pakistan with their two toddlers in the middle of the night to buy survival in return for a life in exile in Saudi Arabia. "It must've been something all the big, powerful people despised," my five-year-old self thought. "Interesting . . . we're all somehow alive and doing fine."

My ten-year-old self, covered from head to toe in an ultraconservative Arabic garb, holding tight to my mother's hand, walking and dodging strange men's nasty stares. Sitting cross-legged on princely rugs in the vast, serene, open spaces of Haram-al-Sharif, observing rows of women in black and men in white, now heads on the ground, now standing upright, now hands on the knees, connecting with their creator on command. Makkah looked to me like an exotic and spectacular world of contradictions, a place where I clung to any opportunity to form, rather than find, an independent identity. With manufactured dreams and opinions, which the big people might honor or despise, I began to love the feeling of freely floating in thin air, right above the borders of right and wrong as defined by a people, charting out my own rules of good and evil. We returned to Pakistan after eleven years, when democracy was finally restored.

"Duck, *now!*" my father exclaimed to all of us in the backseat. I peered out the window, terrified. A growing crowd of angry young men, with clubs and arms. The driver hit the gas pedal. None of us said much. We didn't play our favorite tunes. Just waited for the shrill silence to dissolve. Once we left the outskirts of the city, Karachi, we left the home we had built with half a decade of savings, yet the air felt more breathable again. Ethnic violence between the Sindhi-speaking and Urdu-speaking populations had reached a crescendo. Families were stopped, commanded to say words only Sindhis knew how to pronounce, and depending on which side the other side was on, were harassed, mugged, and often enough, shot on the spot. That year, the year I turned thirteen, we ended up making a life for ourselves by my father's village, Akri, in a town named Badin. Some five hours away from the civilization I knew, Badin allowed our parents a life they had been wanting to come back to—one where, through their chosen profession, they could care for the sick and helpless who have no place else to go. We children were home-schooled and determined to prove to the world that we could and would go places. I always liked intellectual exploration, but it was in the solitude of a life with virtually no visitors to host or places to visit, no cliques to try to fit into, and no norms to sport, that I fell in love with education for the sake of exploration and illumination of the mind. With squealing chirps of rodents as my backdrop and a gentle feeling of suffocation on warm summer nights, I'd sit on my bed and imagine my fifty-year-old self giving interviews, reflecting on a lifetime of achievements, a Nobel Peace Prize winner one night, CEO of a conglomerate that brought the country to prosperity another, while carefully name-dropping some of the world's best universities, usually Harvard, that I was supposed to have attended.

I graduated from Cornell with a major in human development; married a wonderful, wise person who speaks Urdu and cannot pronounce those words only Sindhis are supposed to say; took a job in consulting and, in the wake of the dot-com bust, got laid off within nine months; and then fast-tracked my career with a company I fell in love with, Microsoft Corporation. Microsoft allowed me the freedoms to chart my destiny and be rebellious with reason. Outside of my job as a product manager, with strategic business management and P&L responsibilities at age twenty-six, I headed up Microsoft's women's employee group, representing over five thousand members and twelve thousand female employees around the world—and in the process fought for simple rights that questioned age-old company policies that did us no good. I felt I made a difference. That it mattered that I was there.

I traveled to the pits of Sindh and the brinks of Pakistan and Kashmir, working for an education not-for-profit and a microfinance organization. This was not part of my strategic life plan. No form of nonprofit was. During my third week of Harvard Business School, I was forced to take a medical leave of absence and rejoin the program almost ten months later. Unemployed in the United States, between a work and student visa, and eager to make something of the days handed to me, I took the first flight to Pakistan so I could force myself into a corner to do something I would never otherwise have done in my now interesting-on-paper life. I found myself among half-naked children running on the streets, with glimmers of rebellion in their eyes and dreams of doing something they will one day be truly proud of. I visited my cousins in our village, whose eyes and smiles reminded me of my four-year-old self, and that the life I was living now was alien to me as a child. I saw my aunts and uncles, who didn't know what or who Harvard is or even how to spell that word, who had likely never owned an independent thought or harbored any reason to reason.

Crack of dawn. I was driving Mona, a dear friend, to Akri. No one outside my family—none of my friends, nor my husband—had ever visited my family in Akri. She had flown in from the United Kingdom after a brief conversation about whether she would join me in founding an organization that would plug into communities around the world, give them the option and ability to think for themselves, and create better alternative realities. We stood in the heart of my village—in front of children young and old. With glazed eyes in an inaccessible world, the older ones looked through us. We met with the village elders. They complained about lack of education. About the government. About the state of the country and how we're all heading toward disaster. They complained, and my heart sank in my chest. I felt privately and acutely embarrassed.

And then we met the little ones. Girls and boys five, six years old, in their orange *shalwar qameez* and big, wide-open eyes. Some with their hands on their mouths covering their giggling teeth. Others elbowing their neighbors, pointing at us. I stood in front of them all, taking in the distinct energy in the room. Mona threw a question to the room, "So, can anyone tell me what you want to be when you grow up?" A little voice at the back said out loud, "A heart surgeon." Mona and I stared at each other. Other voices joined. "A teacher—for the little children," said a little girl, fixing her head scarf. "A lawyer, like in the movies, to arbitrate justice." We found that for the little children, the realities of Akri and of their destined life in this village had not yet set in enough to convince them how unreasonable their dreams sounded. Images of young Bill Gates flashed before my eyes—with big, round eyes, and too much energy for his slender little body to hold in, saying, "We will have a computer on every desk!" Gates morphed into Sam Walton, who faded in and out with Warren Buffett. "We will make a school for you here," I blurted out to little Atta, "so you become all that you said." "Really?! Here? When?!" he exclaimed back. And we never looked back.

Thedreamfly.org, the organization we founded that day, exists to bring together communities in conflict to coinvest in each other's success for a better common future, one where drive for personal distinction, appreciation of differences, and thoughtful, independent reasoning prevails. It exists to create a human connection that's inviolable by culture, religion, and politics. We chose business and education, not charity or literacy, as the means to achieve this goal.

I was on one knee, looking at young Nazeem through the eye of my SLR camera. We had gone for a stroll in the village and I wanted to capture the moment. "Remind me what you want to be when you grow up?" He smiled at the camera, looking calm and confident; he must've grown several inches since the last time I had seen him with Mona several months ago. "Last time I wanted to be a pilot but I now want to be a scientist." I was moved. You, Nazeem, are why we're doing what we're doing, I thought to myself, and looked to find my voice. "That's fantastic! Do you know what kind of a scientist?" Looking straight in my lens with his beautiful smile that belied his words, Nazeem said, "Ones that know how to make bombs. So I can bomb India." And you *are* why we're doing this.

August 2008. I had returned to HBS, completed my first year and I was now standing on the ground inside the dreamfly school in Akri. I could hear uncontrollable excitement and energy everywhere. Kids were laughing, signing, playing, learning. My throat kept lumping up with overwhelming emotions of excitement, astonishment, and gratitude. I stepped into Class One, Section Blue. The class seemed to be having a discussion about whether kids should ask the teacher for permission before they have to step out of the class. "If anyone can go at any time, there will be no rules," one said. "That's a good point, but why do we need rules?" asked the teacher. The class paused for a moment. And my eyes immediately teared up. They weren't just learning A-B-C's and 1-2-3's. They were . . . thinking. "Maybe to avoid chaos?" said another student, "because sometimes when there are no rules, every man thinks he's the boss." The class fell into a fit of laughter and applauded. I was seeing the HBS case study method in action in Akri in Class One. We weren't imparting knowledge to our children, we were merely inviting them to learn for themselves. As the class settled down for a bit, a hand went up in the air: "Teacher, why did we all clap this time, when we didn't clap when Syed had the right answer earlier to your question?"

We are now looking to take dreamfly to Afghanistan. Adopting a for-profit business model that can help us ensure that our efforts can be self-sustainable and self-propelling, we want to establish an organization that outlives its founders. We are using technology and social networking to sew the seams between communities at war, giving each exposure to the world outside the one they most comfortably fit in—connecting Pakistan with Afghanistan with the United States, humans with humans, really, regardless of where they live or stand.

Graduating from HBS, I didn't explicitly consider going into the not-for-profit sector. Neither was I thinking I was going into the for-profit sector. The incredible freedoms that come with floating across and above boxes—the boxes of business and social good, of cultures we must fit in, of beliefs we must abide by—and the courage and power to look through sacred norms, that's what I care to build into myself and the world around me.

I decided to come back to Microsoft Corporation, to a rebel organization within the company that runs internal groups like external start-ups unhindered by the large-company mentality and practices. We're looking to break a few rules, fall on our faces, pick ourselves up, learn, reason, and march ahead. I take my dreamfly spirit to work and my work ambitions to dreamfly. I take my ability to manage with near-zero resources to my Microsoft start-ups and my business savvy to Afghanistan. And my anxious energy to do more, my fervent desire to make an impact, my unsystematic at-the-edge-on-the-border-of- boxes thinking to everything I do.

More and more, I feel, we must define ourselves by who we are, our deeply personal naked self, and what we want to do, rather than by which professional hole the peg fits best. And we must find our way to our vision through our own crooked path, exposing possibilities we never imagined might exist.

I don't know where the fullness of my life will take me. If I will become that CEO. If I will win any accolades. If I will die when I'm forty. But I know I want to live a life that gives people reason to reason; to pause and question the comfortable assumptions, to form and inform beliefs, and never give up common sense for common opinion.

Learning from Kibera

Nonprofit Lessons for Business from East Africa's Largest Slum

RYE BARCOTT cofounded Carolina for Kibera in 2001. He graduated from Harvard with an MBA and MPA, is a TED Fellow and a World Economic Forum Young Global Leader, and works at Duke Energy. His first book, *It Happened on the Way to War: A Marine's Path to Peace*, was published by Bloomsbury in April 2011. He is passionate about participatory development.

"*Vipi beshte?*" I asked over Skype. Something was wrong. Cantar's voice was tense. "What's up?"

"*Si poa hapa. Hakuna panga iko Uchumi,*" he replied from Kibera in Swahili, referring to Kenya's largest grocery store. "It's not cool here. There are no machetes left at Uchumi."

It was January 2008, and Kenya had just held a disputed presidential election.[9] Kibera was an ethnic fault line, a slum in Nairobi, Kenya, where more than three hundred thousand people resided in an area the size of Central Park. In the next thirty days, more than ten thousand residents would be displaced, and the medical clinic a widowed nurse named Tabitha Atieno Festo had founded with a $26 grant would treat more than a thousand patients wounded by gunfire and *pangas*.

I was in my first year at Harvard Business School. It was Christmas break, and I was preparing to return to Kibera to welcome a delegation from the Bill & Melinda Gates Foundation to Carolina for Kibera (CFK), the organization I founded in 2001 with Tabitha Festo and the community organizer Salim Mohamed to build a better generation of African leaders.

"It might not be good to bring the Gates people," Cantar, our sports program officer, warned.

I did not want to cancel the trip. We had courted the Gates Foundation for two years, and they were interested in how our model of participatory development could be used to prevent violence and empower youth living in abject poverty worldwide. However, Cantar and I had worked together for over eight years. I trusted him. I had learned from him, and he had learned from me. That was the key to participatory development, an approach that is rooted in the conviction that solutions to social problems must be driven by the affected communities, not outsiders.

I cancelled the Gates Foundation visit. The following day Kibera's largest church was looted and set on fire, igniting weeks of vicious bloodletting and ethnic cleansing.

I had decided to attend HBS to better understand business management after having founded and helped lead CFK as a volunteer while serving on active duty in the U.S. Marine Corps. CFK needed better management practices, having grown from a start-up reaching two hundred children in its inter-ethnic sports program to a fully integrated leadership development program involving more than thirty-five thousand residents. I arrived at Harvard thinking nonprofits had more to learn from business than vice versa.

My business education has since suggested to me the learning can go both ways.

I think there are three broad areas where business best practices can greatly assist nonprofit organizations like CFK: cost-benefit analysis, strategic planning, and accounting.

Nonprofit managers typically need to take into consideration factors that cannot be easily quantified, such as community support. Nevertheless, *cost-benefit analysis* is a powerful way to think through trade-offs systematically. Over the past year CFK has implemented basic cost-benefit analysis at a programmatic level. The results have been encouraging. Our program officers have found that cost-benefit analysis is a tool that helps surface healthy debates and keeps us grounded and focused on our core mission, which is to help create a better, more ethically guided generation of African leaders from an unlikely place—East Africa's largest slum.

An excellent business education can also equip nonprofit managers with useful tools for *strategic planning*. Many of my nonprofit colleagues think they need to hire expensive outside consulting firms to manage the strategic planning process, and they fear that their organization will lose operational flexibility and initiative once a plan is complete. I held similar viewpoints before I attended business school. I now see strategic planning as a vital and dynamic process that should be prioritized in an organization's growth. Too often nonprofits such as CFK simply fall back on the "founders' stories" for guidance. Founders' stories are important. They are part of the culture of an organization, but they are not a strategic plan. When effectively conducted and used, strategic plans help organizations maximize their impact.

Finally, many nonprofit managers with whom I've worked have never been formally educated in *accounting* and thus cannot properly supervise their finance departments. Most of my classmates at HBS took only one accounting course during their two years, a first-year course called Financial Reporting and Control. That class taught the basics, and although it was not a favorite class among my peers, it was among the most important courses that I took. I entered business school without the knowledge of how to prepare and read financial statements, and these are skills that most, if not all, managers need.

Shortly after the postelection violence in Kenya threw the nation into turmoil, the real estate bubble burst and the U.S. economy imploded. It was a unique time to be at business school, especially a school like Harvard, which had educated many of the CEOs whose firms destroyed staggering amounts of value, and who came under the fiercest public criticism for their failed leadership. It was in this context that I revised my initial presumption that nonprofits had more to learn from business than vice versa.

Nonprofit best practices can greatly assist business, and they merit more examination at business schools. Specifically, there are at least two broad areas where nonprofits may offer substantial insight for corporate executives and entrepreneurs: values and stakeholder outreach.

The financial crisis occurred in part because American firms were guided by poor *values*. CEOs sent the wrong messages when they incentivized productivity primarily though financial bonuses. In any industry, nonfinancial factors should be more powerful motivators for employee retention. This is true even for employees who were primarily motivated by financial gain when they first joined the business. Nonfinancial factors are cultural, and they include pride in the product delivered, the strength of firm identity, unit cohesion, and the integrity of the organization. Exceptional nonprofits have their values aligned with their missions and rely on nonfinancial incentives to keep their employees and volunteers motivated. At CFK, for example, our teenage members must participate in community clean-ups in order to compete in inter-ethnic soccer tournaments, and winning teams receive soccer balls and uniforms, not financial rewards.

Second, business should learn not to overemphasize shareholder value at the expense of broader *stakeholder outreach*. Donors are the nonprofit corollary of shareholders to business. Exceptional nonprofits ensure that their donors are not prioritized over their other stakeholders. This can be challenging, because many donors exert pressure on nonprofits to alter their service delivery. For example, CFK once received an offer from a foundation to build a vocational school for older women. The initiative would have detracted from our mission and core competency of youth empowerment. We turned it down. It was a difficult decision, because the grant was large and would have provided a substantial contribution to our overhead. Business executives also must make difficult decisions to balance shareholder demands for profit maximization with their duties to serve a broad base of stakeholders. Best practices in nonprofit management can assist businesses in better measuring and evaluating their impact and contributions to all of their stakeholders.

I finally had a chance to return to Kibera during spring break in 2008. Although I continued to volunteer much of my life to CFK, the violence made me question what we were actually achieving. The most ravaged parts of Kibera reminded me of Fallujah, Iraq, where I had served with the Marines in 2005 and 2006. The buildings around our youth center had been reduced to charred rubble. I became depressed looking at the damage, and after a day I confided my feelings to my cofounder Salim Mohamed, who was CFK's executive director.

"What are we really doing, man?" I asked Salim.

"Bro, even me, I have to ask myself the very same question," Salim replied. "But it's the tough times when we have to push, and let me tell you something that gives me hope. When things were really bad, the community united."

"What do you mean?"

"You know, thugs, they came here. They wanted to take our stuff and burn our buildings. The community though, it stopped them. They protected this place. A group of mamas and youths faced those men with their *pangas*. They risked their lives for this place."

Salim's words gave me peace of mind. We will never be able to measure the depth of community support for CFK displayed through the actions of an anonymous group of residents. Their actions were profound, and I interpreted them as an indicator that we were doing the right things for our most important stakeholder, our reason for existing—the community.

As much as Harvard Business School made me a more effective nonprofit manager, my experiences in Kibera did much more to equip me with the core values and skills that will keep me grounded as a leader as I pursue a new stage of my career, building and growing companies in North Carolina that exist to serve American communities.

I feel fortunate to have been able to work across the public, private, and nonprofit sectors at a young age, and I aspire to continue to incorporate such a balance throughout my life. The solutions to our world's toughest problems, such as the growth of megaslums, require full engagement and collaboration from each sector, and we have no time to waste.

Commerce and Culture

Combining Business and the Arts

Originally from Lansing, Michigan, **CHRISTINA WALLACE** now lives in New York City where she is the cofounder of Quincy, an early-stage online women's professional apparel company. She holds a BA in mathematics and theater studies from Emory University and an MBA from Harvard Business School. She has worked as a professional musician, actress, theater director, and arts administrator at organizations including Theater Emory, Georgia Shakespeare, Actors Express, the Schwartz Center for Performing Arts, and the Metropolitan Opera. Contact her through www.christinamwallace.com.

I arrived at the T stop in Central Square on a stiflingly hot day in August 2008 carrying a rucksack overflowing with dirty clothes and smelling like a Latin American hostel. Although I had just endured the heat and humidity of Nicaragua, there was something about the air in Boston that day that felt heavy as I walked the mile from the station to the Harvard Business School campus, white sand leaking through the seams of my pack and dusting the pavement with each step. In just three days I would start the Analytics Program at HBS, which would prepare us "nontraditional" students to begin our MBAs in September.

I was certain I was about as "nontraditional" as they come. I had studied first as a classical pianist and cellist, then as a mathematician and actress, and I had a tattoo of a Fibonacci spiral on my right shoulder blade. I was sure I wouldn't fit in. But that didn't matter. I was on a mission to figure out what business had to offer the arts.

My life in the arts began early, when, at the age of five, I insisted I begin piano lessons so I could be just like my big sister Stephanie. Music quickly gained a prominent place in my life. After a decade of lessons, master classes, competitions, and recitals, I decided to spend my last two years of high school at Interlochen Arts Academy, a preconservatory arts boarding school in northern Michigan. It was there that I realized I did not want to make my career as a professional pianist. I loved music, and it would always be a part of my life, but I longed for something different.

So I went to college instead of conservatory and spent four years diving into number theory and discovering theater. I fell in love with Paul Erdos, Richard Feynman, Richard Greenberg, and William Shakespeare; with cryptography, directing, dramaturgy, and Mersenne prime numbers. I toyed with a career in theater or a PhD in math, but knew neither was a great fit. With experience in music and theater and a brain that delighted in quantitative problems, the true match for me was arts management. It combined my artistic passion with a love of planning, producing, strategizing, and communicating. After internships with two theaters in Atlanta and a one-year fellowship with the Schwartz Center for Performing Arts at Emory University, I was hooked. I moved to New York to see what it was like in the "big leagues." On a whim I applied to a job at the Metropolitan Opera and, unbelievably, I got an interview. I was speechless. The Met isn't in the big leagues; it's in a league all its own.

In my interview for a rehearsal associate position with the Met, my potential supervisor and her boss made me promise that I would not try to change a thing in my first year. The fact that this request did not trigger a flashing neon warning sign is a testament to how ingrained and pervasive that attitude is in many of our cultural organizations—and how anxious I was to simply be part of such a legendary institution. Peter Gelb, who had served for a decade as president of Sony Classical, had just been named the new general manager of the Met. It seemed like the dusty institution was poised for a renaissance. Surely 2006 would be an exciting year for a young person to help revitalize one of the country's most important arts institutions.

The HR manager thought otherwise and did his best to scare me off. He said the days would be long, the pay terrible, and the pressure unyielding. He said I would not be promoted until someone died or retired, since people rarely left the company for any other reason and openings were scarce given that the Met was long past its growth phase. I would have the worst job in the house, he insisted, and be stuck there for a while. I took it anyway. I was certain I could make a difference.

Yet on my first anniversary with the opera, leaving work frustrated by my ineffectiveness for the fifth time that week, I wondered if this was what a career in arts management really meant. I had completed my one-year trial period and was excited to share my ideas to innovate and transform the stodgy Rehearsal Department. There were processes that could be streamlined and structures that could be created to systemize much of the repetitive and error-riddled work streams. The department had one central database with 90 percent of the information we needed to access over the course of the day, yet we repopulated that data into schedules by hand, increasing the likelihood of human error along the way. We ran the same handful of reports every week by marking up documents with a highlighter and adding figures with pencil and paper, burning through hours behind a desk that could be better invested in face time with the artists. We spent the bulk of our day in our "command center" buried in a corner of the administrative wing while most of the rehearsals were going on three floors below.

Yet when I approached my manager and the head of our department with ideas to improve our processes, my proposals were deflected one by one: there was a certain way that things were done here. I just didn't understand the customs yet. Making suggestions, it was pointed out, was not in my job description.

This culture seemed at odds with the strides Gelb was making at the helm of the Met. In his first year as general manager he had focused on reinvigorating the repertoire with new theatrical productions, reconnecting with the public through a provocative outreach plan, and establishing an innovative new-media strategy that ultimately set the bar for all other arts organizations. His sharp business acumen was unquestionably foreign to the velvet-cloaked halls of the Metropolitan Opera. The speed with which he enacted his ideas felt like Mach 5 in a company that was still using typewriters in many departments through the end of the twentieth century.

Just two months after officially taking the reins in 2006, he opened the theater to the public in an unprecedented event by holding a free open house for the dress rehearsal of Anthony Minghella's production of *Madama Butterfly*. Partnering with a longtime board member, he launched a rush ticket program with $20 orchestra seats available two hours before curtain for most performances. To celebrate the season's opening night in September, Gelb simulcast the performance both on the Web and on the big screens in Times Square. Days later he announced a dedicated Met channel on Sirius satellite radio, and by Christmas the Met was broadcasting a live performance of Julie Taymor's *The Magic Flute* in high-definition video to movie theaters around the world.

It seemed so easy for innovation to blossom at the top of this prominent institution, but from where I sat, I felt like I didn't have a voice to contribute to the momentum. Gelb's passion from atop was translating into an external revitalization, but it wasn't affecting the internal culture one whit. And I wasn't the only one whose passion was dwindling. The few Met employees under the age of forty were growing frustrated and leaving in rapid succession. Moreover, this wasn't just affecting the Met; my colleagues in comparable roles at other cultural institutions were feeling similarly disillusioned. An entire generation of passionate nonprofit kids was transitioning out because they felt they had so much to offer, yet no one was willing or able to harness their zeal. Surely there was something I could do about it. There had to be.

I briefly considered master's programs in arts management but quickly realized it wasn't the "arts" I needed to learn—it was the "management." I wanted to learn the best practices of companies that are ultimately responsible for a bottom line. So I applied to business school.

My subsequent experiences in business have confirmed my belief that private sector frameworks, tools, and best practices can fundamentally contribute to the social sector, even the performing arts. In my HBS class on managing high-performing nonprofits, we read a case study on the Edna McConnell Clark Foundation. This innovative foundation offers grants to support organizational development, insisting that nonprofits prioritize structural health alongside program expansion. In general the philanthropic capital markets still penalize nonprofits for significant overhead costs, but it is heartening to see one leading foundation acknowledge that overhead is essential to the development of controls, processes, and human capital. Overhead like employee training and mentoring is what allows nonprofits to create a pipeline of leadership and establish succession plans. Clearly defined processes and well-developed controls strengthen organizations, providing employees with necessary resources and setting them up for success in achieving their mission.

I've also been inspired to learn about the significant growth in the forprofit social enterprise space. Cochairing the 2010 Harvard Social Enterprise Conference exposed me to companies that are eradicating diseases, increasing access to financial services, and supporting at-risk youth with more success than their nonprofit counterparts. In many cases the profit motive can support a social agenda by encouraging innovative business models wherein the people controlling the cash flow (usually by buying a good or service) are the same constituents receiving the benefits of that enterprise. This stakeholder alignment translates into a more sustainable funding model than exclusive reliance on government or foundation support, replacing a charitable relationship with a customer relationship.

To be clear: social enterprise is not about balancing the double bottom lines of social impact and profit as though they are equally important. Profit, in these sectors, is ultimately a means to achieve social impact, not the end itself. But it is a mechanism to encourage growth, innovation, and evolution.

On an even more basic level, however, I learned that businesses really do aim to create value. In the traditional sense, they create value for their owners or shareholders. But they can do so only by encouraging the types of ingenuity and entrepreneurship that impact the broader world. Translating and adapting business frameworks and best practices for the social sector means leveraging these resources to create value for society. From this perspective it becomes absolutely necessary for leaders in the social sector to utilize business tools, not only to create innovative enterprises but also to scale high-potential organizations to maximize social impact.

Over my two years at HBS I learned that there isn't simply a place for businesspeople in our cultural institutions; there is a desperate need for them. The integration may be difficult since there is currently little dialogue across the nonprofit/for-profit divide, but it is in our best interests to foster such collaboration.

Peter Gelb began that collaboration when he brought to the Met the marketing and media savvy he developed while at Sony Classical. There is no doubt that the "new Met" has been wholly transformed from the audience's perspective. But there is more that can be done internally. The cultivation of human capital should be one of the company's priorities, by mentoring and coaching employees to think beyond their job description and understand more than just their corner of the company. And the Met is not alone.

Moreover, in an organization that spends about 75 percent of its operating budget on payroll, the Met must consider how sophisticated planning techniques and other applications of technology could transform their costs. Adapting tools and analysis from the business world could improve the coordination and utilization of their large union groups and help reduce the need for expensive overtime. With seventeen unions and a century of data to analyze, the impact of such tools could be substantial.

It seems like an eternity since I plodded that first time from the subway in Cambridge to my new home at HBS, but my experiences have led me to believe ever more firmly that business is how I can help build and sustain the vitality and accessibility of arts institutions in a world that needs them more than ever.

Iraq, Afghanistan, and the Business of Peace

JAKE CUSACK is a former Marine Corps officer who served in Iraq as a sniper platoon commander and intelligence officer from 2005 to 2008. He will graduate with a joint degree from the Harvard Business School and Harvard Kennedy School in 2012, and has written extensively about entrepreneurship and economic growth in Afghanistan. He is passionate about economic development in conflict zones.

My idea of war in Mesopotamia was so steeped in mythology that I felt the laws of gravity might be upended when I landed as a marine in Al Taqaddum, Iraq, on Christmas Day 2005. I thought I was being transported into a world of legend, populated with heroes and filled with pageantry amid chaos. But I soon learned the difference between my abstractions and reality.

I found the same laws of physics that applied to me growing up in Michigan applied in Fallujah. There was no particular romance or mystery as to how battles were won or why people died. Small projectiles ripped into skin in combat the same way twisted metal cut through flesh in a highway car accident. Fighting the insurgency was blue-collar work, sweat and tedium under a hot sun. Hours of patrols, census-taking, and conversations with local elders over warm tea were punctuated by the briefest moments of extreme violence.

I was woefully clumsy navigating a war so unlike the one I had imagined. Two months into my first deployment, I remember standing with another Marine lieutenant on a rooftop in a city of over twenty thousand Iraqis. Both in our early twenties, we were the senior officers present, working

for the security and welfare of the city. We discussed the current problems: complaints from the city council, closed markets, illicit trades, the
virulent imam, unreliable electricity, and undrinkable water. I realized
that while I knew how to employ a machine gun or call in air support,
I was completely unprepared for the full spectrum of modern conflict.

Economic factors were fundamental to the surprisingly base logic un-
dergirding the war. Profit—not just nationalism, religious fervor, or need
for honor in battle—motivates behavior under even the most anarchic of
circumstances. In Al Qaim, a dusty Iraqi town on the Syrian border, a
local tribe became one of the first to turn against Al Qaeda in 2005. The
tribe was driven neither by patriotism nor by fear of an extremist Islamic
state, but by its desire to regain control of lucrative cross-border smuggling routes.

On another hot summer day two years later, I sat in a meeting of senior Iraqi leadership discussing problems in the Ninewah province. Little
of our conversation actually stemmed from typical security or military issues. Instead, the topics were the price of refined and unrefined oil; infrastructure at the points of entry; taxation schemes; the relative health
of agricultural commodities. I was the only one present who wanted to
talk about foreign fighters or illicit weapons smuggling. Everyone else
was concerned with business.

In the peak of the insurgency, senior military leadership advocated a
"carrot and stick" approach to bringing the populace to our side. But initially, our sticks were frail and our carrots were stale. We found we could
never win an intimidation battle with the insurgents: if Iraqis gave information to us, Al Qaeda would come in the night and kill their families;
if Iraqis passively cooperated with Al Qaeda, we might be able to detain
them for two weeks. Too often, our enticements were equally weak: to an
unemployed Iraqi, pencils and soccer balls for schoolchildren or a few
meal packages tossed from a Humvee seemed at best platitudinous and
at worst insulting.

We eventually realized that robust funding and effort at the lowest levels could show a road to a more tolerable future—one with electricity,

jobs, and education—than the lawless bloodletting that Al Qaeda's Islamic State of Iraq offered in the territory it controlled. Although the endless raids and captures of insurgents were important, I saw subtle political and economic shifts rapidly yield more significant results. The infamous Sunni "awakening" that turned Al Anbar province against Al Qaeda went beyond local leaders finally banding against foreign fanatics—it was also a jobs program, pumping millions of U.S. dollars into the hands of military-aged males who had formerly been our foes.[10]

In 2009, I returned to academic study with a desire to gain new perspectives on the interaction of business, governance, and security at the edges of chaos. After subsequently finishing the first year of the joint MPP/MBA program, I spent the summer in Afghanistan. A fellow student, Erik Malmstrom, and I hoped to explore private sector growth and constraints in the country from the perspective of the indigenous businesses. We worked to find Afghans who had stayed clear of the easy short-term money suckled from international forces and instead launched more sustainable ventures in industries like carpets, dried fruit exports, and light manufacturing.

Landing in a war zone as an independent researcher was a jarring departure from my time as a marine. At first, I felt almost naked without a bit of body armor or the camaraderie of fellow armed men. In tense situations, my hand moved unconsciously to my right hip, grasping for the 9-mm Beretta that was no longer there.

But I soon felt far more comfortable wearing local dress than I ever did with Oakleys and fatigues. I relished spending hours in conversation with locals in their homes without having to mentally count down the time it would take for the insurgents to set an ambush or lay an IED outside. I even enjoyed it when Afghans refused to speak to me—a leveling of roles that had not generally been possible when I showed up for meetings carrying a semiautomatic weapon.

Time spent with businesses was also more uplifting than my old pursuits hunting "high-value targets." Although the summer of 2010 was a tumultuous time—the relief of General Stanley McChrystal, rampant intelligence leaks, and a growing chorus labeling "failure"—I left more optimistic than I had ever felt about a conflict zone. The reminders of war were still there: the owner of a flour mill in a large city near the Iranian border answered a question about his company's growth by dividing it into "before and after I was kidnapped" (he escaped and moved to Kazakhstan for a year, shutting down a portion of the business). But good businessmen are by nature optimistic about the future—their money is tied up in it, after all—and their entrepreneurial enthusiasm and willingness to invest was contagious.

Even in Kandahar, where the local Pashtun tribesmen who accompanied me to meetings carried Glock pistols under their long dress—not just for my protection, but for theirs—I found enterprises still growing. The risk, substantial of course, could be overrated. The chairman of Afghanistan's first insurance company explained to me how they had gradually been able to lower the annual property premiums they passed on from Lloyd's of London from 12 percent to around 1 percent. Though the governance and regulatory framework could be massively unpredictable, outsiders generally overestimated the actual physical threat to normal business.

As in combat, the test of a chaotic environment revealed character. Some businessmen were entrepreneurial in the worst sense, staging attacks to drum up business for their security company or monopolizing control of scarce resources for personal power. But this made the fortitude of others all the more impressive: a television station refusing to bias its news coverage despite relentless political pressure; a clothing manufacturer employing hundreds of women; a custom-made carpet manufacturer providing jobs to thousands of rural families; a supplier forgoing a contract rather than paying a bribe.

After six years in and out of conflict zones, I have learned that people can continue to respond to economic incentives in rational ways, even in the most dangerous of circumstances. Outside forces conducting ambitious interventions desperately require private sector expertise in order to reconstruct failed states. Nascent local government leaders need to remember that businesses—their success staked to overall stability—can be an invaluable support.

An infusion of private sector talent could benefit our national security apparatus. Specifically, I can offer a few examples of what government might learn from a private sector mind-set:

- **Focus on ensuring predictability and stability to enable economic growth.** Contrary to expectations, neither physical security nor corruption is the primary constraint on business in Afghanistan. Instead, over and over again, entrepreneurs complained about the overall uncertainty of the business environment. Tax structure, custom tariffs, local power brokers, American force posture, financing, government officials—all were in constant flux. Just like in Western markets, uncertainty is even worse than a large but specific downside. When given a specific threat, business can adapt or hedge by shifting operations, becoming more liquid, or paying bribes (a form of tax). As one of the most adept businessmen told me: "The problem is not the variables themselves, but the variability of the variables." International forces can help mitigate such uncertainty by making public long-term policy commitments, providing advance purchase financing, and incorporating private sector considerations into even low-level military planning.

- **Be willing to make long-term investments.** Ironically, I found the American government—which should be looking toward long-term, regional implications—to be absurdly short-term in orientation. Quarterly reporting deadlines and year-long deployments lead to a culture where everyone is looking for the fix that will pay off on their watch. This in turn makes the businessmen focused on the quick dollar (often from trading), when they otherwise would be willing to make three- or five-year investment (in fixed-capital production facilities).

- **Allow reasonable profits.** Despite working on behalf of a country that was built on capitalism, some in the State Department and

USAID (U.S. Agency for International Development) seem fundamentally uncomfortable with the idea that a good business will enrich its owners. They sometimes seem to perceive profit as illegitimate and immoral, and feel that the best small business projects should verge on socialism. This has created a culture where Afghans applying for a grant hide the "profit" part of their business plan because they think the donors will not support an enterprise that may reward the owners. Interestingly, the reverse is true for contracting in the security, transportation, and construction sectors, where international forces turn a blind eye to blatant rent-seeking and windfall returns.

- **Abandon failing projects.** Unlike a business, which will cut its losses and move on, each layer of a traditional development project has no incentives to acknowledge failure. Elegant reports with glossy pictures substitute for real performance. Donor, implementer, and beneficiary often maintain the facade of obviously flawed projects because evaluation is based on money spent—"burn rates"—and vague social metrics.

From the other perspective, Western business can find it both financially and socially rewarding to be a partner in the rebuilding of a sustainable economy amid conflict. There are lessons the private sector might find useful for doing business in chaotic countries:

- **Do not make risk assessments from media reports.** Western companies often significantly overestimate the physical security risk and avoid even safe areas of Afghanistan. At this very moment, Turkish, Chinese, Lebanese, and other investors are seizing business opportunities because they are more realistic in their assessments. If Westerners travel and act in a low-profile manner, some areas of Afghanistan seem safer than some American urban centers.

- **Vertically integrate and replicate missing government functions internally.** In the absence of contract sanctity, the best way to know the transport trucks for your goods will always show up is to own the trucks. Bereft of government protection, industrialists are forced to replace government functions with their own. Effectively, they develop internal police forces (Ministry of Interior), external protection (Ministry of Defense), independent communications, electric and water infrastructure, and so on. This actually can be a sustainable business model, so long as the profits are sufficiently strong.

- **Ensure security by working with the community.** The largest company in Afghanistan, Roshan Telecom, used to hire outside security contractors to protect its numerous cell towers. Faced with rising costs, they switched to a model where they paid local villagers to guard the towers, and offered incentive benefits for the community. The new "socially responsible" initiative resulted in lower costs and improved security.

- **Be proactive in finding entrepreneurs and investing in local human capital.** In a conflict climate, the men who show up at your doorstep asking for investment money often cannot be trusted, as they are often locals who have become expert at gaming a donor system. It is better to identify the sector you are interested in, then go scour the countryside for the entrepreneur already making progress in that area. Once you find a good one, keep investing—human talent is the hardest to find and the most irreplaceable factor. Those who rely too much on outside consultants discover that as security worsens, the outsiders leave and will not return except for exorbitant fees.

I find my classmates at Harvard, with significant business expertise, unaware of how much their skills can help in our current global struggle with terrorism and our efforts to rebuild failed states. The tools of national security are far more diverse than those of the military or even development aid. The capacity to build a secure world will not be found only in West Point or unleashed from afar by unmanned technologies. Now, more than ever, the call for service in national security can be answered by everyone.

Business in the World

How Corporations Can Be Change Agents

KELLI WOLF MOLES worked in investment banking at JPMorgan in New York before graduating from Harvard Business School with the class of 2011. Kelli is founder and CEO of Project Spark, a nonprofit that promotes sustainable philanthropy and organizes volunteer trips. Kelli is passionate about helping businesses give employees greater purpose through public service.

In 2006, my husband and I took our honeymoon in Africa. We went on a safari, and then spent two weeks volunteering at an orphanage in Uganda. Nine months after our trip, while working in investment banking at JPMorgan, I began to feel ill. For two weeks, I refused to take time off from work, trying a few outpatient visits to remedy my flulike symptoms. Finally, I went to the emergency room. With a team of ten to fifteen doctors surrounding my bed, I was diagnosed with an advanced form of malaria. This deadly disease had lain dormant in my body since our return. My tests showed a life-threateningly low white blood cell count, and the doctors determined that my spleen had ruptured and was pouring toxic blood throughout my body.

In my darkest hours, I found myself drawing on my faith. I had to believe that something positive would come from this, and looking back, this experience changed my perspective forever. My brush with death reminded me that life is short. I realized I want to change lives and influence people more than I want power or wealth. Wall Street is an exciting and challenging place to work, but making a positive impact on communities and individuals is equally important for bringing meaning to my life.

Soon after I recovered, I began raising funds and awareness for malaria prevention. After raising $5,000 for malaria nets in 2007, I was asked to host a booth at JPMorgan's volunteer fair and speak on a panel about my project. I quickly realized how many of my colleagues also appreciated the fact that life should not be taken for granted and were interested in leveraging business to change the world.

Business and its leaders play a powerful role in shaping society. This has always been a core belief of mine, and it is the reason that I chose a career in business. In my travel to more than forty countries, I have seen firsthand that businesses and corporations are often more powerful than governments. Whether you believe that business is only for profit maximization, or that it has a broader role, it is undoubtedly a force producing many effects—both positive and negative—in the world.

After talking with my colleagues and friends, we organized a group we called Project Poverty to serve two goals: (1) to raise money for sustainable development projects and (2) to organize trips to developing countries to see the work firsthand. In the first year our team planned six events, from a three-on-three basketball tournament to a cocktail hour. JPMorgan supported our work in many ways—from featuring us as a "Project of the Month" to matching donations to helping with publicity of our events. It was great to see the positive results when competitive businesspeople unite toward a common goal. The friendships and camaraderie we developed through Project Poverty stuck with us as we worked through challenging client situations.

After the success of our fund-raising, we wanted to take Project Poverty further. We suspected the investment of "sweat equity" into the clinic's construction would help us all connect with our cause. My first visit to Africa had changed my life, and I knew the same would happen to my colleagues. In September of 2008, thirteen professionals, including five coworkers from JPMorgan, traveled with me to Ghana. We spent five days carrying stones and mixing cement by hand to build a health clinic.

Since that time, Project Poverty has brought forty-five people to developing countries and raised over $100,000. Of the people who have gone on Project Poverty trips, all have found their lives impacted in very different ways. Many of us learned about ourselves and the world during our time abroad, and brought the insights and stories back to our jobs and clients. Managers today have to understand the diverse, interconnected world we live in while still paying respect to national pride and cultural sensitivities. More than ever before, we will be managing global teams with people very different from ourselves. Understanding and appreciating other cultures and people more deeply makes it easier to work together.

Soon after that trip, I also got involved in a program called Bankers Without Borders and served as one of the inaugural volunteers. This is a program set up by the Nobel Prize–winning Grameen Foundation to utilize private sector resources to make a difference by helping the poorest of the poor. JPMorgan gave me time off and sent me to Africa to serve as a project leader for a technology pilot at a microfinance institution. Using banking skills halfway around the world was an interesting learning experience. I learned as much as I helped, and came back with new ideas and a greater appreciation for banking in emerging markets.

I believe this tendency among large corporations and professional firms to devote more resources to giving their employees life-changing experiences in the public and nonprofit sectors is both growing and incredibly valuable to the firms themselves. The company I am now working with, McKinsey & Company, offers opportunities for interested professionals to take sabbaticals, and through various secondments and externships, consultants are able to take time off to pursue their passions.

To keep a dynamic workforce, these options are important. These types of programs truly set employers apart. They attract talent, motivate employees, and transform workforces. Not only do they show commitment to employees and provide meaningful and valuable options, but they also demonstrate cutting-edge thinking, a willingness to try new things, and flexibility. All of these options then equip employees to become more thoughtful, engaged leaders.

In my experience with Project Poverty, Bankers Without Borders, and McKinsey, I've noticed a few patterns in the way managers and organizations have successfully imagined and executed these public service programs. A few of the key elements each program seems to contain are partnership with first-class organizations, easy and accessible options for involvement, senior leadership support, publicity of events and impact, and inclusion in a formal review process:

- *Partnering with first-class organizations* allows companies to do what they do best, while lending talent to nonprofits that are best in class at fulfilling their mission. Bankers Without Borders allows the Grameen Foundation to join forces with those working in traditional banking areas. Many of these public service organizations have formalized programs that limit the administrative burden for companies building new programs. These organizations often have successful models that can be leveraged for everything from selecting volunteers to choosing projects. Partnering with these top organizations also provides employees the best opportunities to learn and to develop new skills to bring back to the workplace.

- *Easy and accessible opportunities* for employee involvement are also key. It is a big commitment to take time away from personal obligations and an already busy workload to participate in volunteer activities. The volunteer fair my company held over lunch enabled me to recruit employees interested in getting involved with Project Poverty. Providing opportunities such as volunteer fairs, lecture series, benefit happy hours, and companywide service days allows employees to find out more and consider further involvement. We found that shorter events over lunch or breakfast encouraged employees to stop by without making a large upfront time commitment. This also broadens the reach of the programs and allows greater awareness and participation.

- As with any major corporate initiative, *senior leadership must buy in and be personally committed* to ensuring the success of the programs. Senior leaders who are excited about the public service programs spark enthusiasm from employees. Executives must be flexible and willing to support employees' involvement. Senior involvement helps to work through any problems with the initial implementation of the program and ensures it is institutionalized for years to come.

- *Publicity of events and impact* is crucial to communicating the success and importance of the work with a broader audience. When Project Poverty was selected as Project of the Month, we were featured in the company newsletter and on the website. A short video and pictures were included to show firsthand the work being done. This kind of publicity provides a platform to share the impact not only with employees but also with customers and clients. With the rise of social media, there are many low-cost ways companies can showcase the work being done and garner further support for future initiatives.

- Last, inclusion of the employee's involvement in the *formal review process* also helps to build a successful program and a company culture that promotes participation in volunteer opportunities. This is usually done as a "back page"—additional information to accompany the core performance review. It showcases employee leadership and involvement in company programs outside of the basic day-to-day activities. It shows a true commitment on the part of the company to encourage employee participation. It also provides additional incentives for those considering whether or not they will have the time and the ability to volunteer in addition to their current jobs.

Corporations are vast and often untapped resources for sustainable solutions to the world's greatest social and economic ills. I have learned this lesson firsthand through my fund-raising work and my current role in management consulting. Companies that support and empower employees to take on challenges they care about will win in the long term. We will bring our experiences out in the world back to our jobs, while developing loyalty to the companies that are determined not just to make money, but to leave a positive footprint along the way. As I learned through my brush with death—life is short. Each day should be treasured and our talents used to their highest purpose. Imagine the impact of more companies lending top talent to good causes. Through partnerships and public service programs, we have the opportunity to leverage business to play a positive role in society.

David Gergen

Adviser to four presidents, Director of Harvard's Center for Political Leadership, and Senior Political Analyst for CNN

David Gergen discusses a new, cross-sector generation and what the increasing convergence of the public, private, and nonprofit sectors will mean for the world.

David, over the course of your career, you have interacted with a lot of influential leaders—of previous generations and of the current generation. What do you see as some of the primary differences or similarities between those groups?

There are some similarities. The leaders of past generations whom I have known led incredibly demanding lives. They had to put in long hours, often at the expense of their families, and they had to dig deep into complex questions—often not knowing what the answers would be. Complexity is not new. It comes back to us in different forms, but it's not new for leaders. Another thing that hasn't changed is that leaders have always had to have a set of values and to be deeply rooted in values. The context has changed but the importance of integrity, courage, and fair play has not changed—over time or across countries.

But there are also notable changes in the context of leadership today that place fresh demands on young leaders who are emerging from business schools and other institutions of higher learning. For one, the pace of change has quickened dramatically in recent years so that young leaders today have to be much more adaptable than leaders of my generation. It's unimaginable now that if we were faced with a missile crisis coming out of Cuba—or today, in Iran—that any president would have thirteen days to resolve it. Modern technology and other changes demand that you act much more quickly. And a modern president wouldn't be able to maintain the privacy that Kennedy had.

Henry Adams famously wrote in his memoirs that the nineteenth century was when things really began to speed up. Prior to that, what the father did was what the son tended to do, and what the grandson tended to do. But in the nineteenth century, things started moving more rapidly, and now in the twenty-first century, we've reached warp speed. You have to have much broader, wider bandwidth to deal with it.

In my generation, you tried to be an expert in a field. You might, for example, be an international relations specialist focused on Sub-Saharan Africa.

Today, you must know not only international politics but also international economics, health care delivery, issues related to education, and so on. Knowledge has spilled out of individual fields and there's much more need for knowledge across fields. Universities today are developing more and more interdisciplinary studies. Someone coming out of businesses is expected to understand the government and the civic sector. And inevitably, people are finding their careers span sectors far more than they did in the past. Now there is a real premium on an education that allows you to build foundations across sectors.

This is not to say that an individual doesn't need some specialized knowledge. I still think it pays rich dividends for a leader to have at least one or two areas in which he or she has made a deep dive. To be a generalist who skims across things on the Internet or depends on another person's knowledge is insufficient in today's world. You can't simply rely upon the competence, knowledge, or backgrounds of those who work with you or report to you. As you rise to leadership, the decisions that come to you are always very close calls. They're often 51/49 and you find that your advisors are divided about them. Somebody has to make the ultimate decision. And that requires a person who has training or at least a capacity for judgment that goes beyond "front porch" understanding. George W. Bush, for example, was a man of integrity but often had divided advisors and had to make decisions on his own about things he hadn't really had the chance to study deeply.

So you're driving toward a point here about the increased bandwidth
that a lot of young leaders need to have, both because of the pace of
change and because there's so much interaction now between the
different sectors?

I think that's right. They're all in partnership now: the civic sector, the
private sector—you know, companies today operate internationally and
have to be worried about issues of sustainability, and inevitably that
brings them into close contact with NGOs. And then the web of
regulations—government regulations and government engagement—is
growing. Companies have a lot of international bodies to deal with and
an increasing number of financial rules and regulations that impact
them. You can't operate a modern environment as a corporate leader
without having a very clear appreciation of that. A lot of leadership
studies talk about leadership as a matter of concentric circles. The
inner circle is the individual; the first circle out is the people in that
leader's organization or the team. Most of our earlier studies focused
on those two circles. Now we concentrate on a third circle as well, and
that is working outside your team, with leaders of other teams, and
with other organizations. You increasingly have to learn how to align
yourself with others in order to tackle the major problems.

It seems like you're driving toward different skills younger leaders will
need in a cross-functional world. Do you think there are a lot of skills
that are transferable between these sectors?

There are definitely some skills that are transferable. For example, a
capacity to work with and to lead through the Internet is transferable.
You see that with social media in Egypt. It's also extremely important
for politicians running for office, as we learned with Barack Obama.
And social media has become important for corporations to understand as an offensive and defensive tool. Corporations are ill-designed
to defend against online attacks. They are in the situation that if they
make one mistake or they leave themselves vulnerable, then suddenly
a mass movement can be organized against them on the Internet.
They're scrambling to figure it out. But corporations are also

scrambling to figure out how they can use the Internet offensively. Starbucks, for example, has developed a network of people online who have come to appreciate its special culture. Other companies in the apparel industry use the Internet to have interactions on questions on fashion. There are a lot of imaginative uses that could cross the sector boundaries we've been talking about.

You're kind of driving to some of the differences between sectors, too. Are there things that you think the sectors can learn from one another? We've seen deficiencies in each sector in its own way over the past decade or so. And I think that young people are acutely aware of that, particularly in business. Are there key lessons to learn?

You have to learn across sectors. For example, the pioneers who are really challenging the status quo in public education are rarely public employees. They tend to be coming out of the civic sector. And certainly government has a great deal to learn from business about efficiency, technology, and setting concrete goals and achieving them. Think of health care in the United States. We pay twice as much as any other mature economy and get less for it. There's a widespread feeling now that the health care industry has to learn from the competition that exists in the business sector. And that people who come out of business schools can make excellent hospital administrators and directors. They might also make very good school administrators. Look at the number of cities now looking to MBA graduates and lawyers to help run public schools.

Are there examples where you think leaders in the public sector or the nonprofit sector could make a big and positive change in business the same way you're highlighting the ways in which businesspeople might be able to come into sectors like health care and education?

The transfer is not as easy as it looks. I can't remember a senator becoming a CEO in recent years. There are some things that don't transfer there. But yes, I do think that business can learn a great deal from some aspects of work in government or nonprofit. A CEO in a field like health care may, from years in a NGO, understand what a patient may need or what a society may need and from there, figure out how to make money doing it. I was just talking with Coca-Cola two weeks ago and had dinner with their advisory board and sat with the chairman of the company. Coca-Cola is now deeply engaged in sustainability projects in which they make money. They've got whole areas where they're working with farmers and developing new ways to produce things—their bottling, for example—and they're finding that these are profitable enterprises. It goes to the heart of what Michael Porter argues—that a growing number of companies are finding ways to solve societal problems and make money at the same time.

Renewable energy is potentially one of those areas. In that case, many of the people solving the energy problems are coming from universities, coming with ideas just as they did with the Internet. A lot of those ideas came out of government. As you know, the Defense Department was the originator of the Internet. And that created a whole industry. And now there are areas where energy research is going on, sponsored by government in major universities like MIT. Twenty percent of the allied key faculty at MIT now work in energy research. There are also private companies that are in the renewable energy field that have great promise.

Can I ask a question from the young business leaders' perspective? You're talking about all the ways in which companies are beginning to interact more fruitfully and more consistently with the different sectors . . .

This is not entirely new. If you look at where the real growth areas have been, they have often been clustered around major research universities, whether in Silicon Valley, Austin, the Research Triangle, or the Harvard-MIT area. They all have this synergy that occurs among knowledge workers who cut across sectors.

If you were a young businessperson now, but you did have some kind of passion for the other sectors, how would you get involved? Through universities? Through internships? Is it through their extracurricular activities? Or through sustainability programs within companies? Are there ways you see young people, especially in business, beginning to get involved in those sectors outside of business—in the public or nonprofit sectors where they can make an impact?

I think it begins in the university days. You open yourself to trying to understand not just one field but to develop secondary interests in other fields. I do think it's important to exit your formal education with an area in which you're strong and you've really gone deeper. But I think in today's world, it pays to have a secondary field or even a third field that may or may not be related. You may find somebody who majors in physics but also has an interest in the arts. She can suddenly start making connections across them that may seem unlikely at first but may actually turn out to be more helpful than they look. I think of our friend Sidney Harman, who passed away in his nineties. Sidney was a renaissance man who believed that CEOs probably ought to hire poets because they think outside the box. I think that someone who comes into the business who graduated in the arts and then goes on to business school has got a very strong background. If you have time and are inclined, it's good to get a double major or joint graduate degree far more than it was when I came through. I went to law school and if I were coming through now, I would probably get a law or business degree but then look for a joint degree in another field—maybe in public policy. I would definitely think about trying to get that dual degree.

In business, you have to manage your career. If you're a young rising star, it's wise to have some exposure beyond your own area and not get too specialized too early. You certainly have to make your mark somewhere. And that often requires you to pare down and really go deep into some area of the company and be content spending three to five years doing it in order to build something or create something. I think it's really important to get your hands dirty and understand that things get more complex as you get deeper. And I think that's valuable work. What is important, though, is even as you professionalize yourself, to maintain a curiosity toward life so that you're continually reading, learning, growing. You know, the best businesspeople I've met—I'm incredibly impressed by how much they read, and not necessarily just in their fields. David Rubenstein [co-founder and managing director of The Carlyle Group] probably reads fifty books a week. I'm astonished, really. I don't see how they find the time to do it, but I do see that it broadens them, and I think they see themselves as on a learning journey. Les Wexner [founder, chairman, and CEO of Limited Brands] is a veteran CEO who built a retail empire, but he's still very much on a learning journey.

One criticism of younger leaders today is that they sometimes lack focus—the ability to drive deeper or maintain an attention span. Are there any words of caution you would have for young leaders?

Don't be afraid of failure. The metaphor for my generation was "climbing ladders"; the metaphor in your generation is increasingly "riding waves." You have to ride waves as they go. You're often going to find them collapsing underneath you, and you have to ride the next one when it comes. That's the nature of careers today. Companies come and go quickly. People are CEOs for only—you know, a twinkling of an eye—and then they have to start over. And you've got to be prepared. I don't know what the latest numbers are in the Department of Labor, but a few years ago they were projecting that someone graduating with a degree today would hold at least seven or eight jobs over the course of a lifetime—three of which would not have been invented when they graduated from college. It just goes back to bandwidth and adaptability. One must be prepared to take risks, to take the fall, pick yourself back up, and start again. It is also important to build some financial security very early if you can, so that you have reserves and can afford to take risks. When you're doing the start-up, you know, it's almost a badge of honor to have a couple of start-ups that fail. But if you're going to do that, it helps to have some financial reserves to fall back on.

And so you're driving a little bit toward dealing with the obstacles, especially dealing with failure. A lot of young people, particularly in business, have been a little discouraged by the difficulties of the past five or six years as we have been coming of age. Do you have a word of encouragement or hope for this generation as we try and move forward, and especially as we try and correct some of the difficulties that we've encountered politically and economically?

We're entering a period that will be one of the most unpredictable, fast-moving, and toughest we've ever seen. But at the same time, it's one of the most fascinating because so much is uncertain that if you choose to lead, you can have a tremendous impact on reshaping the future. For those of us who are older, one of our greatest regrets is that we may not be here to help and to see how this turns out. I think we're just at one of those hinge points in history in which mankind can go in more than one direction. And it's the younger generation that really could shape what those answers are, what direction we should take. We talk about people in their twenties being the leaders of tomorrow. But with everything we're seeing now—especially on the streets of Cairo and elsewhere—I believe that people in their twenties can and should be the leaders of today.

CHAPTER 2

Globalization

Embracing the Global Generation

*I find that because of modern technological evolution and our global
economy, and as a result of the great increase in population, our
world has greatly changed: it has become much smaller. However, our
perceptions have not evolved at the same pace; we continue to cling
to old national demarcations and the old feelings of "us" and "them."*

—The Dalai Lama

The scene of a typical Harvard Business School classroom in the
1950s would seem rather peculiar today. For one thing, there were no
women. The MBA class would be composed mostly of white American
men, dressed in business suits and taught by a male professor. Fast-for-
ward to 2010. Displayed on the walls of first-year classrooms are the flags
of countries from around the world, representing each member of the
class. You'll hear a plethora of accents. More importantly, if you listen
closely, you'll learn that the educational and professional experiences that
these students bring to the classroom also span almost every country and
region. Globalization has become as commonplace in MBA programs as
in business itself.

The next generation, more than others, is taking advantage of the
learning opportunities globalization provides. Instead of simply using
their formative years to develop their professional skills, young people in

business have used globalization to gain practical experience earlier in their careers, learn more about different cultures, and ultimately, learn more about themselves. Like it or not, globalization is now an inescapable part of the emerging millennial zeitgeist, whether this means work experience in a multinational company, participation in addressing global problems such as climate change, the pursuit of new ventures abroad, or connection to an expanded international network.

According to the IBM Global Leaders Survey, when respondents were asked to name the top factors that would impact organizations in the future, globalization garnered the most votes, with 55 percent of students ranking it number one. In contrast, CEOs voted globalization the sixth most significant factor. In the same survey, students were 46 percent more likely than CEOs to identify "global thinking" as a crucial leadership skill in the coming years.[1]

In short, the next generation views globalization in a fundamentally different way—and this has ramifications for companies, governments, and international institutions around the world.

Can Globalization Build Better Leaders?

Working in an international setting has become the new normal for young leaders. In our MBA Student Survey, respondents had worked in an average of 3.8 countries, including their country of origin. International students tend to have worked in more countries—MBAs born outside the United States had worked in an average of 5.3 countries, versus 3 countries for those born in the United States (figure 2-1).

After pursuing international opportunities early in their careers, young MBAs expect to have worked in even more countries by the time they hit their midthirties. Our respondents expect to work, on average, in 4.6 countries within ten years of graduating from business school. Forty-eight percent intend to work in 1–3 countries, 32 percent intend to work in 4–6 countries, while 10 percent would like to work in 7–9. Once again, country of origin also matters in choosing how global one's future career

FIGURE 2-1

Today's MBAs seek global experiences

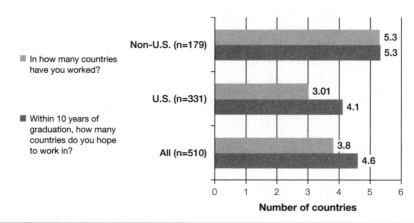

- In how many countries have you worked?
- Within 10 years of graduation, how many countries do you hope to work in?

Non-U.S. (n=179): 5.3 / 5.3
U.S. (n=331): 3.01 / 4.1
All (n=510): 3.8 / 4.6

Number of countries

will be: those born outside the United States intend to work in an average of 5.3 countries in the next ten years, compared to 4.1 countries among those born in the States. As a result, this generation of managers will have more global aspirations and experiences than any in history. This comes with its own challenges and opportunities.

The first challenge is the complexity that a boom in global business creates. Globalization, particularly trade liberalization, doesn't always move forward in a straight line. Despite the explosion in trade, with more than two hundred free trade agreements signed in the last two decades alone, the global economic crisis has brought about renewed fears of protectionism.[2] Yet despite the current gloom, it's hard to ignore the staggering explosion in the number of multinational companies around the world. There were approximately 79,000 multinational companies around the world in 2006, up from 7,258 in 1970.[3] And their leaders are seeing a very different global economic environment from the one that marked the past four decades. In the 2010 McKinsey Global Survey, 63 percent of more than 1,400 executives expected increasing volatility to be a permanent fixture of the global economy.[4] And in the IBM Leaders Survey, students pursuing MBAs were 28 percent more likely than CEOs to believe that the new economic environment is increasingly complex.[5] Inevitably, young people will play an important role in helping these new multinationals navigate uncertain global markets, especially in demographically young regions like India and Southeast Asia.

One respondent in our survey summed up the next generation's sentiments about globalization nicely: "Leaders will be forced to unify groups with greater and greater diversity. They will ask for sacrifice from men and women who have rarely been asked to give up much. They will be required to explain issues that are growing in complexity and scope with the same simplicity as leaders have been required to do in the past."

The second challenge is increasing and enriching the global exposure of young leaders early in their careers. This is crucial in helping them to get comfortable with uncertainty, and to grow the knowledge, skills, and networks to thrive in a world filled with it. The general importance of working abroad to develop one's skills seems to be more important among international MBAs. Eighty-two percent of non-U.S.-born MBAs agree or strongly agree that "by working abroad, I have learned new skills that will be valuable to my career," compared to 60 percent among American-born MBAs.

Young people will also have to address the crises of identity that globalization inevitably creates. Globalization has influenced young leaders' sense of identity in two ways: by helping shape common values that transcend national and cultural divisions, and by taking them out of their comfort zone and forcing them to learn more about themselves.

Growing up in a time of ubiquitous globalization and connectivity, today's twenty-something manager has developed values that transcend country or culture. As one of our respondents said, "Leadership will increasingly be attributed to improving the lives of others around the world. By the end of the twenty-first century, one's actions will be judged more on [their] impact, on what we call 'externalities' today. We will get better at determining the value of these externalities, and this will have to be a priority for any leader." What's fascinating is that as young people around the world develop a shared sense of global citizenship, they've also become more astute students of local and unfamiliar environments. Consider the cases of contributors such as Andy Goodman, who grew up in the United

Kingdom and helped the government of Qatar establish a new educational program, or U.S.-born Christopher Maloney, who worked in Rwanda. Their global perspective is built around a series of local experiences.

Global experiences have also become a crucial way for the next generation to develop a sense of personal purpose. In the MBA Student Survey, 61 percent of respondents agree or strongly agree that "working in different countries has helped me learn more about myself and what I plan to do in the future" (see figure 2-2). This holds more true for MBAs born outside the United States, as they are 42 percent more likely to agree with this statement than those born in the U.S. Part of this is driven by global educational opportunities. In 2005, there were 2.7 million foreign students enrolled at tertiary educational institutions around the world. And though traditional sources of foreign students such as Hong Kong, Japan, Korea, and Malaysia are expected to plateau and eventually decline, "sunshine" markets such as India, China, and Chile are expected to pick up the slack and drive the growth of mobile international students.[6]

FIGURE 2-2

MBAs find immense benefits in working abroad

Percent of respondents who agree or strongly agree with the following statements

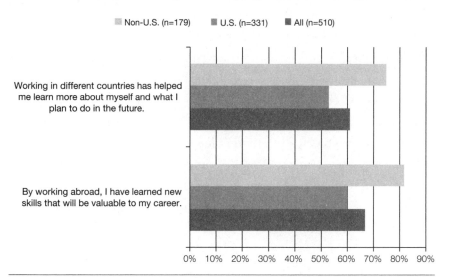

The third challenge is adapting to the shift in global political and economic affairs—the "rise of the rest." While it's been fashionable to say that globalization is no longer driven solely by the West, nobody really knows for certain how a multipolar world will take shape. This shift has enormous consequences. A unipolar world is shifting to a complex multipolar global economy. Chinese and Indian companies have been aggressively expanding overseas. Indian companies announced more than a thousand M&A deals, valued at $72 billion, between 2000 and 2008.[7] Chinese companies, meanwhile, are buying foreign companies from Africa to Singapore to gain access to precious oil, gas, and mineral resources to fuel the country's expansion. The share of developing Asia in global GDP has more than tripled to 23 percent in 2010, compared to 7 percent in 1980.[8]

Young MBAs see this trend. When asked which countries are the most important for businesspeople to understand in the next ten years, respondents of the MBA Student Survey voted China the overwhelming favorite, with 63 percent decisively ranking the world's most populous country first. India came in a distant second with 11 percent, and other developing countries were frequently highlighted.

The rise of the rest undeniably requires integrative work across functions, cultures, and classes. Young leaders will have to adapt to places where extreme poverty is spurring new ways of creating value through the role of private enterprise in delivering public infrastructure such as water, energy, and health care, or minimizing externalities such as pollution and social inequality. When asked openly on how leadership will change in the twenty-first century, learning to manage in an interdisciplinary way emerged as a recurring theme on the MBA Student Survey. As one student summed up nicely, "I think that leaders will be forced to work globally in a way they haven't before—requiring leaders to understand and adapt to different cultures, manage teams and relationships that span the globe, piece together divisions and companies that operate under completely different environments."

Bridging Two Worlds

An India Story

SANYOGITA AGGARWAL leads business development at Dev Bhumi
Cold Chain Ltd. in Delhi, India. She received her MBA at Harvard
Business School in 2010. San talks about the decision to return to
India after studying abroad and the surprising, often counterintu-
itive, lessons she's learned in bringing global best practices to a
traditional family business.

Upon graduation from Cornell, I had to choose between two paths. One was
to work for Morgan Stanley in New York; the other was to work in our family
agribusiness company in India. Most of my best friends were going to be in
New York, and Morgan Stanley offered a traditional path to prestigious institutions for higher education. On the other hand, I also longed to be home. It
was a personally hard decision to make. But in the end, I chose India.

India was not only my home; it was also the new land of opportunity.
It was poised for explosive growth in the coming decade, the place where
we would witness societal change unfold. With the second-largest population in the world and retail giants like Walmart and Carrefour zeroing
in on India as the "next big thing," there was no doubt in my mind that
the future here would be full of promise and optimism. This was a far cry
from the India of the 1970s, which suffered from political instability,
hyperinflation, high unemployment, and decrepit industries. The bright
optimism in India in the first decade of the twenty-first century mirrored
that of the United States in the 1950s. And it was contagious.

So, I decided to work in Delhi with my dad in his agribusiness company,
Dev Bhumi Cold Chain Ltd. The company is a complete one-solution
provider for farm-fresh produce, starting at the farm and ending on the
supermarket shelves. I was beginning to look forward to the experience.

Confronting Reality at Home

When I started working with my father, I was expecting it to be familiar territory. I was hungry and passionate to do big things in an environment I thought I understood. Brimming with ideas, bursting with ambition, and full of confidence, I had no inkling of the troubles ahead. The next few months brought reality home for me.

The company was entrenched in the "family business" way of working. In other words, employees were not evaluated on any performance metrics, work was carried out in an ad hoc manner, and there was a lack of organization and systems. Many thought that the business of fresh produce was fit only for men. Women would never be able to adapt. Consequently, I was the only woman in the company. Not only did some of the old senior management object to my coming to the office, but some of the new female staff that I hired faced a lot of heat. One of the new female MBAs hired for marketing faced significant opposition and noncooperation from various fronts, and eventually she quit. Furthermore, many in the company disproportionately valued experience over education. My American education was seen as an obstacle rather than an accomplishment. My "new" ways were despised, looked upon with suspicion, and labeled as impractical.

One of my very first projects was to set up a mineral water plant at the company's Himalayan facility. This project had been sidelined due to skepticism and contention within the organization about its future benefits. So when I decided to conduct a feasibility study to conclusively decide the potential, there was widespread dissent, touting this exercise as a waste of energy and company resources. Every activity I undertook for this project met with hostility and noncooperation. Halfway through the study, my budget was completely withdrawn for a few months because I was told that the company resources needed to be dedicated to core activities.

Four months into the job, I was seriously considering quitting. What made me stay?

Establishing Roots, Making a Commitment

Indian agriculture has long suffered from outdated pre- and postharvest technologies as well as antiquated systems. The average yield of apples for the Indian farmer, for example, is approximately 5 metric tons per hectare, compared to a whopping 60 metric tons per hectare for his European or American counterpart. In addition, an estimated 40 percent of fresh produce is lost in value and kind due to the lack of cold chain infrastructure in the country. Despite these dismally low yields and the staggering wastage, India continues to command a 10 percent share of the global production of fruits and 13.7 percent of vegetables. The opportunity is simply mind-boggling. With the right systems in place, India could very well become the "fruit bowl" of the world. A complete cold chain infrastructure that starts at the farm gate with procurement facilities for the farmers; takes the freshly harvested produce through the entire chain of cold storage facilities, uses refrigerated trucking, packaging, and palletizing; and delivers fresh produce into the hands of the end consumer would elevate India to the world platform in agriculture. However, one of the biggest obstacles to achieving this objective is educating the Indian farmer.

To do so, our company started the Yield Improvement Program. The objective of the program was to work closely with farmers to introduce higher-yielding varieties of fruit and educate them on the latest pre- and postharvest technologies, in conjunction with following food safety protocols and promoting sustainable agriculture. During one of our initial visits to the Himalayas, while conversing with the locals, one farmer said, "We absolutely love this program and are fully on board with you. If your intentions materialize, generations to come will never forget you." This left a lasting impression on me and at that point, I realized the immense impact this program could have on the farmers in the area and, eventually, the entire country. I believed that the goals I was pursuing reconciled the profit motive with the right underlying social objectives. I fell in love with what we were doing, and this outweighed the daily predicaments I faced in the workplace. So, I decided to stay and confront my problems head on.

Changing the Status Quo

I learned several important life-changing lessons, lessons that hopefully will be relevant to anyone hoping to do business in India, working in a family business, or entering an unfamiliar market.

First, I witnessed firsthand how change is always resisted. The best way to make change is to first understand the reasons behind the status quo, then become a part of the system, gain people's trust, and make the change slowly but steadily. It's easy to approach problematic situations thinking that most things should be changed from the ground up, as fast as one can. But I realized that confrontational attempts at change are the most damaging. Most of the time, there aren't any real reasons for this stance except for the manager's hubris to leave his mark quickly. When I got past my youthful naiveté, it dawned on me that the most meaningful changes must be initiated at a slower pace.

In my particular case, to address the sensibilities of the staff, I started wearing only Indian attire to the office. Once everyone got comfortable with me, I slowly changed to Indo-Western clothing and then to my normal Western outfits. For the female staff, I decided to hire candidates already known and trusted within the company. For example, we hired the daughter of an existing staff member, and since she already knew most of the people in the company, she found it much easier to adapt and fit in. Most of the senior management, who had previously resisted all female hires, considered her like their own daughter. Hence, they were more protective of her and cooperative in helping her understand the work and the systems.

I learned that local conditions can lead to very different and unique solutions. In the United States, for example, I would never have considered this approach for fear that my action be termed as favoritism. But it worked wonders in my Indian situation. This woman quickly grew very comfortable working in the difficult environment, and the staff soon acclimated itself to her. This ultimately opened the door to new female hires who now had not only a more receptive organization but also a ready mentor.

Second, I learned not to fall prey to a one-size-fits-all philosophy of leadership. Unique problems always call for unique solutions. For example, in my initial months in the company, I came to realize that our employees placed a strong emphasis on relationships with clients and suppliers, and less, or none at all, on quantitative analyses. Business decisions were often made on the basis of old associations and relationships, and completely without any NPV or IRR calculations. Thus, the most important leadership skill I've learned—and would encourage my peers to learn—is to be sensitive to the intricacies of the situation at hand.

I soon realized that an amalgamation of both quantitative and relationship-driven approaches would lead to a "best of both worlds" result. Coming from a strong educational background in quantitative business management, I found focusing on relationships baseless and immature. But I soon realized the immaturity of my own thinking. There was no black-and-white answer to this. No one way of working was better than the other; the two were simply different. The Indian way of working relied heavily on a "trust" culture, and a lot of business was conducted based on good faith. One glaring example of this was what I saw in the fields while talking to farmers during the procurement season. Huge multinational mammoths were out to procure from the same fields and the same farmers at higher than market rates. Despite the monetary advantages, the farmers somehow preferred to sell to us. Logically, this made no sense. When asked, one of them replied, "It's because we have faith in you. We have worked with Dev Bhumi for many years and we know you would never cheat us. Money is not everything and our relationship is based on a lot more than just rupees."

Last, I learned interesting lessons on how to adapt to a family business environment, a situation that I foresee several of my peers face as they return to Asia, where family-owned and -controlled companies are the norm. Working in a family business is not only about the bottom line, but also about legacy and emotional attachments. Many projects in family businesses are driven more by the founder's passion than by purely economic reasons. The founders often invest their personal wealth and life into building these businesses, and many of their memories are associated with the grueling efforts they put in.

Family businesses have been and will continue to remain important drivers in India's economic future. They account for roughly 65 percent of the economy's GNP and for 75 percent of the employment in the country.[9] The new generation inherits the responsibility of taking the business much further than the previous one and needs to earn the credibility and respect of its peers and employees. I learned that working in a family business also requires a very entrepreneurial attitude, especially in interacting within the company.

In my case, as the fourth generation in the family business, I was expected to hit the ground running from day one. My challenge was more than just problem solving; it was also getting buy-in from the staff, proving to them that I was capable of the responsibilities handed to me. The first approach I applied was to start small with projects that could be completed in a short period of time. Small projects allowed me to have a lot of interaction with different groups of people and better get to know them and their problems at work. This increased our comfort level of working together and we soon transformed from a group to a team.

As the next generation transitions in, it becomes important to thoroughly understand the undercurrents of the business. In family-run companies, often the staff members are equally committed and passionate about the business and share the founder's values and principles. The next generation needs to demonstrate the very same ideals that represent the foundations of the company. One of our company ideals is to provide for better living to all staff members through higher education opportunities and extracurricular experiences. I initiated English classes at the office for staff who were not fluent. We also started the policy of paying for complete school education for children who showed high academic performance in school. All this helped the staff to realize that I was just as committed to them as they were to our company.

In retrospect, the decision to continue on in India turned out to be one of the most fulfilling commitments of my life. It was here that I learned what doing business in the real world truly means, what it means to be a part of the system and yet be an agent of change, and what it means to become "comfortable being uncomfortable."

QatarDebate

Education, Civic Engagement, and Leadership in the Arabian Gulf

ANDREW GOODMAN graduated from the Harvard Business School in 2010 as a Baker Scholar. Before attending HBS, Andrew cofounded QatarDebate, a civic engagement initiative that aims to develop and support the standard of open discussion and debate among students and young people in Qatar and the broader Arab world. Andrew's story helps young leaders appreciate the importance of cultural intelligence, the right partnerships, and a pipeline of local leaders in building ventures in unfamiliar markets.

If you had asked me when I started college in England if I expected to find myself two years later in the midday heat of the Qatari desert, being filmed balancing precariously atop a camel with a Scottish man in a kilt, the answer would probably have been no. The state of Qatar is a tiny desert country at the tip of the Arabian Gulf. A conservative Muslim country, ruled by an emir, it is home to 1.6 million people and the world's third-largest reserves of natural gas, from which the country derives its prodigious wealth. Before the summer of 2007 it was certainly not a place I had ever imagined commuting to every month during my final year at Oxford and the first year of my MBA at Harvard.

It was a passion for education that drew me to the Middle East. Qatar is richer per capita than Luxembourg or Switzerland, but its scores on the PISA tests, which assess students' educational literacy in math, reading, and science, are comparable to those of the former Soviet republics of Azerbaijan and Kyrgyzstan. In historically failing many students, Qatar's education system is by no means unique. However, unlike most other countries with very poor educational outcomes, Qatar has a rare combination of advantages: the leadership, willingness, and funding to implement genuine education reforms.

From the early 2000s, the emir, Qatari government, and Qatar Foundation embarked on an ambitious education reform program. From these reforms came substantial changes in both secondary and tertiary education. At the secondary level, reformed, charter-style "independent" schools were created that used a new syllabus and were accountable for their results to a Supreme Education Council. At the tertiary level, Qatar Foundation invested billions of dollars to develop an "Education City" that housed the branch campuses of six leading U.S. universities and numerous other education initiatives.

An Unusual Job Interview

My time in Qatar began in the summer of 2007 with an unusual job interview. Alex Just, a colleague from Oxford, and I were invited by Ali Willis, an executive director at Qatar Foundation, to spend ten days in Qatar, working with students to improve their debating, civic engagement, and critical thinking skills. At the end of the ten days, Alex and I were asked to attend a meeting with Her Highness Sheikha Mozah Bint Nasser Al-Misned, the Queen Consort of Qatar and, in her role as chairperson of Qatar Foundation, one of the leading education reformers in the Middle East. We were told simply to expect the unexpected.

At the meeting, we suggested that Qatar Foundation create and fund a national organization to work with students and teachers within the Qatari education system to improve critical thinking and civic engagement. Our background had been in competitive debate, where teams of students would compete in national and international competitions to hone arguments and marshal evidence to support an assigned position on a variety of moral, political, and social issues. We believed that this type of training—at that time mostly alien to the region—built skills, civic engagement, and a connection to a global community of high-achieving students. Such a national organization could therefore be based initially around a culture of debate and discussion, gradually expanding to incorporate other elements and pedagogies.

As we flew back to the United Kingdom following the meeting, we reflected that Qatar was a fascinating country, and despite our preconceived notions about conservatism in the Arabian Gulf, a large number of the students we had met seemed to embrace the concept of debating important political, moral, and social issues. We knew, though, that governments and national foundations were not generally in the habit of entrusting millions of dollars of funding to unproven undergraduates.

It was therefore a surprise when Ali called us in Oxford a few days later to say that Sheikha Mozah had recommended that Qatar Foundation fund our project, and that we should make arrangements to start work immediately as program directors . . . in Qatar. Alex and I would be working under a mandate to fill just a small piece of Qatar's broader educational puzzle—student engagement and critical thinking—creating a national organization that would foster an emerging culture of debate and discussion among students in Qatar, with the hope of developing the country's "leaders of tomorrow."

QatarDebate

Over the eighteen months after our initial meeting, Alex and I, under the direction of Ali and with the support of Qatar Foundation, created and managed a national civic engagement initiative for Qatar that would become known as "QatarDebate." Life took on a surreal rhythm, writing undergraduate essays in the rain and gloom of the Oxford winter one day, and the next, pitching the importance of debate as an educational tool to education ministers from around the Arab world in the heat of the Qatari capital, Doha, living out of suitcases and working from Qatar Foundation's headquarters, airport lounges, and our university dorm rooms.

In its first eighteen months of operation as a not-for-profit start-up, QatarDebate worked with more than three thousand students and teachers in thirty schools and universities in Qatar. We delivered a curriculum to students that encouraged them to think critically about the world, contest complex concepts, and challenge political and social beliefs. Schools and universities formed debate teams that constructively and often heatedly discussed policies from censorship to negotiating with terrorists to Islamic dress on a weekly basis. At an international level, we created, selected, and coached the first Qatari national debate team, which went on to break records at the World Schools Debating Championship as a first-time entrant. We distributed curriculum materials on debate and civic engagement to partners in more than fifty countries, including every state in the Arab world. We even successfully bid to host the world championships in Qatar in 2010, exposing Qatari students to some of the brightest young minds from more than forty countries, including the United States, Israel, and Mongolia.

We were given access to former heads of state and education ministers from around the Middle East to explain the importance of debate and citizenship education, and provide a blueprint for similar national programs in their countries. In the media, we brought student debate to prominence on the often controversial satellite channel, Al Jazeera, and were featured in an award-winning documentary that premiered at the Tribeca Film Festival in New York. Sitting in a cinema on the Lower West Side and observing New Yorkers watch Qatari, Iraqi, and Syrian students engaging in an intellectually rich discussion of U.S. policy in the Middle East since 9/11 on screen is an experience that I will never forget.

Launching a Start-Up in the Arabian Gulf

The experiences of launching and operating QatarDebate highlighted several of the challenges that come as part of launching an organization as an outsider in an unfamiliar environment.

How to organize. The relatively simple process of creating an LLC, public limited company, 501(c)(3), or registered charity is typically taken for granted in the United States and Western Europe. In an emerging market like Qatar, the process of creating an organization presents often over-looked challenges and pitfalls. To create a new charity in Qatar requires paperwork, time, and approval from the government. We launched QatarDebate within an existing organization, Qatar Foundation, and as a result were able to start operations immediately and benefit from the foundation's funding and goodwill. In contrast, even major multinationals entering Gulf markets as new entities find themselves waiting several months for the required documents and permits to be approved. However, to position your new entity within or in partnership with an existing organization is to be bound by additional policies, procedures, and protocols in the longer term. Young managers confronted with the realities of an unfamiliar market must find balance between speed to market and freedom of operation, or be fortunate enough to find a rare partner that offers both.

How to bridge cultural divides. Within our first few weeks in Qatar, it quickly became apparent that there was a gulf between the fundamental paradigms of U.S. and Qatari education. When our Western-educated trainers entered the classroom, one of the first questions they faced from Arab students was simply, "What is debate?" To many students, the concept of critically discussing important political, moral, and social issues was entirely new. Alex and I were often unsettled early on when confronted by culturally "different" events—in one instance a highly educated woman wearing the *niqab* (face veil) and yet strongly advocating that this choice was a woman's right and an expression of freedom. We quickly learned that the Arabic word *inshallah* (God willing) had a multiplicity of meanings, and often wondered if specific divine intervention was required to accelerate meetings, permits, and procurement orders. Managers in emerging markets must draw a mental line between those cultural differences they will embrace and those things on which they will stand firm.

How to measure impact. Observing the academic progress of students who had been through QatarDebate's programs demonstrated in *our* minds the ways in which the coaching improved their critical thinking, structure, and English fluency. To prove impact, though, we needed to develop a much more rigorous assessment process that tracked cohorts of students over time. Young managers in emerging markets should be aware that they will have to modify their existing assumptions about research and tracking. Market research in the Gulf is thought to be at least twice as expensive as in Western markets, and traditional survey methods face severe constraints. When entering a market in the Gulf, organizations need to have rigorous KPIs (key performance indicators) to avoid spending large amounts with limited ability to prove impact, but managers also need to be specific up front about what meaningful data they will actually be able to collect, sometimes departing from standard metrics and getting creative about what measures might provide a reliable proxy for some other outcome that they are not able to observe directly.

How to lead. When it comes to leadership in the Gulf, we found that small is often beautiful. By working with students in a relatively small country, we genuinely had the potential to change the way those young people will think about the world in the future, for better or for worse. Those students whom QatarDebate spent hundreds of hours coaching, now imbued with a new set of tools with which to evaluate the world, will very likely become the key decision makers within business, government, and society in Qatar. When observing those multinationals who had been successful in Qatar, we saw a similar phenomenon. Successful companies who had entered the market brought experienced expat staff, but over time, the most successful companies hired a small number of very talented locals into genuine leadership development schemes. These Qataris were given incredible amounts of training and exposure, and they were told to aspire to be the future CEOs and executives at those multinationals. Less successful firms complained about a dearth of local talent, but the market leaders set about generating their own local talent pipelines from the very beginning.

How to transition. For a national organization to become truly sustainable in a world in which individual leadership is only ever temporary, it needs to be run, at least in part, by nationals. Expatriates can bring significant expertise and dynamism, but they will never quite be able to match local managers in cultural insight, local knowledge, and a desire to make their lives in that country. Resistance to this reality is dangerous—the Gulf has historically seen many examples of the vicious cycle in which expats fear losing their positions in the longer term and therefore act to maximize short-term gains. Locals in turn perceive foreigners as concerned more about their short-term gains than long-term sustainability. Handing over control of QatarDebate's day-to-day operations and watching a new, Qatari leadership team embark on a new and different path was extremely challenging—QatarDebate was after all something that we had created—but it was the right thing to do to create a truly national organization.

Leaving Qatar

My time in Qatar drew to a close in July 2009 as the full transition to a Qatari leadership team for QatarDebate concluded, and I decided that I would return to the United Kingdom after completing the MBA. I look back on those eighteen months as my first leadership role—a plethora of incredible enriching, rewarding personal experiences. Many of the challenges faced were similar in nature, although definitely not in scale, to the challenges faced by countless case protagonists that I have subsequently encountered during my two years at HBS. With hindsight and the imparted wisdom of various cases and scenarios, I would certainly make many decisions differently. However, Qatar "made real" for me some things that had been lost over the course of the seven hundred or so MBA cases.

As I sat with a Qatari friend on Doha's Corniche on one of my last evenings in Qatar, watching the sun set over the Arabian Gulf, we found ourselves discussing the fascination modern business education in the United States has with "leadership." Leadership in the Gulf and beyond, my Qatari friend concluded, required the serenity to accept the things you cannot change, the courage to change the things you can, and the wisdom to know the difference.

Emerging Social Enterprise

Learning the Business of Agriculture in Tanzania

KATIE LAIDLAW is a consultant in the New York City office of the Boston Consulting Group. Prior to joining BCG, Katie was a senior associate at the Parthenon Group and served as executive director of Inspire, Inc., a nonprofit organization that advises community-based nonprofits. She is passionate about international development and future growth in public-private partnerships.

Deo, the local government agriculture officer assigned to Mhonda, directed me to sit in a red plastic chair as farmers entered the weathered brick structure in the center of the village. Mhonda, Tanzania, was my first stop along a series of village visits to gather field data through farmer group interviews during a summer internship with TechnoServe, a U.S-based international nonprofit focused on poverty reduction through economic development. TechnoServe hired me to work independently on a three-month study to analyze the fruit and vegetable markets of Tanzania. After a seven-hour truck ride over freeways, dirt roads, mud trails, and mountainous terrain, I was excited to continue learning about the business of agriculture in Tanzania firsthand from farmers.

I smiled at each farmer who entered the meeting space. They stared back at me with facial expressions exhibiting everything from cautious optimism to anxious skepticism. They were not yet sure of what I wanted or offered. I noticed how each farmer arrived with his or her own smoothed sitting stone. Seeing them sitting perched upon stones in seemingly uncomfortable, crouched positions, I felt instantly self-conscious about my thronelike chair. I then nearly committed a serious, albeit unintentional faux pas by attempting to lower myself discreetly to the dirt floor to join them. Deo quickly corrected my move before I fully sat down by simply stating, "Visitors sit in the chair. You must sit, you are a visitor."

Feeling a bit flustered, I quickly reviewed my questions for the group interview. The purpose of my project was twofold: to identify opportunities within or beyond the existing supply chain that could result in increased farmer income, and to submit a completed grant proposal in order to access funding for the implementation of any proposed plans.

For me, this opportunity to gain international field experience across private, nonprofit, and public sectors through TechnoServe was a dream. Social enterprise, the pursuit of innovative opportunities to create social value through market mechanisms, is one of my personal passions. I knew that this three-month experience would be a short-term entrée into a lifelong, multisector career at the intersection of business and social change.

Assembling the Puzzle Pieces

The data I gathered through farmer interviews informed the creation of a pro-forma profit and loss statement for growing and selling fruits and vegetables throughout the year. Starting with a baseline financial perspective, I brainstormed ways to change assumptions of cost and revenue drivers, with the goal of increasing farmer income. In addition to the more specific data inputs, farmer group interviews also answered questions about their savings rates (low), up-front seed and fertilizer input costs (high), and investments in more sophisticated processes like irrigation (low and rare). Due to the seasonality of planting and the lack of access to savings or banking, I could not directly ask farmers how much money they had made in profit in the past year. Instead, I cobbled this data together by analyzing what was planted and harvested throughout the year, typical high and low market prices, and what volumes were actually grown and sold.

Data collected in each village helped to narrow my focus on farmers producing primarily *mparachichi* (avocados) and *nyanya* (tomatoes). And thus, my "guacamole plan" was born. I honed in on the differences between these two fruits and suggested a comprehensive plan to support groups of farmers through pilot programs in two distinct farming regions in Tanzania. I supported TechnoServe's Tanzania country director to complete a grant proposal to a large U.S. international development funding agency identifying the need and income increases possible through interventions with avocado and tomato farmers. As the grant proposal served as a summary of my field findings to date, I started to recognize other peripheral constraints to operating in the international nonprofit space that impacted my understanding of the sector.

Patience, Not Speed, Is Required for Results

Constraints on time, human capital, or funding (or all three) are common across the private, public, and nonprofit sectors. While success in the for-profit sector is often measured by stock performance, progress in the nonprofit sector, particularly international development, can be more challenging. Stock prices change in real time. Measurable gains in tomato production or avocado quality require a longer runway to implement change and measure impact, and adjustments in perceptions, culture, and expectations in emerging economies are even more ethereal.

I was surprised to discover that most global aid programs are built upon the expectation of three to four years of funding, often with no renewal. This funding approach is severely disconnected from any longer-term goal of institutionalizing improvement. Just as many development programs hit their stride in meeting goals, funding ends, leaving a well-designed idea half-tested and uncertainty around what truly "worked."

The nonprofit sector plays a unique role in global capitalism. It is not predominantly concerned with campaigning and election as in the public sector, nor subject to the scrutiny of private sector shareholders. It is, instead, a useful go-between. The sector provides a way to work with and within global markets and local politics to encourage real, on-the-ground change. But the nonprofit sector, particularly in the field of international development, will need to increasingly free itself from the constraints of short-term financing to achieve lasting impact.

Applying Lessons from One Sector to the Other, and Vice Versa

At the end of my time in Tanzania, I felt confident in what I had learned from my experience as well as in what I had contributed to designing a program for agricultural economic development. This experience confirmed my own hypothesis that future leaders will be better equipped to tackle the problems of tomorrow by being successful in operating across geographies and sectors today. Leaders must also recognize that there are no longer silos but, rather, continuous opportunities to achieve greater social good through collaboration.

Throughout my time in Tanzania, I relied upon skills from my private sector training, my previous nonprofit sector involvement, and my willingness to learn and understand new approaches specific to the international development community. The opportunity to work in agriculture provided me with new information and perspectives that I have since applied in other industries. By establishing a consistent company relationship with a single organization or encouraging employee choice, for-profit businesses today can benefit from expanded employee perspectives gained by working in a nonprofit or public sector arena, in very unfamiliar environments.

The same benefits of global, cross-sector involvement can result when nonprofits seek for-profit or public sector resources as a complement to their internal capabilities. Though I lived and worked in Tanzania for a brief time, I felt that my final outputs contributed to longer-term knowledge and resources of TechnoServe. Nonprofit leaders today can fill gaps or further challenge their organizations by looking beyond their sector and benefiting from short-term engagements with public and private sector organizations.

Investing Time and Resources for the Changing Global Economy

Upon returning to the HBS campus, I served as a copresident of the Social Enterprise Club, the student-run umbrella organization offering programming and networking opportunities for HBS students interested in this intersection of market mechanisms and the social sector. The Social Enterprise Club continues to grow in membership and is currently one of the largest clubs on campus. This membership metric demonstrates the increased awareness by business school students of the personal value of doing good in one's community *and* doing well in one's professional life, concurrently throughout a career.

During the start of my fall semester, I learned that the proposal submitted for this avocado and tomato project had received a multimillion dollar grant. It was a deeply fulfilling and satisfying outcome. News of winning the grant reminded me of so many distinctive memories of my summer traversing along the highways and dirt roads of Tanzania's Southern Highlands. My awkward and uncertain start in Mhonda village, seated in a red plastic chair, was a distant but wonderful reminder of future possibilities to tackle some of our society's largest problems through the intersection of private, nonprofit, and public resources. And young people like me can find an enhanced sense of purpose through pursuing them.

Global Citizen Year

Learning from the World

ABIGAIL FALIK is the founder and CEO of Global Citizen Year and a recognized expert in the fields of education reform, international development, and social innovation. For her work as a leading social entrepreneur, she has received awards from the Draper Richards Foundation, the Mind Trust, and the Harvard Business School. Abigail has made a commitment to using global immersion as a way to equip the next generation of leaders with the empathy and insight needed to overcome twenty-first-century challenges.

Today, fewer than 1 percent of American college graduates have ventured beyond the wealthiest environments to meet any of the world's 4 billion people living on less than $3 a day, according to the Open Doors report sponsored by the U.S. State Department. Without firsthand experience with the global majority, how can American leaders possibly expect to lead with global skills and insight?

Early Journey, Lifelong Commitment

When I was sixteen, my sense of self and the world was blown open when I spent a summer in a rural Nicaraguan village. Living with a host family, I learned to speak Spanish and make tortillas by hand, spent my days working in the fields, and taught English in the community's schools. And while my motivations as a do-gooder high school student were initially to provide some form of "help" to a community plagued by material poverty, it didn't take long for me to realize that my hosts were far from victims to be pitied. Instead, they were resourceful, persistent, and better attuned than any well-intentioned foreigner to what was really needed to lift themselves out of poverty.

Energized by my first experience working abroad, I called the Peace Corps to see if I could join when I graduated from high school. When I was told to call back in four years, I was struck by the incredible irony that our country allows young people to wield a gun in military service at age eighteen, but requires a college degree or significant work experience to join the Peace Corps.[10]

I was determined to find a way to continue learning from the world. Without these experiences, how could my higher education be relevant to life outside the classroom?

As an undergraduate at Stanford, my coursework focused on poverty, inequality, and international development. Always eager to test what I was learning in my classes in the real world, I took time off midway through college to return to my host community in Nicaragua and support them in developing their first library.

Armed with grant money and Spanish language books, I arrived in Nicaragua with what seemed like a simple goal: to help bring to life a community's dream of building a library. What transpired, however, was far more messy and challenging than I could ever have imagined. Soon, I was the forewoman on a construction project in a culture and language that weren't my own. The daily obstacles ranged from navigating political faultlines to secure the permits for our new construction site, to waiting for days on end for the rains so that we could mix the cement foundation.

My learning that year was incalculably more valuable than anything I had gleaned in a classroom. The experience was so profound that it left me with a question that I've now spent my professional life trying to answer: how different would the world be if every young American had experiences like this?

Years later, after a decade spent working across the nonprofit sector in the United States and abroad, I found myself increasingly disillusioned watching good intentions and resources fall short in the face of intractable social challenges. It was when one boss told me to rein in my ambition and begin to "think smaller" that I realized I needed to go to business school. With my vision for using education to drive social change on a global scale squarely in mind, I hoped to learn how to build a high-impact enterprise where "nonprofit" would describe our tax status, but not our management style.

Global Citizen Year Is Born

Just before graduation from HBS, I entered the Pitch for Change competition—an annual event that features the most promising new social ventures from around the world. With an impassioned elevator pitch, I proposed something outrageous: that someday, every American student would have an opportunity to spend a "Global Citizen Year" working in the developing world before college.

When I won first prize in the competition, I was shocked and humbled. Most important, the experience served as a critical moment of commitment. From the excitement in the nine-hundred-seat Burden Auditorium, I could tell that this wasn't just my idea anymore; instead it was a vision that had resonance far beyond me. In that moment, I realized that my calling as a leader is to help catalyze a transformation in how America prepares its young people for effective leadership in our globalized world.

We all have a sense that today's youth have not been well prepared for college or for a twenty-first-century global workforce. The statistics are striking. Fewer than 9 percent of anglophone Americans develop fluency in another language (compared to 54 percent of our European peers), and just 1 percent study abroad (and of those who do, two-thirds don't venture beyond Western Europe). In a world where economic recession, climate change, and poverty transcend geopolitical boundaries to affect us all, how can we possibly expect to overcome these challenges if we can't work effectively—and collaboratively—across borders?

One year after graduating from HBS, I had raised over $1 million from leading venture philanthropists—individuals and foundations looking to maximize the *social return* on their early investment—to launch Global

Citizen Year. I built a founding team, and together we launched a pilot program with an inaugural cohort of Fellows—young people from across the United States who had the courage to buck the cultural pressure that moves our youth straight along the conveyor belt from high school to college. Instead, each deferred admission from schools ranging from Harvard to Evergreen State, with the aim of taking their education into their own hands and out into the world, then starting college the following year with a clearer sense of purpose and a more global perspective.

Our founding Fellows came from diverse geographies and varied socioeconomic and cultural backgrounds, but they were united by their passion and potential as leaders.

In September, as their friends were heading off for their first weeks in college dorms, our Fellows came to the Bay Area for our inaugural U.S. Training Institute. We introduced them to leaders across the public, private, and social sectors, and helped them develop a framework for understanding the experience they would soon embark on overseas. During the U.S. training, the Fellows had to reflect on two core questions that would help focus their learning objectives in the months ahead. The first was external: What are the causes of poverty? What approaches are most effective in improving peoples' lives? The second was internal: What is my authentic style as a leader? Who am I when I'm so far from my comfort zone? What is it that really makes me happy? While these may seem like obvious questions for a young person, for the most part, this type of inquiry is systematically excluded from the conventional high school and college curriculum.

From here, our Fellows traveled in teams, each guided by a youth development professional we hired and trained to be a "team leader," to their country posts in Africa and Latin America. The first month was in an urban center where the group members acclimated to their new context while engaging in an intensive language immersion and cross-cultural orientation. Next, the Fellows moved to more rural communities, where they were paired with host families and apprenticeships—work placements that matched their interests and skills with the needs of the community.

In Sengalkam, Senegal, an aspiring doctor spent a few days a week shadowing a traditional healer, and the other days working in a public pharmacy and a private clinic. In Seibkotone, Senegal, another Fellow revived the school's library and unpacked the box of U.S. government–donated computers that no one knew how to set up. A few weeks later she was holding workshops to teach teachers to use Google and Wikipedia for the first time. In Santo Tomas, Guatemala, another Fellow worked with a women's group on nutrition issues, and supported the development of a community garden.

Our Fellows had netbooks and flipcams, and throughout their experience corresponded regularly with K–12 classrooms and communities in the United States. Stateside, as interest in their work grew, we helped ensure that our Fellows' experiences touched the lives of their parents, peers, and a broader public through partnerships with Current TV and op-eds in the *Huffington Post* and *New York Times*. A change of mind-set may begin with our Fellows, but ultimately, we hope they will create a ripple that reverberates across America.

In May 2010, our first class of Fellows returned home—transformed in their sense of themselves and the world and hungry to start their college careers. They spent the summer sharing what they had learned about their guiding questions through presentations in classrooms, blog posts, and publications in their hometown papers. In the fall, they headed off to colleges across the country, having developed the passion and perseverance that make the difference in college, careers, and life.

With this first year's success, my vision is emboldened and we are now on track to triple the size of next year's cohort, with the aim of engaging ten thousand Fellows annually by 2020. We are working to do more than build another exchange program—our aim is to catalyze a movement that engages colleges, companies, governments, and social enterprises around the world.

As our effort gains momentum, Global Citizen Year can fundamentally restructure the way young Americans learn about and engage with the world. By supporting emerging leaders at the moment they are most ripe to new ideas, growth, and exploration, we can awaken their true potential. Our Fellows enter college knowing what they want to pursue, why, and how to use their education to have an impact in business and public service—for our nation and our world. Over time, we will build an undeniable force: a pipeline of new American leaders with an ethic of service, the fluencies needed to communicate across languages and cultures, and the ability to work at the interface of the public, private, and nonprofit sectors to build a more peaceful and prosperous world.

Broader Lessons for Business Leaders

At its core, good leadership requires empathy, and empathy requires first-hand experience. If we aspire to develop global leaders, then we must also understand the breadth and diversity of experiencing people, places, and problems that we won't otherwise experience if we stay close to home.

As Global Citizen Year prepares the next generation of leaders, American corporations can—and should—be equipping our current leaders with the empathy and judgment they need to make effective decisions in a globalized world. Following the lead of programs like IBM's Corporate Service Corps, a growing number of companies have developed programs that enable employees to live and work in the developing world as a means of learning about new markets, building internal capacity, and supporting employee retention. But this kind of experiential learning must become the norm, not the exception. GE should send product designers to rural communities to truly understand which technological innovations are—and are not—appropriate in improving lives at the bottom of the pyramid. The Gap should send product managers to work in the plants where their clothing is being produced.

Not until we walk in another's shoes can we truly feel others' hopes and fears, and have the wisdom to know what it would mean to work together toward a common cause. One day, we will have redefined effective leadership training to include firsthand knowledge of people, languages, cultures, and solutions that can only be found beyond our borders. Simply put, we can't afford not to.

The Business of Reconciliation

How Cows and Co-ops Are Paving the Way
for Genuine Reconciliation in Rwanda

CHRIS MALONEY works as a management consultant on projects for
public and private sector clients across Africa, especially in agriculture, health care, and policy. A native of New York, he holds a BA in
economics and African/African-American studies from Stanford
University, and both an MPA/International Development and an MBA
from Harvard University. In reflecting on his experience in Rwanda,
Chris realizes how unfamiliar environments abroad can lead one to
reevaluate traditional notions of business risk and social return.

It was late at night, and I was tired. Perfect timing for my inner consultant to become narrow and critical. I had come up to Rwanda to look at
ways in which the main agriculture challenges in the country were being
addressed by both the government and foreign donors. I was knee-deep
in documents, sitting outside on a typically breezy, eerily silent Kigali
evening. As I read through the reports, my mind started raising red flags
on two programs in particular:

- The "one cow per poor family" program intended to get every poor
  family in Rwanda a cow—thereby increasing the amount of milk,
  protein, and fertilizer available to the average family, which
  sounded good on paper.[11] But this was in the most densely populated country in Africa, where almost everyone was poor (living on
  less than $1 per day) and stuck on tiny hillsides. How on earth
  would this work? There were few people with the skills to care for
  the cows, little land for grazing, little land on which to use the new
  source of fertilizer, and little credit to allow the farmers to expand

their farming activities once they had the cow—it was hard to see how this program could be sustainable.

- In the government's action plan, the co-op approach seemed to be the main way of solving problems—a tough way to go.[12] For farmers to move beyond subsistence, they need to be able to buy the right inputs to grow more and access the right markets to sell more. Co-ops are one way to do this (form a group to access credit for inputs and sell products in bulk), but they are notoriously messy and hard to sustain. There are challenges with misaligned incentives, poor leadership and management, and too many stakeholders. Individual entrepreneurs, on the other hand, were more what I was used to seeing in African agriculture transformations—individuals who would have private sector incentives to work with farmers to help them access inputs, and aggregate their output to help them access markets in bulk and get better prices for everyone. But such entrepreneurs seemed to figure only vaguely in the Rwandan government's plans, and I couldn't figure out why. Why take the riskier co-op approach?

My mind started to wander. As with everything in Rwanda, one cannot ignore the 1994 genocide, in which Hutus, the largest ethnic group, systematically slaughtered a million Tutsis in one hundred days under an extremist Hutu government. This led to the displacement of millions of Rwandans, both Hutu and Tutsi, before Tutsi rebels came in and stopped the genocide. This was a brutal time, involving machetes and constant fear, where friends and neighbors somehow switched off their humanity for four months. This hotel where I stayed—the Serena, Kigali's main business hotel—was called the Hotel des Diplomates during this awful period. The Diplomates was the antithesis of the Hotel des Mille Collines, which was right down the road, and now famous from the movie *Hotel Rwanda*. As opposed to the Mille Collines, which had served as a sanctuary during the genocide, the Diplomates served as the genocidal Hutu government's headquarters as the Tutsi rebels eventually closed in on Kigali. It was here at the Diplomates where district governors of the Hutu extremist government were ordered to update the ministers on how fast their "work" was progressing—that is, killing all the Tutsis in their home regions—and where many grisly executions were carried out on the top floors. But now, sixteen years later, I couldn't even fathom such a thing. The hotel had since been bought, gutted, and transformed into a modern facility that could have been anywhere in the world. Today the place was sterile, and it was comfortable. And just below this shiny surface, it was filled, like everything in Rwanda, with the ghosts of the past.[13]

How does a country begin to put such spirits to rest? Perhaps, amazingly, the way the government was going about its agriculture transformation activities was one such way. As I thought about these programs, and as I pressed for more feedback in interviews with various people around Rwanda over the subsequent days, I realized that both the cow program and the co-ops were trying, perhaps, to use business as a means of reconciliation. To me, it was a startling idea.

Spending some time in the rural villages and meeting with farmers themselves painted the picture for me. After the genocide, many villages' lands had to be completely reconfigured as many families had been killed, or fled, while other people, sometimes totally new, came to the village for the first time. In a few places I visited, genocide victims were given plots of land right next door to someone who had been a perpetrator of the genocide, thereby encouraging some form of reconciliation since they had to see each other every day. It was not easy. One woman I spoke to, who had lost most of her family, simply said, "It's very hard, but he is my neighbor." How does one rebuild in a setting like that? It was here where I began to see that the cow program had a part to play in this story. A program rule in many places was that the first calf of the cow must be given to a neighbor. In this way, the cow program was not just a subsidy or "gift from the government," but rather an asset with a strong future value that brought neighbors together and gave strength to families where so much had been lost. This gift of the first calf was incredibly significant. A cow, it turns out, can often provide a family with just enough cash to access higher education, and have a steadier, more diversified diet, among other benefits. As I began to understand it, the gift of a cow could change lives, as it would work across families, and help, in some small way, to aid in reconciliation—if nothing else, it would certainly help bind neighbors together.

Rebuilding communities was the other big challenge. The fractured villages needed something to pull them together—not just at the family-to-family level (as was being done with the cows), but at the community level. This is where the co-ops came in. As tough as they are to build, manage, and sustain, the role of co-ops in a Rwandan village was more than just helping farmers improve their income. Looking closer, I saw that the co-ops would give farmers a common sense of purpose, an incentive to *want* to work together and achieve a positive outcome. A co-op changed the lives of farmers economically and socially. It could be a critical tool for pulling a community together and provide an incentive for it to rebuild itself. It also avoided the appearance of favoritism. If the government was seen as supporting one individual entrepreneur over another in some of these places, the fractures in the community could grow. But the co-ops could avoid all of this, as they would first pull the community together, and maybe at a later point spur more individual entrepreneurship.

Stepping back, I realized the co-ops and cows were important in ways that no IRR (internal rate of return) or competitive strategic analysis could measure. I learned that, as with so many things in Africa, the context was everything. It is hard to put a number on the "value" of reconciliation, but it is here where measures like social return on capital and deeper cost-benefits would be critical. Indeed, the amount of effort that would be needed to make "one cow one family" and the co-ops work would be high, but the value it could create was socially tremendous, and something I might have missed had I not gone into the villages themselves, or thought more deeply about the programs' unspoken motivations. You wouldn't see any explicit reference to reconciliation in the dry, official policy document. Instead of thinking of the cows and co-ops as too risky, in fact I realized it was this high amount of risk that could possibly guarantee a very high return—one that went far beyond monetary value, but helped families confront the horrors of the past, and reconcile entire communities.

For me, the lessons from this experience are twofold. First, business can be used to create incentives not just for economic return, but also for social return. This is happening all over Africa and across the world, but Rwanda was the first place I saw business used as a cornerstone of such broad social transformation. Second, it is not always easy to see this idea of "social return," nor is it easy to quantify. The risks of "social business" are high, and likely require some economic cost to capture the value of increased social return. Efforts need to be placed on understanding how to mitigate these risks to maximize the social return, and shed new light on what might have originally been a questionable business case. For young managers seeking to grow global careers, this implies several things:

- First, working in environments completely different from the ones you are used to requires you to push harder to understand the context and keep an open mind. Though difficult, you must think through the project from the point of the view of "the other side," looking at all the players' motivations and incentives, or else you might miss the whole point. No one ever explicitly told me these projects were about reconciliation—my realization came through getting out into the field and interacting with a range of people, from individual farmers to political and social experts. What would the government want? A country put back together and moving forward. What did the villagers need? A stronger social fabric and a way to start lifting themselves out of poverty. Using this lens, I began to see how these projects were using business to achieve such outcomes.

- Second, because projects in areas with profound social challenges may have positive externalities that are hard to quantify, the *process* may be as valuable as the end product. While the programs are rolled out, the "cow annuity" and the small businesses formed by the co-ops bring families, neighbors, and communities together.

Therefore, when weighing the risk of a particular project in such a situation, one must consider all of the possible effects that might come out of the process of implementing it—and what might happen if it is *not* implemented. This then needs to be weighed against what the project will ultimately create, to see if the trade-offs between the various costs, risks, and returns are worth it.

- While perhaps stating the obvious, when you work in socially troubled areas, there is a high risk of failure. Alternatives to achieve the implicit outcome (in this case, reconciliation), as opposed to just the explicit outcome (income generation for poor farmers), should be explored up front, to see which approach makes the most sense. From the cows to the co-ops, many of the programs I saw in Rwanda are risky and difficult to implement. But the social return I believe is worth the risk, and we need to shift the focus to ways to increase the likelihood of success and to solve the execution problems during roll-out.

What I love about working in Africa is that I am constantly reminded that I don't know what I don't know, and that with every project there is something more to learn, a new perspective to add to my toolbox as I work on various projects around the continent. In the end, I cannot guarantee the cows will turn Rwanda into the next Wisconsin, nor can I guarantee that every co-op will run smoothly. However, I do believe that the process of working through this venture can help put many of Rwanda's ghosts to rest.

INTERVIEW WITH . . .

Dominic Barton

Global Managing Director of McKinsey & Company

Dominic Barton talks about his own global experience, what globalization will mean to organizations and young leaders, and how businesspeople can use global experience to improve themselves and their organizations.

As a firm with a global footprint, McKinsey has nurtured an organization that cuts across cultures and boundaries. How have McKinsey and its clients responded to globalization over the past several decades?

In the late 1950s, we began to help emerging multinational companies expand their presence in Europe, South America, and parts of Asia. We also began hiring global talent (at some scale) in key universities in the U.S. and Europe. This helped to set us up for globalization over the next fifty years. Over the past several decades we have broadened our geographic footprint (now fifty-five countries with the opening of our Nigeria office in November 2010). In fact, McKinsey—and many of our clients—have responded to globalization by expanding physical presence to where demand opportunities are in key geographic nodes around the world and by becoming locally relevant in each of those nodes. We have also pursued a global or "one firm" culture—a common standard across geographies for our client service approach (e.g., all clients are clients of the *firm* and not the local office—we serve our clients with global teams and bring to each of them the most relevant parts of our global knowledge); global training; one language; our talent development approach (e.g., all partners are elected globally and have been from the beginning; a strong encouragement of mobility between countries throughout one's career—I have personally lived in seven countries on all major continents while at McKinsey), which encourages a global perspective; and our remuneration approach (e.g., one firm global profit pool).

In your experience, how has globalization affected the careers of today's young managers? How is this different from the previous generation of managers?

Managers today are playing and need to be equipped to play in a significantly larger, more diverse—but interrelated—and fast-moving playing field. They need to understand the broader world context in which they are operating—rather than just their immediate surroundings. This applies not only to new potential "demand" markets, but new sources of supply, innovation, and talent. For many, if not most, industries, disruptive change and innovation is as likely to originate from across the globe and adjacent businesses as it is in just the local market, and managers will need a wide field of view that includes deep awareness of global trends. Technology has a role to play in making emerging managerial challenges easier. There are also new decision-making and oversight skills to learn to ensure that the challenges associated with globalization and increased volatility and risk are met.

Young managers will also need to be much more versatile and mobile. Of course, overseas "chapters" in a career will be a much more prevalent part of career development for a far greater portion of leaders than in the past. However, versatility will need to go much farther—including the ability to work more seamlessly across public, private, and social sectors. The challenges we see in a globalizing world (for example, job losses in developed economies) require the strong collaboration of business, government, and social sectors. I think that young mangers should seek out opportunities to work across those areas—in effect becoming "tri-sector" athletes over the course of a career—and some parts of the world do this more naturally, such as India, China, South Korea, and Singapore.

Finally, for all mangers, the bar for depth of knowledge and the ability to work across cultures continues to rise in a globalizing economy. It is not sufficient to be the best within a market or region. In today's world, young leaders must have relevant expertise and skills in a multi-country setting.

In what ways does global experience early in a businessperson's career help him or her become a better leader?

Global experience early in one's career can be likened to a "leadership accelerator"—developing a broader understanding of cultures and of decision-making and team-building approaches, as well as the challenge of what can be built from a "standing start," enhances leadership "muscle." Global experience early on forces one to challenge basic assumptions—for example, what is important to customers; what is important to talent; how to get things done—skills that are important for innovation and improving performance anywhere in the world. These managers will understand the cultures and values of partners outside their home country—making them more effective in building relationships everywhere. They will also develop bonds with suppliers and customers that are much harder to achieve at a distance. I spend a lot of time encouraging CEOs to take their boards into emerging markets to see in-person the changes taking place. The earlier that businesspeople can get to grips with the communities in which their customers live, the more likely that they will successfully lead companies that serve those customers well.

There are broader macroeconomic benefits as well. Workers overseas often act as ambassadors for their home country—making connections and opening pathways for other business leaders in their home country.

What are the skills and experiences that managers and organizations should nurture in their young business leaders that will enable them to succeed in tomorrow's global marketplace?

One of the most important, but least valued, skills is the ability to put oneself in the shoes of others. We have been living in historic times with continued—and often disruptive—changes from all sectors and all parts of the globe, creating a constant stream of new possibilities.

In this context, leaders should seek out experiences outside their own country to understand dynamics, trends, and approaches that could create opportunities and challenges for their businesses.

Cross-sector perspectives can also be very helpful. Retailing and technology, health care and telecom, banking and consumer goods are all examples of industries where connection and cross-experiences will benefit young leaders. Even today, many CEOs get a lot of value from connecting with leaders in industries unrelated to their own.

Young leaders also need to be constantly open to change—seeking and even stimulating continuous experimentation with new technologies, new products, and new business models. One of the hardest things for any of us to do is to let go of business models that have proven successful in the past. Leaders need a "healthy paranoia" that will keep them on a high state of alert for new possibilities. By constantly questioning assumptions and orthodoxies, we can avoid becoming too comfortable with past success models. As the rate of change in the world increases, leaders need to learn to do this even more aggressively than their predecessors.

Finally, leaders need to learn how to anticipate and prepare for risks. The volatility we have experienced recently will become a more normal part of how we operate. The sources of risk for any organization can be quite different and wide-ranging. Spending sufficient time with key stakeholders and people in the organization that directly serve them—especially key customer segments—is very important.

You've traveled extensively throughout your career. What was your own global journey like, and what have you learned from it?

I have been very fortunate to have worked with McKinsey clients on six continents, and to have witnessed firsthand the growth of Asia as an economic powerhouse while living in Seoul and Shanghai. My confidence and excitement about Asia's economic future comes in part from that experience of having called the continent my home for the last twelve years. I have learned a lot about learning. In many of these country experiences, I felt like I was starting over again and, while painful and stressful at many times, I think one benefits a great deal from these experiences. I learned a lot about relationship building—in several of the countries, I did not speak the local language but had to learn how to communicate effectively and "read" people—in fact, I think I developed a deeper sense of "radar" than I ordinarily would have if I had not moved around so much.

You've spent a significant part of your career in China. What can Chinese companies and business leaders learn from the rest of the world? What can the rest of the world learn from China?

For Chinese companies, it is crucial to recognize that strategies and organizational models that work well in China will not necessarily work in other parts of the world; in particular, talent models and decision-making processes will need to be quite different. Adapting to the world beyond China's borders is their biggest challenge—they need to understand and respond to the diversity of other markets; not only customers, but employees, competitors, and regulators.

For companies from outside China, the learnings are very similar. For example, you would be surprised how often executives assume that China is a single market—and indeed that most Chinese consumers will view a product or service in a similar way. Of course, the reality is that China is far from homogenous. Companies coming into the Chinese market for the first time need to understand its tremendous diversity, and build this into their strategy. For example, in consumer goods sectors we often advise our clients to think of China as twenty-two distinct markets. For many, this will also mean creating a second headquarters in China and substantially "beefing up" government relations as a means to becoming an insider in the country.

What are the most important lessons that American business leaders can learn from the process of globalization and from their global business partners?

The coming decade will be the first in two hundred years when emerging market countries contribute more to growth than developed ones. Leaders of American businesses need to prepare for dramatic changes to the world in which they operate.

We will see 900 million new middle-class consumers driven by these shifts. Their demand for goods and services will reshape industries. It is far from clear how companies will serve that new demand successfully, and I expect consumers in developing markets to put tremendous pressure on companies to innovate. Similarly, technology brings near-instant connectivity and innovation continues to rise alongside connectivity as consumers have a global field of view and a multiplicity of choices.

Ideas and innovation occur all over the world, and globalization will push the pace of innovation to increase further. While the U.S. will remain an important individual economy, American businesses will need to figure out how to go after these 900 million new middle-class consumers—often challenging major orthodoxies to meet new preferences and provide high-quality products and services at significantly lower price points. Many businesses will also need to significantly rethink their talent and talent-development models—both to access great talent in different parts of the world and to develop an even deeper bench of globally minded leaders. Finally, American business leaders, like all others, are going to need to be comfortable with and learn to thrive with levels of uncertainty and volatility we have not seen in recent times.

Are there any words of caution you'd offer to the next generation of global leaders? Are there any words of encouragement?

The next generation of leaders will have the opportunity to deal with exciting and quite different challenges than their predecessors—all in a context of a globally connected and constantly changing world.

They need to have both a "long lens" and a "short lens" and keep both in constant balance. A long view keeps careful watch on where the world is going and makes investments accordingly. At the same time, the short view enables one to be nimble and move quickly in the moment— adapting to sudden changes and capturing pockets of opportunity.

The next generation of global leaders should nurture curiosity and seek new experiences as much as possible by traveling, working across cultures and even sectors, connecting and forming relationships across country borders, absorbing new perspectives—especially beyond Anglo-Saxon ones—and reading broadly. Information, ideas, and innovation come from many sources, and they should develop as many "source spots" as possible.

Finally, I would encourage leaders to develop their "resilience muscle"—there will surely be shocks, challenges, and failures along the way. We all need to get back up on our feet when (not if) we are knocked down—our research shows that more successful people and leaders actually experience more "bad luck" than less successful people—and reach out for more experiences, especially international ones!

CHAPTER 3

People

Leading in a Diverse World

Variety is the spice of life.

—William Cowper

O ne of the striking facets of modern business is the incredible diversity of the people—customers, colleagues, suppliers, and competitors—with whom we now interact. On a day-to-day basis, businesspeople engage people of every race, religion, color, creed, and personal preference—and while this variety can prove difficult to navigate, it's also equipping young leaders to operate with agility, humility, and individuality.

Businesspeople, of course, have always had to lead diverse groups. Historically great cities like Piraeus, Alexandria, and New York were both cultural and commercial centers—where trade brought together people of every race, religion, and ethnicity. The private sector has often flattened class differences and offered excluded peoples a means of participating more fully in society. And, particularly in modern times, the entrepreneurial desire to reach every untapped (and profitable) niche has led to an explosion of various "long-tail" business ventures—from independently produced online music albums to art house movies and organic vegan restaurants.

And despite occasional resistance, workplaces around the world are becoming ever more diverse. On a global level, we may be living in one of the most inclusive times in history. As labor force participation increases and old racial, class, religious, and gender-based barriers are gradually lowered in many regions, the workplace is benefiting from a multiplicity of perspectives. In practical terms, these varied points of view are often quite necessary to reach the equally diverse array of consumers who now purchase goods from multinational institutions. Companies like Coca-Cola must now serve customers of every conceivable nationality, class, and creed. And they have often recognized the importance of this diversity more quickly than global political institutions.

That's not to say these companies are perfect—far from it. Senior executive suites are almost all still dominated by historically powerful groups. In the United States, this means that many CEOs are older white males. In Mexico, it means that very few native people hold executive positions, and in many companies around the world it means an underrepresentation of women.

But the trends—at least on these conventional measures of diversity—are improving. In 1975, for instance, only 11 percent of the MBA class at HBS were women, 6 percent were U.S. minorities, and 15 percent were international. By 1995, women comprised 28 percent of the class, U.S. minorities 14 percent, and international students 23 percent.[1] And for the HBS class of 2012, the figures had climbed to 36 percent women, 23 percent U.S. minorities, and 34 percent international students.[2] Other business schools, like France's INSEAD, are even more diverse (at least by country of origin), with INSEAD boasting a 2010 class that was 92 percent international, with 59 percent of students from outside of Western Europe, and 33 percent women.[3] Those of us who recently attended business school can attest to the dedicated efforts these schools make to celebrate the religions, cultures, and passions of these various constituencies in very authentic ways.

In our own survey, more than 92 percent of respondents answered "agree" or "strongly agree" to the statement, "Increased workplace diversity can lead to better business outcomes." And a majority of respondents selected numerous categories when prompted with this statement:

FIGURE 3-1

Traits to foster in the workplace (percent responding "yes")

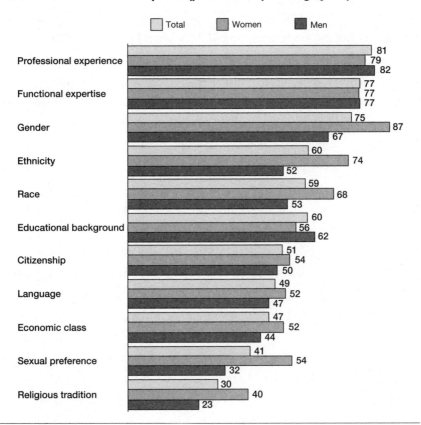

| | Total | Women | Men |

Professional experience — 81, 79, 82
Functional expertise — 77, 77, 77
Gender — 75, 87, 67
Ethnicity — 60, 74, 52
Race — 59, 68, 53
Educational background — 60, 56, 62
Citizenship — 51, 54, 50
Language — 49, 52, 47
Economic class — 47, 52, 44
Sexual preference — 41, 54, 32
Religious tradition — 30, 40, 23

"I hope my future employers seek to actively foster the following elements of diversity in the workplace" (see figure 3-1)

Of particular interest is that these respondents don't simply or even predominantly value racial, ethnic, and gender diversity—but diverse professional experience, functional expertise, and educational background. There seems to be a realization that out of these diverse experiences and identities come the strength of alternative perspectives—and next-generation leaders value those perspectives for the personal growth and professional success they can bring. This kind of diversity is both a challenge and an opportunity.

How Can We Lead in a Diverse World?

So where do we go from here? Certainly, the next generation of business leaders will continue to seek out inclusive workplaces; and they'll likely be more effective at creating them because they themselves are more diverse in almost every conventional sense. But there is a growing belief that these external measures of diversity—particularly race and gender—are insufficient, and that sensitivity training programs are quickly becoming outdated and ineffective. We are also realizing that as important as the diversity of the people you lead is the diversity of your own leadership experiences.

This generation—fed on the aforementioned "long-tail" idea that each person is unique beyond his or her class, race, or gender, having unique tastes and preferences—is instead pushing for greater "wholeness" in the workplace. Alternative work schedules. Part-time or remote employment for mothers and fathers who choose to stay at home with children. Increasing incorporation of various religious and cultural practices in the workplace and increasing openness among employees about sensitive topics. This generation is pushing the idea that no one achieves happiness by cleaving herself in half—one part "professional" and one part "personal." And as technological and cultural shifts increasingly allow such radically individualized diversity, the next generation's leaders will use these shifts to gain a competitive advantage among customers even as they create a fuller work experience for employees.

This shift is perhaps most pronounced among millennial women. According to a recent Accenture survey, 94 percent of millennial women believe they can achieve "work-life balance"—a modern euphemism for happiness and fulfillment in one's personal and professional life. And 70 percent list "maintains work/life balance" as a critical quality of a successful female leader.[4]

But the shift toward individualization is also clear, more anecdotally, in the changes companies are making to accommodate the needs of their increasingly varied workforces. Google has traditionally offered employees "20 Percent Time"—one day per week dedicated to their own pursuits and initiatives; 3M has promoted something similar with its "15% culture."[5] And in 2007 at least, Netflix claimed that it did not even track the hours of its employees.[6] Far from the purview of radical companies in Silicon Valley, similar techniques are employed by the likes of JetBlue, which pioneered a program of at-home call center agents, many of whom were stay-at-home moms, in locations like Salt Lake City.[7]

Some pioneering companies are even embracing religion. Tyson Foods, for instance, created a chaplaincy program—staffing its various facilities with religious mentors who reflect the dominant faiths of workers in their particular regions, and are available to employees of all faiths for counsel. This program would seem eccentric if similar versions hadn't been implemented, in whole or in part, in other prominent companies, such as Coca-Cola, R. J. Reynolds, and Texas Instruments.[8]

And, of course, businesses have often been harbingers of social change on lifestyle issues like sexual preference—many private firms began to offer same-sex partner benefits, for instance, long before same-sex partnership became a prominent political issue. According to the Human Rights Campaign, by 2003, 64 percent of the *Fortune* 100 offered same-sex partner benefits, and by 2009, that number had reached 83 percent.[9]

In short, companies are both expanding what it means to be "diverse" and doing so in ways that attempt to empower employees and offer them greater fulfillment, wholeness, and happiness in the workplace. And the next generation of business leaders is thinking in ever more innovative ways about how to expand these initiatives and lead these varied individuals in the pursuit of common goals.

The following stories address the idea of leading in a diverse world with the benefit of diverse leadership experiences. People are freer to live with greater passion and purpose when they feel more "whole" at work. Over the next twenty years, the best organizations will find ways to harness this incredibly diverse and dynamic talent pool to revolutionize the way they do business.

Nonconforming Culture

How to Feel Comfortable in Who You Are No Matter Where You Are

After five years in the consulting practice, **KIMBERLY CARTER** now works as a senior manager in the Leadership Development Group focused on talent development and corporate university launch for Deloitte. Kimberly earned a BS in accounting from Florida A&M University and a minor in German from Florida State University. She is passionate about education and leadership development.

Imagine walking through the streets of a small town and always being met with stares—most are inquisitive while others are laced with malice. Imagine questioning how someone could seemingly judge your worth or meaning without knowing anything about you. I experienced something like this when I lived in Germany as an exchange student in the early 1990s, a time of heightened hostility toward outsiders. At the time, Germany had an influx of immigrants following the collapse of the Berlin Wall along with a rash of fire bombings and *"Ausländer raus"* ("foreigners get out") demonstrations that expressed a widespread negative sentiment. There were also a number of marches organized to address tolerance and to counter xenophobia. On the surface, many assumed I was an African seeking asylum and employment rather than an African American studying the language and culture. The internal conflict I felt from not always feeling welcome given the color of my skin spurred me to write a poem entitled "Identity" for my high school literary magazine. That experience not only exposed me to the stark realities of modern-day bias but drove me to never let others' perceptions of me limit or determine my path.

Growing up in Mississippi, I was no stranger to prejudice. The impact of discrimination in the United States lingered past the abolition of slavery because certain laws prevented blacks from having the same civil rights (e.g., to vote, to use common restrooms or drinking fountains) as whites until the late 1960s, particularly in some Southern states. My parents experienced segregation firsthand and dealt with systematic injustice; however, those experiences fueled their desire to earn university degrees to create a better life and demand fair treatment professionally. Even after the passage of the Civil Rights Act of 1964, some mind-sets had not changed enough to grant African Americans immediate access to education, jobs, and housing—even if they were overqualified. My family emphasized that education held the keys to equal opportunity. They grounded my life in the idea that you can excel in spite of adversities and still be true to yourself. With a deep appreciation for the faith and sacrifices of those before me, I kept those memories dear as I worked my way up in the business world. Although I initially struggled with the expectations to conform to corporate environments in order to succeed professionally, I soon discovered there should be no real boundaries for diversity in the workplace.

Many of those unspoken expectations and my feelings about them may seem superficial (e.g., always having straightened hair because natural hair is not acceptable, or feeling as if I had to represent the universe of African American females at work since we represented 1 percent of our starting class). But at the end of the day, I had to be comfortable with the person I saw in the mirror and happy with the choices I made. I recognized that companies figured out that the true value for them did not lie in having everyone look and act the same.

Over time, I've come to understand the profound impact of my experiences in Germany, growing up in Mississippi, and traversing the professional world, and translated it into three key principles in my life and career—three things I wish I could have told myself earlier as a young person entering the working world:

1. **Do not be afraid of what you do not know.** Every day, I had to mentally prepare for any number of reactions from others, but that did not keep me from walking out the door and enjoying what

Germany had to offer. Furthermore, I had the courage to make bold moves on my own and not let fear hold me back. For example, the decision to move from the South to New York and work in investment banking after college was considered a big risk. I dared to be the first in my circle of friends and family to embark out of state to work without any nearby support. My great-grandparents long ago made the decision not to migrate the family up North for industrial jobs in the early 1900s and took pride in establishing themselves as pillars in the local community (through teaching and preaching), yet I decided to seemingly break away from my Southern roots. There was an inherent fear that anything could happen given the perceived corrupting influences of the big city. But there also must have been a strand of wanderlust in my genes, because one of my great aunts ventured to California to pursue her dream to dance and act. She somehow made it despite the challenges of her day. How would I know whether I could be successful at my venture if I didn't try?

That does not mean that I do not get a queasy feeling every time I decide to shift directions. But I close my eyes, take a deep breath, remember that the feeling will pass (eventually), and then make the first step. No matter where I end up, the journey has always been worth it and has made me more comfortable with accepting what I do not know in order to continually move forward.

2. **Look for ways to bridge the gaps.** To bridge the gaps between people you have to understand where there are gaps and why. Obvious differences such as race, gender, and age are easier to address given various levels of "diversity training" offered today, but other cultural influences that are often not easily discernible offhand also shape a person's views. Opposing beliefs or mindsets tend to emerge through casual conversations and informal networking. Gaining an awareness of those differences equips you with areas to focus on in order to better relate to colleagues.

I realize that human nature allows us to make assumptions about others when we do not know or understand enough about them. I was perceived as a potential threat by some in Germany because my skin color was different. However, there was almost immediate acceptance if my onlookers discovered I was an American. In fact, I had more in common with them than they would ever have thought. That also translates into the workplace, where far too often I have been the youngest, the only person of color, the only female—or all three.

There are, however, commonalities underneath the surface of those obvious differences. It is too easy to get distracted if you become stuck focusing on what separates you from others versus what connects you. I have understood the value of leveraging the unique skills, talents, and perspectives each person contributes to a team. Having a diverse workplace requires a comprehensive understanding of all facets of an individual to truly embrace the new diversity that transcends generations and a demographic checklist.

3. **Do not forget to pay it forward.** Exposure to completely different environments and social issues has had a transformative impact on me. I grew the courage, confidence, and resolve to make decisions and test uncharted waters personally and professionally. Without that experience, I probably would have still succeeded in my endeavors but remained in the South, in my comfort zone.

I feel it is my responsibility to encourage others by helping them recognize that they cannot grow unless they realize they don't have to fit in any predefined box. I am an advocate for study-abroad programs because of the immense opportunities they offer to expand one's horizons. It opened doors for me that made me a more complete person and deepened the core beliefs and values that make me who I am—regardless of the country, the culture, or boardroom I occupy.

And now that I manage people—primarily those under-thirties who are rising leaders in business—I've developed a few rules of thumb for helping them succeed as well:

1. **Reevaluate how well you know your colleagues and managers.** Learn about each team member individually and their interests versus assuming certain stereotypes or gross generalizations. With the proliferation of information on the Internet and social networking, you can easily find out more about others informally and share experiences by joining and using the sites yourself.

2. **Be open to other viewpoints, and expect to be surprised.** Even though you won't always agree with a different perspective, you can often learn a lot just by listening to alternative approaches to situations. It is easy to think you have "the answer," but life encounters teach us there is more than one solution. Many paths can lead to the same destination. Given an appreciation for history and the experiences of others, you do not always have to reinvent the answer when something has been proven effective in the past.

3. **Understand that although change is inevitable, not everyone adapts at the same speed.** With the evolution of virtual workplaces, there are new ways of communicating and working together. These methods are effective only if everyone uses and understands them. It is just as important to have an awareness about the impact change has on others on your team as it is to understand the change itself. How you respond and help others adapt will demonstrate your capabilities as a leader. And understanding a person's heritage or background can be essential to a deeper understanding of the ways they can understand and adapt to change.

Since my parents first entered the workplace, I have noticed changes that allow me to be bolder with who I am and what I expect from others. Blatant discrimination is not tolerated today. My generation grew up in a fully integrated society and benefited from diverse experiences. I can easily reference many successful role models in business and politics with nontraditional backgrounds. Companies have taken steps to teach employees about diversity and how to handle sensitive situations. They recognize in this age that you cannot mask who you truly are and maximize your productivity at work. Self-awareness and cultural acceptance are critical elements of feeling confident with yourself and treating others with respect.

As business professionals in the twenty-first century, we should recognize that the new diversity encompasses a breadth of attributes not constrained by race, gender, and other stereotypical factors. It requires first embracing and celebrating the essence of who you are before you can appreciate what others bring to the table.

Diversity Day

Whole People, Whole Organizations, and a Whole New Approach to Diversity

JOSH BRONSTEIN has been a human capital consultant since 2005, specializing in talent and change management strategies. Josh holds an MBA from Harvard Business School and a bachelor of science in industrial and labor relations from Cornell University. He is passionate about helping people bring more of themselves to work.

In the first season of the hit television show *The Office*, an episode about "Diversity Day" pokes fun at a tacky diversity training session that teaches employees to become HEROs through **H**onesty, **E**mpathy, **R**espect, and **O**pen minds. The comedic routine highlights the skeptical views most employees have toward an outdated view of "diversity."

When many of us think about diversity, we think about these silly, over-dramatic sensitivity training sessions that have been the subject of such ridicule. We think about nondiscrimination policies that exist on paper but allow the highest-revenue producers to opt out. We think about affirmative action and hiring a greater number of underrepresented minorities or women. Or perhaps we think about the most tangibly strategic efforts in which organizations mirror customer or client segments, such as Hispanic or LGBT (lesbian/gay/bisexual/transgender) marketing efforts, to increase revenues. Most people think about these manifestations of diversity because most leaders who came before us viewed workplace diversity in the context of affirmative action, litigation avoidance, or access to diverse markets. But these views of diversity are evolving dramatically.

In conversations with my peers, I've realized that our generation believes that such diversity practices are simply table stakes. Of course, it's still important to ensure employers aren't discriminating and that individuals are sensitive to the way they treat each other at work. Such practices are necessary, but not sufficient. Our generation wants to lead companies that willingly celebrate a broader definition of diversity in order to galvanize top talent who can deliver better business results.

Value of a Broader View of Diversity

I was twenty-five years old and a relatively new employee. After discussing some time off I was requesting for an upcoming family vacation with "significant others," my manager asked me in a crowded, open team room, "How long have you been with your girlfriend?" I could play the pronoun game and say "I've been with her for two years." Or I could tell the *whole* truth. I grabbed a piece of paper and quickly scribbled "boyfriend—2 years." "Oh, cool," she responded.

In hindsight, I made the right decision. The energy required to hide my identity from those who I assumed wouldn't like it distracted me from the work that I was being paid to do. Since then, being openly gay has only helped me professionally—I've benefited from a stronger sense of community and a professional network that spans functional silos, more confidence when speaking with senior leaders, and the comfort of always being able to use accurate pronouns.

As a human capital consultant and former leader of the LGBT student association at HBS, I've spoken with dozens of general managers, HR leaders, and peers about the role of diversity in a wide cross-section of companies. There are tremendous variations in how diversity and inclusion efforts play out across companies and geographies, but in all of my discussions on the subject my consistent observation has been that diversity is no longer defined by typical indicators such as gender, race, or religion. I've realized it takes a broader view of diversity to foster an environment in which everyone feels comfortable telling the *whole* truth, scribbling—or maybe even *outwardly discussing*—their diverse backgrounds, experiences, and individual situations, even if those attributes don't fit neatly into the categories previously associated with "diversity."

Employers today realize that to remain competitive, they must attract, motivate, and retain individuals from a wider range of experiences, and look for diverse geographic origins, socioeconomic backgrounds, academic experiences, personality types, sexual orientations, generational views, ways of thinking (left brain/right brain, e.g.), and styles of communication. They also realize that by removing constraints that may have deterred applicants in the past, the broadest view of diversity will attract the largest talent pool from which to find the best and brightest future leaders.

By fostering discussions out of differences, we can all challenge the status quo and help our colleagues think outside of the traditional constraints placed on them. Doing so also develops increased intellectual rigor through vigorous debate and a well-rounded ethical compass by avoiding groupthink. The companies that can extend this broader view outside of the United States can also enable enhanced global mobility among diverse high performers.

And let's not forget the human element—a big component of the value proposition for diversity investments and the broader view of diversity, is that it is simply the right thing to do. How hard was it, really, for my manager described above to react supportively? In today's business world, collegial values and supportive, strong leadership go a long way.

Redefining Professionalism

To make this new view of diversity work, our generation is prepared to bring our whole selves to work, being open in the workplace about differences in our backgrounds and feeling comfortable enough to resist the temptation to force-fit ourselves into a preset definition of a stereotypical "professional." This isn't easy or always comfortable for employees or managers, but true professionalism requires incorporating differences in an inclusive way—not hiding them.

In the past, decision-making authority was limited to a few suit-wearing executives, usually white straight males from prestigious backgrounds. As a result, some employees have been guided to act more "masculine," more "straight," or even more "white." Some managers have historically hidden these suggestions under the guise of encouraging employees to act more "professionally." But business is inherently personal, not just professional. Our relationships drive our success. And our individualism drives our relationships.

Now more than ever, work and life have converged. With ever-longer workdays and technology—like Facebook and Twitter—that puts us "always on," we are forced to discuss our work-life balance needs with our managers, and we encourage our employees to do the same with us. Avoiding the subject of a same-sex partner, a child at home, or one's involvement in certain religious activities takes valuable energy away from the work at hand. It can also be considered untruthful.

Rather than fight this convergence between work and life and calling it "unprofessional," as many of our predecessors did, take the opportunity to discuss and embrace personal differences in your professional life. Those distinct qualities that make up your identity, beliefs, and situational characteristics arm you with a very unique perspective from which to view business challenges—and hopefully arrive at less traditional and more value-adding solutions. Lead by example—telling the whole truth about who you are—and encourage your employees to do the same.

Authentic Leadership

As the LGBT Student Association's liaison to admissions, one of my primary tasks was to organize an LGBT open house for prospective students. I knew that the attendees were in for a real treat when Frances Frei—one of the most remarkable, inspirational individuals I've ever met—agreed to deliver the faculty address. As the first openly gay tenured HBS faculty member, Frances spoke about LGBT life at HBS, as well as the academic experience, the section experience, and other subjects. But when the million-dollar question came up—should you be "out" in your application—she brought it back to the school's mission: educating leaders who make a difference in the world. Leadership, Frei has repeatedly argued, fundamentally requires authenticity. And authenticity is tough to demonstrate when you've buried the truth deep in the closet.

My call to action for our generation is simple: be authentic. That means bringing your *whole* self to work, not just those characteristics that you think your employer wants to see. Because as Frances Frei taught me as a teacher and a mentor, being true to yourself and your colleagues will enable you to lead more effectively.

Generation Why

A defining characteristic of our generation is that we want to be recognized as individuals—not anonymous cogs forced to think, act, and dress in the same way.

We see Steve Jobs dress in jeans and a black turtleneck and we wonder why we can't wear an outfit to work that reflects something about our individualism. We saw the meteoric rise of Sarah Palin, embracing her status as a "hockey mom" and articulating the value such experiences would add to her leadership, and wonder why we can't do the same. For the first time in history, our generation has seen countless examples of very successful leaders succeed *because* of their differences, rather than *in spite of* them.

We also believe that anyone who can address a business challenge in a respectful, intellectual, and honest way is acting "professionally," even if it means disrespecting the traditional hierarchy. As a part of this new view of diversity, therefore, organizations must flatten. Young leaders are notorious for impatience. As such, we're empathetic to junior employees who don't want to wait until they reach the top of the corporate ladder to contribute their unique ideas; we didn't want our ideas to be held back by our age, and we don't expect to hold back those who come after us.

Most of us also realize that with the acceleration of technology, some of our knowledge will be outdated by the time we reach the c-suite. For example, it was just a few years ago that texting and social networking were exclusively for social use, making it highly inappropriate for a young employee to text his boss or add her as a friend on Facebook. Today, executives at all levels use text messages and social media to communicate with us. We realize that trends in communication styles must evolve. Based on these experiences, our generation will be even more open to diverse communication styles as they emerge in the years ahead, no matter how foreign they may seem to us by the time we're middle-aged executives.

As the next generation—"Z" or "I"—enters the workforce, we want to engage them early. Organizational flattening is a critical component of generational diversity that will enable us to take full advantage of the youngest and most creative talent pools. We understand the need to do so because we lived through the greatest technological advancement in modern corporate history, and we saw how some of the most successful companies were those who kept their youngest talent relevant.

Managing Differences

But all of this doesn't mean that we should be encouraging everyone to conform to the new definition of nonconformity. For example, Steve Jobs can wear his typical jeans and black turtleneck outfit, but if everyone had to do the same to conform to Apple "culture," employees wouldn't be bringing *their* whole selves to work. If a single woman is surrounded by working mothers and made to feel like an outsider for not having a child at home, then the benefits of bringing *her* whole self to work are negated. If an LGBT-friendly culture becomes so LGBT focused that a straight employee feels uncomfortable bringing *his* whole self to work, the organization will have a serious talent problem.

The new view of diversity requires a delicate balance that enables employees of all talents to bring their whole selves to work and to acknowledge—and work through—the inevitable conflicts that might arise from doing so. The moment an employee feels uncomfortable bringing his whole self to work because others are doing the same is the moment the leader must interject to regain balance. Without such leadership, the business case for this new view of diversity falls apart.

What Can I Do?

As a young leader, there are a number of steps you can take to be on the forefront of the next wave of diversity strategies. First and foremost, lead by example. Bring your whole self to work. Talk about your family—traditional or nontraditional. Bring your background and experiences—traditional or nontraditional—to the conference room table. Your authenticity will be contagious.

Second, articulate to senior leaders how differences drive success. Refresh the business case for your company's diversity investments to focus on bringing the most varied views to the table to foster innovation—which is forward thinking— rather than being obliged to find employees who fill in boxes on your diversity checklist—which takes your organization a step back. As a hiring manager, bring this view to life. Hire truly diverse employees with unique backgrounds and perspectives that will help you grow your business, not just those individuals who will help you to meet your diversity targets.

Third, take ownership over fighting the hierarchy. Diverse ideas flow best when there aren't consequences for sharing them, and hierarchies inherently create such consequences. Plus, the youngest talented employees are also the least influenced by "the way things have always been done" and often have some of the most diverse perspectives. This isn't easy: it takes young leaders to articulate this strategy and cooperative, secure senior leaders to facilitate it. Make the case and push hard.

Fourth, embrace a variety of communication styles and mediums. Organizational communication mechanisms evolve. The more you use emerging technologies for business communications and spread such trends to your peers, the more responsive your organization might be.

Beyond technology, a broad view of diversity takes a range of information processing styles into account when communicating key messages. The most creative and varied styles of communication, rather than the loudest, cut through the information clutter within organizations and reach a variety of people who don't all learn and interpret information the same way; therefore, push your organization to vary communication styles and mediums. At the very least, do so with your own communications.

Finally, reward individuals on your team for bringing their unique perspectives to the table. A few words of praise for having the courage to talk about a relevant personal situation or experience in a meeting can go a long way—and the positive impact can spread throughout the organization.

The business case for expansive diversity is gaining strength—gone are the days when companies hire a few more underrepresented minorities, hold a "Diversity Day," and call themselves "diverse." A diverse workforce of the future will be an innovation machine. Such an organization will be armed with individuals anxious to share their unique experiences, beliefs, and backgrounds to create value.

Help your company stay relevant by redefining its view of diversity to create a truly inclusive culture, and ensure this culture permeates your operations across geographies. Doing so will motivate existing employees by enabling them to bring their whole selves to work no matter where in the world they are, and will attract the best and brightest new talent who want to do the same. As a young leader, it starts with you.

Women and the Workplace

After graduating from Wellesley College, **TASNEEM DOHADWALA** joined an equity sales strategy team at Lehman Brothers. She left to join the Nooril-Iman Foundation, where she executed a program of economic self-sustainment in Myanmar and construction of a medical clinic in Yemen. After graduating HBS in 2009, she cofounded Excelestar Ventures. She reflects on the evolving roles and expectations of women in business.

In my first year at Lehman a respected and successful female senior manager reprimanded my male manager in a meeting. As we were leaving the meeting he told me, "I like my women as I like my coffee—with milk and sugar."

I responded, "But she gets things done." This woman, like so many others in similar positions, needed to maintain a firm approach, but often got stereotyped and ridiculed in the process.

There's little doubt that women now have greater access to the upper echelons of the business world than they did fifty, thirty, or even twenty years ago. The fact that I could respond to my manager's comment without any tangible repercussion is evidence of that advance; but the fact that he even made the comment is a microcosm of the work that remains to be done. Access to the business world for female professionals has too often hinged on conforming to the expectations of male colleagues and managers. In some cases, male counterparts expect women to remain feminine and *not* be one of the guys. In other situations, men expect their female colleagues to conform and *be one of the guys.* It has been the woman's job to figure out what her colleagues and managers are expecting, consciously or subconsciously, and project that as her personality. Regardless of which bias exists, it is almost impossible for a female professional to receive the same level of "brotherly" inclusion.

Further, because of the current constraints inherent in today's business world, women are often compelled to choose between work and family more explicitly than men are. They are not rewarded for efficiently balancing both. As Elizabeth Gudrais noted in the February 2010 issue of *Harvard Magazine*, "Women have undoubtedly made gains in terms of access to business careers . . . But in terms of being able to choose careers they want within those fields, as opposed to having to abandon professional goals for the sake of family, women still have far to go."[10] In many cases, women discover that trying to balance work and family results in a muted professional life. When a woman's scale tips in favor of work, people often assume that work is her only priority. As a result, many women choose family. A survey of 6,500 Harvard and Radcliffe graduates revealed that only 30 percent of female MBAs worked full-time, year-round and had children, while 45 percent of MDs did.[11]

Currently, many organizations accommodate the specific circumstances of female employees. Usually, this involves flexible work arrangements, maternity leave, and day care facilities. Unfortunately, these are peripheral solutions to the lack of gender diversity in businesses, especially at the top. It's incumbent upon the next generation of female business leaders to forge their own rules based on a female-centric value system. Only after the rules of business are rebuilt to incorporate such a value system will businesses truly be able to harness the talent of all their employees. These values involve

- Rejecting the false choice between family and professional success

- Breaking down artificially forced gender roles

- Changing how women view themselves in the workplace

These are difficult issues to discuss because they question deeply held assumptions about the role of women, the nature of meritocracy, and how we reward people in our organizations. Turning conversation into action is a two-way street. Not only must organizations understand what young female professionals hold dear in order to truly capture the value they bring, but women themselves must also strive to better articulate and champion their values in the workplace.

First, the next generation of female leaders must break down the false choice between career and family. Like it or not, for biological and social reasons, women are often positioned as primary caregivers in their families; and that position often involves trading success at work for stability at home. The next generation of women and employers must work to erode this trade-off. This starts with openness. Companies should become more proactive about making female managers available to female candidates to discuss openly how female managers balance family and professional success within the firm. Female candidates must become more comfortable raising these questions explicitly. When I interviewed with the CEO of Care.com, Sheila Marcelo, she described several instances of Care.com employees *proactively* balancing work and family. For example, she told me that the CTO worked from Greece and the head of business development took every Friday off. It seemed to me that her willingness to allow employees to create their own work experience enhanced their commitment, work ethic, and productivity. Unfortunately, in the current context, female candidates often do this more covertly, asking other women who work in the company about the "rules" around balancing family and work. Candidates shy away from asking about what they can expect of the quality of their personal life because they feel that they will be adversely judged. Companies can start to implement this openness by instructing HR professionals and managers who conduct interviews to describe the various degrees of flexibility available to the candidate and directly ask the candidate what they need to achieve work-life balance.

They of course shouldn't be adversely impacted for prioritizing both the personal and the professional. Rather, women should be rewarded for successfully balancing both family and work (as, incidentally, should men). Women should feel free to bring their "authentic" selves to work— whether that concept of self involves family or not—and employers should create space for those discussions.

Second, in addition to valuing women's ability to nurture both work and family, organizations must make efforts to break down artificially forced gender roles and create organizational sponsorship for women. Often, these are projected by senior management—where the ranks of women are still remarkably thin. Whether a manager's female subordinate assimilates seamlessly with her male counterparts or asserts her femininity is irrelevant. The matter of significance is that she is able to have her own personality. The proximity afforded to "one of the boys" should also be offered to her. Although women and men are currently both successfully mentored, climbing the ladder demands more than mentorship; it requires sponsorship. This issue was covered extensively in a *Harvard Business Review* article whose title stated the problem: "Why Men Still Get More Promotions Than Women":

> All mentoring is not created equal, we discovered. There is a special kind of relationship—called sponsorship—in which the mentor goes beyond giving feedback and advice and uses his or her influence with senior executives to advocate for the mentee. Our interviews and surveys alike suggest that high-potential women are overmentored and undersponsored relative to their male peers—and that they are not advancing in their organizations. Furthermore, without sponsorship, women not only are less likely than men to be appointed to top roles but may also be more reluctant to go for them.[12]

Embracing and utilizing sponsorship is especially important early in a woman's career. A recent study demonstrated that nearly a quarter of women leave their first job because of a difficult manager, while only 16 percent of men do.[13] Because many managers are men, there seems to be an almost subconscious tilt toward being less of a sponsor or "champion" for young female employees—and, while other factors could be at play, this may have a lot to do with why women feel so frustrated with their managers early in their careers. Companies interested in greater and deeper female participation should address this concern head-on, training managers on what it means to be a sponsor, and making sure that women receive such sponsorship the day they walk in the door.

Finally, young women in business must actively participate in the process of rebuilding existing workplace rules, as described earlier. They must reflect and be honest about trade-offs they are willing to make in both their personal and professional lives. This can be hard, in light of the scarcity of jobs. I was interviewing in 2009, an abysmal year for most job seekers. I decided to put together a list of requirements that could help create balance between work and family, and as a result, significantly narrowed my list of potential job opportunities. I did not want a job that demanded never-ending hours, required travel more than 50 percent of the time, and demanded tremendous after hours networking. I looked for a job where some employees were already experimenting with work-time flexibilities and some work could be done remotely and independently, rather than being dependent on going to the office. Though constraining, I was candid with myself and what I valued. I was fairly assertive and conscious of trying to be open with my employers. However, I was not idealistic, as I knew there would be many times when work would demand more from me than home would. Those would be the times when I could not be home in time to read to my son before bedtime. I was certain that there would be many business needs that could only be met in person, demanding travel. Fundamentally, work and family require trade-offs. And as long as both dimensions of my life made room for each other, both would thrive.

Despite what I thought was a sense of realism, when I was applying for jobs I still found myself trying to conceal my pregnancy. I bought suits specifically tailored to hiding my bump. Rather than use my ability to balance both my professional aspirations and motherhood as a testimony to my drive, dedication, and ambition, I suppressed it. In retrospect, I was disappointed in my approach. Only when we are comfortable with ourselves and what we value will others begin to embrace our very real needs. If we conceal our personalities and the multiple facets of our lives or conform to a dysfunctional status quo, organizations will never realize that changes must be made. I felt that being open about my pregnancy would immediately diminish my chances of winning the opportunity as it would give the interviewer the impression that work would always suffer as second to family. I believe if we eliminate the false choice between work and family, women will no longer feel the apprehension I did.

To truly rebuild the current system of values and see a meaningful change in the current workplace ethos, more women in this generation need to be assertive about what they need at work. Women need to emphasize that motherhood does not make work a lesser priority. Rather, female business professionals aim for both dimensions of their life to excel. Managers of companies that truly embrace work-life balance, such as Care.com, and allow employees to create their own workplace experience should speak out about what they are doing and the benefits it brings. Some practical advice for managers of companies that still lag in work-life programs: begin talking to your subordinates about the trade-offs in *your* life. This should encourage them to start sharing with you. Ask those team members who have families how they manage, especially when times get too hard. If you, as a manager, speak to them, the fear of lack of acceptance will slowly dissipate. Not only encourage team members with families to experiment with programs that are being offered, but try them yourself and then talk about it. The employees who excel at both family and work should be publicly celebrated. Ironically, many business professionals are already successfully balancing work and family, but we do not hear about it because it seems that no one cares to listen.

If we want to see more gender-balanced executive suites, if we want to see greater freedom for men and women to embrace dual roles as professionals and heads of families, and if we want to see a more inclusive set of rules that offer female professionals to be their authentic, whole selves at work, we must take active responsibility for building on the successes of the past several decades. Rebuilding workplace rules around the life realities of *both* men and women is the challenge for the new generation of leaders and professionals.

Joyful on the Job

A Generation Pursuing Happiness at Work

BENJAMIN SCHUMACHER is from Lexington, Kentucky, and studied psychology at Washington University in St. Louis. Ben has worked in management consulting for Deloitte Consulting, McKinsey & Company, and Instituto Exclusivo in La Paz, Bolivia. He holds an MBA from Harvard Business School and finds happiness working with education-oriented nonprofits.

The unyielding sun melted into the horizon, finally relenting after a sweltering, sweaty day of work in the horse farms of central Kentucky. My hands blistered and my throat parched, I let my shovel fall to the dirt and knelt under the shade of an ancient sycamore next to my fellow irrigation installation crew members, Ariel, Manuel, and Abenamar. Our fifth, oldest, and most experienced member—"Tio" ("Uncle")—walked to the garage to input the final settings in the irrigation system controller. The evening was closing in on us, and we had scrambled to successfully finish installing a residential sprinkler system before it was too dark to work any longer. Digging trenches, laying pipe, and setting sprinkler heads for twelve hours straight is no small exertion, but there's a special gratification when a team can point directly to the fruit of its labors. From the garage, Tio flipped a switch, and as the system sprang to life with rotors blasting across the lawn and smaller heads gently misting the gardens, the five of us exchanged grins of satisfaction. We were happy.

This experience at Bluegrass Irrigation, my family's business, is one of the earliest that got me thinking about happiness on the job. How was it that my parents, entrepreneurs who had no formal business background or training, could create an environment where Tio, Ariel, Manuel, Abenamar, and I could find happiness, but the company's client who would fly in on his helicopter to monitor our progress seemed so perpetually unhappy? Or, if we are all in agreement that we'd like our bosses, coworkers, and subordinates to be happy (not to mention ourselves), why is happiness so often elusive in the workplace?

I believe it is not the idea of promoting happiness in the workplace that presents conflict to most people. It is the idea of trade-offs: when to prioritize others' happiness over yours or future happiness over immediate pleasure. In a managerial context, leaders of organizations must make these decisions frequently: how often an employee is allowed to work from home or how much time off to write into company policy, for example. Given the ubiquity of structures in the workplace—cubicles, where to sit, what to wear, scheduled hours in the office, scheduled years to the next rung on the corporate ladder, and so on—it is no wonder that a mental trade-off is manifested: how much time and happiness do I devote to the success of my company and how much do I keep to myself?

But is this traditional trade-off between employee happiness, managerial happiness, and a company's financial success as robust as it is perceived to be? I had the chance to explore this question inadvertently during the summer of 2009 in La Paz, Bolivia, where I worked at a local language institute, Instituto Exclusivo. After getting over the initial shock of the altitude (12,000 feet above sea level!) and settling into the hustle and bustle of La Paz's Sopocachi district, the institute tasked me with improving student retention rates. Fresh off two and a half years of operations consulting, I was eager to put my skill set to work. I honed in on the student-teacher relationship and observed several suboptimal practices: teachers weren't coming to lessons on time, new technologies made available by the institute were not being leveraged for lessons, and the retention rate after students' first lessons was particularly low. Like any eager consultant, I immediately set to work devising a performance-based incentive system meant to tweak specific teacher behaviors. Bonuses would be given to teachers who were punctual, who implemented technology into lessons, and who consistently kept first-time students coming back for more. However, while getting to know the teachers more personally during my time at the institute, I began to observe an intriguing relationship: teachers who were happy working there, such as three I met—Patricia, Rudy, and Helen—tended to be the top performers. Their students sang their praises, they eagerly adopted new technologies, and they contributed disproportionately to the profitability of the institute. The unhappy teachers tended to be more transient employees whose students consistently complained about their lack of preparedness and commitment, and who disproportionately contributed to the costs of the institute in the form of hiring costs, lost students, and unquantifiable detriment to the institute's brand.

Upon making this observation, I took the logic chain one step further: if good performance is associated with happiness, what was intrinsic to the institute that made these employees happy? In some cases, it was the opportunity for teachers to arrange their lessons according to their own busy schedules. Patricia worked in a chemist's lab during the day and preferred giving lessons early in the morning or later in the evening. In Rudy's case, it was the camaraderie of sporting activities such as *futsal* (five against five soccer with a smaller, less bouncy ball) that were organized through the institute; and for teachers such as Helen (who migrated from the Netherlands to La Paz in 2006), the institute's common room was clearly the teachers' primary space for socializing throughout the week with friends. The point is that whether intentional or not, certain practices of the institute contribute to employee happiness by integrating the "whole person" into the organization, and this, in turn, appears to contribute to greater productivity in the institute's employees as well.

Although the empirical correlation between employee happiness and productivity is still being researched, job satisfaction has been shown to be positively linked to productivity.[14] HBS's own Teresa Amabile has found that happiness in the workplace provokes greater creativity.[15] To me, it also seems intuitively true that I work harder when I'm happy. We all can relate to putting an "extra 10 percent" into an enjoyable activity or toward a commitment to someone we respect (the flipside, of course, appears equally probable: the resentment I feel toward an unsavory task is compounded immeasurably if I'm generally unhappy with my work environment). The question, then, is what can corporate leaders do to increase happiness within their organizations, and, notably, what are some leading-edge companies already doing?

The answers come in various forms and are certainly not as straightforward as a bigger bonus or more vacation time. I believe that for my generation, the notion of the "whole person" is central to finding happiness in the workplace, and thereby giving our best efforts toward the objectives of our employers. A "whole person" is one who feels comfortable bringing his or her authentic self to work each day, especially in a technological world that breaks down barriers between the professional and the personal. A "whole person" is able to integrate the rigorous demands of his job with the rigorous demands of his life—and work more passionately and purposefully as a result. There are a number of tools managers can employ, and young leaders should demand to promote the concept of the "whole person," thus creating a happier, more productive workspace.

First, we should attempt to *formalize flexibility into how employees perform their work*. This is all the more important to a generation of marital partners who both hold jobs outside the home. A former employer of mine, Deloitte Consulting LLP, has chosen to implement what its creators call "Mass Career Customization" (MCC). One way MCC plays out in practice is to allow employees to "dial up" or "dial down" certain aspects of their careers. This could include the amount of time spent traveling, the location from which one works, or something as fundamental as hours worked per week. I have a friend who is employed by the Washington, D.C., office, lives in New York, and currently has "dialed down" to half-time work in order to pursue her passions as an author—all with encouragement from top management. Deloitte has bought into the idea that the retention of top talent is worth keeping its top talent happy.[16]

Recently, this trend toward career flexibility has even manifested itself in the public sector. The Human Services and Public Health Department of Hennepin County in Minneapolis has implemented its own version of MCC, known as ROWE or "results-only work environment." Defining features of ROWE include location flexibility, clearly defining desired results, and, most provocatively, completely optional meetings (the idea being if the purpose of the meeting is worthwhile, it will be attended). Custodians of the program have cited tremendous productivity gains in activities such as processing incoming mail.[17]

Second, we should *seek to provide an outlet for employees to make a positive impact on people they care about,* thus bolstering the traditional employee-employer relationship to a level that yields deeper levels of happiness and purpose. In his book *Just Enough: Tools for Creating Success in Your Work and Life,* HBS professor Howard Stevenson refers to this as "significance" and defines it as a core component to "enduring success" in life. I was fortunate to work with a Boston-based nonprofit called Young Entrepreneurs Alliance (YEA) that offers this type of program to its corporate sponsors, and it is essential to their value proposition. YEA is a business-ownership program that seeks to alter the trajectory of at-risk teens. As part of its corporate sponsorship program with companies like Staples, YEA receives cash donations; but it also organizes structured learning sessions where Staples employees create training programs for the participating at-risk teens. This has obvious benefits for the teens, but for Staples, it also happens to boost employee morale, promote teamwork, and even serve as a training ground for its workforce. I believe this volunteerism in a team-based setting—supported by management—can be a powerful force in the fostering of general employee happiness through performing "significant" work.

Third, we, as rising leaders, should *consider organizing a physical fitness program.* As I discovered in my undergraduate research, exercise is connected with happiness—psychologists refer to it as "subjective well-being"—because it burns cortisol (associated with anger or fear) and produces endorphins (associated with euphoria).[18] Evidenced by the success of organic, sustainable foods, or even brands like Vitamin Water, a substantial segment of our generation is putting fitness on a pedestal—and I believe it behooves today's executives to recognize this priority. Some organizations are doing well on this front. Deloitte provides a health and fitness subsidy, a monthly newsletter with healthy lifestyle tips, and annual flu shots to all firm members.[19] Both Deloitte and another consultancy, Bain & Company, host annual World Cup soccer events.[20]

Finally, while happiness is admittedly an abstract concept, this does not diminish the importance of managing it. Since "that which gets measured gets managed," I suggest managers attempt to *track components of employee happiness over time*—and address concerns directly when they are voiced. One aspect that attracted me to McKinsey & Company is that the firm measures happiness both on a consulting project level and at a firm level across offices. On projects, a biweekly survey is sent to each project member that gauges reactions to statements such as "I am excited about my experience on this engagement," "Our working team functions well and there is an atmosphere of trust and mutual respect," and "Overall lifestyle is manageable on a sustained basis." Managers closely track survey results and adjust team dynamics accordingly. At the enterprise level, firmwide surveys gauge relative happiness levels at each office. It may not be a coincidence that the happiest region in the firm is simultaneously one of the most profitable.

In retrospect, perhaps my parents were precocious in the design of our family's small irrigation business. Employees are paid a wage above market rate that they send home to needy families, thus performing the "significant" work of positively impacting those they care about; the job certainly requires physical fitness, as I discovered by the sycamore tree long ago; while sunlight hours aren't very flexible in terms of work hours, at least breaks and lunch schedules always are; and my parents have been successful in establishing an informal culture of monitoring employee happiness and actively addressing concerns. If the employees at Bluegrass Irrigation can be happy, so can the employees at any organization, and I believe that understanding, promoting, and measuring employee happiness will be paramount in transforming the workplace for our generation.

People Leadership from Baghdad to Boston

SETH MOULTON graduated from Harvard College in 2001 and served four tours as a Marine Corps infantry officer in Iraq, two as a platoon commander and two as a special assistant to General David Petraeus. In 2011, he graduated with a joint degree from Harvard Kennedy School and Harvard Business School. He is passionate about service and bringing his experience in the Marines to bear in the private sector.

Tom Brokaw, author of the iconic *Greatest Generation*, a tribute to the men and women of our grandparents' era who fought in World War II, looked at a group of young Americans in 2003 and said, "This is the next greatest generation." But he wasn't looking at a group of Harvard or Princeton graduates, or at a group of business or technology leaders, or at a championship sports team. He was looking at a battalion of soldiers in Iraq. There he saw young Americans so dedicated to the ideal of service that they were actually putting their lives on the line to serve. They didn't just speak of service, or believe in service—they were actually *doing* it.

I was one of them, serving in Iraq, and transitioning to the business world hasn't been easy. At twenty-three, I was intimately responsible for the lives of forty young Americans, and also responsible for life-or-death decisions affecting those we met on the streets of Iraq. Settling into a classroom seat at Harvard in many respects felt boring, inconsequential, and self-serving in comparison.

But it wasn't as I expected. I thought I would return from five years serving in the Marine Corps to a crowd of unappreciative classmates, thankful that they were well ahead of me on the path to personal wealth. Harvard, after all, didn't even allow ROTC on its campus until recently.[21]

But instead of receiving a cold shoulder, I was pleasantly surprised by the respect the community showed my fellow veterans and me. Many of my peers were even envious—not of the horrors I had seen in the war or of the diminutive size of my bank account—but of the fact that I had experienced something so consequential early in life and that I learned something unique about leadership in the process. Every day I made decisions that profoundly impacted the lives of young Americans, and of Iraqis. Even the staunchest opponents of the Iraq War scarcely had the impact on the lives of others that I did on the front lines. And those experiences forged in me and in my fellow marines a sense of pride and camaraderie in our work as well as an appreciation for the difference that individual leaders can make.

So why give up that sense of purpose and service to head into a world defined by profit-seeking and self-interest? Sometimes I have to step back from the emotional pull of the war to remember that while, sadly, fighting wars is critical to our national survival, it is not what America is fundamentally about. America is a free country that thrives on the backbone of its free economy. It is a country built by individuals engaged in free enterprise, and our economic history is by far more important than our military history. I am proud to be a veteran of our country's armed forces, but I am anxious to be a part of this other fundamental part of America as well. Business requires good leadership, just as the Marine Corps does. And as I transition from the Marines to the private sector, I hope that I'll be able to take some of the lessons I learned in combat to my colleagues in the boardroom—even as they teach me something about what it takes to power an economy that keeps our country strong.

In the Marines, I learned that good leadership is about two fundamental things: accomplishing the mission and taking care of your men. Accomplishing the mission is straightforward: it's something every leader needs to do, and America could not have built the great companies of the twentieth century or won its battles overseas without business and military leaders who knew how to get things done.

But the real key to success in leadership is doing it in a way that also ensures the survival and success of the men and women who work for you. Sometimes I think that much of our business community has forgotten this lesson—as Wall Street has become infamous for its excess, companies have emphasized short-term results over long-term investment, and the gap between executives and labor has only increased.

For me, "taking care of your men" in wartime was simple when it was just the forty young men in my platoon. But soon after the invasion, I found myself leading not just a platoon of marine infantrymen but a neighborhood of Iraqi men, women, and children. Suddenly, all eyes turned to young Lieutenant Moulton when it came to solving local crime and paying the police, restoring electricity, and explaining what the Americans intended to do with the Iraqi Army we put out of a job. The impossible diversity of the task was daunting.

Business leaders face a similar mandate when their influence extends beyond their companies into their communities. At the big General Electric plant not far from where I grew up, good management requires not only providing competitive wages and reliable health care for employees, but also stewardship of the marshes and waterways that flow past the plant. Indeed, it is leadership beyond your mandate, taking care of not just your subordinates but your community, that often defines real success. What would Rockefeller mean to us today if he had kept his money to himself, or who would know the Kennedys if they simply enjoyed their house on Cape Cod? Bill Gates is an obvious contemporary example, somebody whose passing fame as this moment's wealthiest person now has the potential to become lasting fame for what he is doing to fight world health problems. He has lived most of his life amassing a personal fortune and bringing productivity to the workplace; now he is saving thousands of lives. Businessmen and women would do well to remember that whether through service, sacrifice, or simple philanthropy, most of the greatest business leaders in history are remembered not for what they earned, but for what they gave back.

Finally, there was a third leadership lesson I took from the Marine Corps that perhaps wasn't as important as the first two, but upon which the success of the first two often depended. That was the importance of exercising humility, and it was something I relearned countless times in the war. Faced with new challenges every day that I could not anticipate, overconfidence was sure to lead to failure, so I had to listen a lot, learn from both my most senior commanders and most junior men, and never rest on past success. In my little neighborhood south of Baghdad just after the invasion, my translator, a former officer in the enemy I had just fought against, became my most trusted advisor. So many times when Iraqis and Americans alike looked to me for answers, I turned to Aiyid. He was a humble man himself, for despite being a proud colonel in the Iraqi military, he drove up to me in a minivan—a man half his age and half his rank, and his former enemy—to ask for a job and volunteer to help. The humility we showed to each other was the foundation of whatever success we had together in serving the people of that neighborhood, and it has defined our friendship ever since. In a business world that has become known by the hubris that led to scandals like those that brought down Enron and WorldCom, as well as the recession of the last few years, I have to believe a similar humility would serve our economy as well.

The challenge for me—for each of us—is to take what I have learned through my own set of diverse experiences and use those lessons to become a part of forging a bright future for our country, a future defined not just by the profitability of our companies but by the role those companies play in the welfare of those they serve. When America's "greatest generation" returned from World War II, they led the nation from the home front into the greatest period of growth and prosperity the world has ever seen. Today's veterans of Iraq and Afghanistan stand alongside veterans of Teach for America, the Peace Corps, and other civilian service veterans as part of a much smaller minority in a country that values service, but doesn't always serve. I hope that this new generation of veterans who bring their own diverse experiences to the business world can have a positive influence on the American business that makes our country great, offering leadership that is guided not just by the prize of success, but by the ideal of service.

INTERVIEW WITH . . .

Deb Henretta
Group President, P&G Asia

> Deb Henretta talks about the importance of purpose and diversity at P&G, the defining characteristics of next-generation leaders, and how businesses can best adapt to utilize their strengths.

How has the concept of diversity evolved at P&G? What are the biggest changes in the company's approach to diversity?

While not always called diversity, P&G has been involved with diversity since its founding days when the P&G founder James Gamble supported education of U.S. minorities. Over time, it's taken many forms. Historically, the initial focus was on representation numbers for several groups. In more recent years P&G is focusing not only on diverse representation, but also *inclusion* so that every employee feels valued and included, so that they can perform at their peak.

What are the challenges that you face in leading a multicultural P&G organization in Asia? What have you done to address these? What works and what doesn't?

Having a multicultural organization is a strength. The fact that our twenty-one thousand employees in Asia belong to sixty-one nationalities is a clear advantage as we try and bring to life our purpose of touching and improving more consumers' lives in more parts of Asia more completely. Today, we serve 2 billion Asian consumers across forty-three markets, and this number is growing. It is critical that we reflect this diversity among our employees to be able to serve our consumers effectively. However, it is indeed important to institutionalize systems and processes that harness the best of this diversity while ensuring that we remain consistent with our global purpose, values, and principles. For this we have adopted an approach that we articulate as "As common as possible; as different as needed."

So while our success drivers, appraisals, and all key trainings are standardized and globally deployed, we also focus on critical and uniquely Asian capability needs. These are related to the effectiveness of Asian leaders to lead the diverse, multicultural teams within Asia and influence their global counterparts outside Asia.

More than any other part of the world, leaders in Asia have to constantly adapt their leadership style to inspire and motivate each of the diverse cultures and countries that comprise Asia. Using a single leadership style will prove insufficient given the differences in culture, motivations, rewards, and definitions of success in the different countries. Only leaders who can understand and adapt to these local cultures will grow into truly successful pan-Asian leaders. At P&G, we have established a multicultural program that equips our Asian leaders with deep understanding of how cultures work in a business context and, equally importantly, with skills to "style switch" as they interact with employees from different cultural backgrounds.

What new forms of diversity are emerging in such a vibrant and fast-changing part of the world?

Asia is home to one of the youngest populations in the world. This has led to a whole new demographic that we call Gen Y and define as those under thirty years of age. In P&G Asia, every one in two employees is a Gen Y'er. Frankly, this changes many things. Gen Y employees have very different attitudes compared to, say, my generation. I see this shift having three clear characteristics, which in turn spur a chain of effects at the organizational level:

1. **Y-Not:** Gen Y employees question status quo. They like challenges and they will not accept a no simply because their manager tells them so. In a way, this is great because it gets the more experimental and innovative thoughts into the room and forces the organization to embrace change faster than it would have otherwise.

2. **Y-Fi:** The second impact of the rise of Gen Y as a demographic is an increase in digital diversity. To them digital is not a skill that they need to adopt. They *are* digital. Their immersion in Web 2.0 and technologies is seamless and holistic. This forces the larger organization to speed up its own digital journey to being digital native. In P&G, we have formalized reverse mentoring programs where Gen Y employees induct older, more senior leaders into the digital way of life.

3. **Y-Go:** Gen Y employees like mobility and flexibility. Nine to five doesn't work for them. That doesn't mean they are any less productive. In fact, they are used to being connected 24/7 and can prove to be much more productive if you let them do it their way. At P&G, we have programs like flextime and work from home that try to accommodate this aspect of the Gen Y personality.

A lot of people are writing about the concept of "joy" or "happiness" at work. Do you think that thinking broadly about diversity can help people find more wholeness and happiness at work?

This goes back to the impact that Gen Y employees are having at the workplace. Traditionally, we used to find that most of us have two identities. One that we brought to work, and the other that we kept outside. We find that Gen Y has an integrated identity that is consistent between workplace, home, and society. For example, their concern for the environment or social responsibility is not extraneous to who they are as a marketing or a finance employee in the office. So they not only want to make a difference themselves, they want to know that the company they work for is also making a positive contribution. Similarly, they expect to be able to spend adequate time cultivating the different sides of their personality and not be at the office working late nights. So, they have clear expectations of work-life balance. We have tried to take all of these expectations to create a holistic Employee Value Proposition (EVP) that goes much beyond the traditional compensation and benefits approach. The P&G EVP, which was awarded the 2010 Asian Human Capital Award, consists of six pillars, including such intangibles as "pride in company," "relationship with manager," and "work-life effectiveness" in addition to the more defined ones such as "fair and competitive reward" and "learning and development."

I believe that such an EVP builds in such expectations as joy and happiness.

You see a lot of young leaders in your organization, and it's arguably a more diverse generation than any in recent memory. But are there any blind spots that this generation has about diversity? What should they look out for?

I think the answer to that is balance. As I have said, generational diversity is great because it forces us to embrace change faster than we may have otherwise. However, it is important to hold on to the good practices that we have arrived at today and be guided by time-tested principles. For us, our purpose is that guide.

We have lived by it for 174 years—that's nearly ten generations! Our purpose is to touch and improve lives, now and for generations to come. Our growth strategy today is inspired by this purpose: to improve the lives of more consumers, in more parts of the world, more completely. Today we serve over 4 billion consumers; our goal is to serve 5 billion over the next five years. That means we will have to serve all types of consumers, in all parts of the world irrespective of what the personal blind spots of a younger generation of employees may be.

What challenges remain for women in the workplace, and how is this changing over time? What has P&G done to address this?

Globally, issues such as the balance or integration of work and home life continue to be a challenge not just for women, but for men as well. We have put in place various programs for workplace flexibility to help provide alternatives and choices for employees to alleviate the challenge of managing the blend of their work and home life.

How do you see the future of diversity initiatives, inside and outside
of P&G? What will a truly diverse organization look like twenty years
from now?

> For P&G, our principle-based purpose and approach to diversity will
> continue, aiming to foster a culture of inclusion with respect for all in-
> dividuals. We want to attract and retain diverse talent throughout the
> organization, and support our employees by providing a flexible envi-
> ronment that enables them to perform at their peak. We expect diver-
> sity and inclusion to be effectively and sustainably integrated into
> P&G's DNA throughout our people processes and accountability sys-
> tems as well as our external and internal partnerships. We recognize
> that everyone is unique in their background, whether it be gender,
> geography, physical challenges, or ethnicity. We want to touch the
> lives of our employees one person at a time. Enabling our employees
> to share their diverse skills, passions, and experiences will enable us
> as a company to leverage their talent to the fullest and give us a com-
> petitive advantage to deliver against our growth strategy and touch
> more consumers' lives, in more parts of the world, more completely.
>
> Simply put, everyone valued, everyone included, everyone perform-
> ing at their peak.

CHAPTER 4

Sustainability

Integrating Preservation and Profits

The first rule of sustainability is to align with natural forces,
or at least not try to defy them.

—Paul Hawken

Sustainability is a widely used word with nearly infinite meanings. The consensus view, however, is that sustainable development incorporates the notion of meeting the needs of the present without compromising the ability of future generations to meet their needs—particularly, in the modern context, environmental needs.[1] Despite the definitional chaos, young leaders are acutely aware of the challenges we face on the environment and other issues of sustainability and are keen to address them in long-term ways.

In our MBA Student Survey, the results were encouraging. Sixty-four percent of those polled agreed or strongly agreed with the statement, "The majority of corporations will have a sustained dedication to environmental sustainability and alternative energy over the next 20 years" (see figure 4-1).

Clearly, the business community has become attuned to the concept of sustainability, and young leaders of today are confident that sustainability—as a topic and a professional pursuit—will only grow in

FIGURE 4-1

Most MBAs believe corporations will support environmental issues

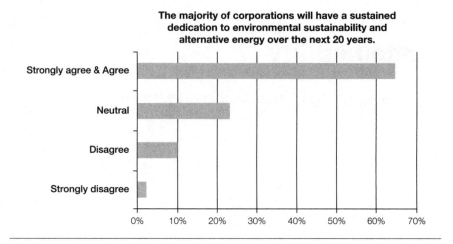

The majority of corporations will have a sustained dedication to environmental sustainability and alternative energy over the next 20 years.

importance. So how do twenty-first-century managers and organizations harness these young leaders' passions and energies, and how can aspiring young businesspeople chart a career that includes an emphasis on sustainability?

From Awareness to Intelligence

While the baby boomers have been concerned with raising environmental awareness, today's leaders are focused on environmental intelligence. Moving beyond the days of community-funded curbside recycling programs and expensive energy-efficient lightbulbs, we are seeking long-term, self-sustaining solutions that benefit entire populations, not small niches that can afford to pay. In short, we are focused on breaking the traditional trade-off between environmental and economic impact to create mass change, realizing that we will never change the world unless we eliminate the trade-offs inherent in traditional sustainability. We're also seeking to avoid the predicted shortages in energy and natural resources by finding new, cheap, and renewable ways to power the planet.

The evidence behind the environmental intelligence movement is profound. For example, a recent Deloitte/Michigan State University survey showed that millennial consumers are not willing to pay a premium for hybrid vehicles simply because they are environmentally friendly.[2] However, a hybrid vehicle with proven fuel efficiency (as measured by gallons per mile) was extremely attractive to the vast majority of participants. One participant summed it up well: "Figure out how to save the environment without charging me more, and I am all for it."[3]

Our own survey supports this claim. When we asked what product attributes mattered most, students ranked cost as the most important, with "environmentally friendly" ranking second (see table 4-1). In the era of environmental intelligence, economics matter.

So what does this balancing act mean for organizations trying to attract young leaders? It means catering to the 96 percent of 18-to-25-year-olds who aspire to work in a greener office.[4] It means evolving communication strategies to emphasize the economic benefits of "going green." And it increasingly means transitioning from traditional vehicles (nonprofits, donation-based awareness, and big-budget marketing campaigns) to the vehicles of our generation (FOPSEs, or for-profit social enterprises, consultative strategies, and interactive social media) to create compelling environmental economics.

TABLE 4-1

MBAs' rankings of project attributes

Imagine you are considering purchasing a hybrid vehicle for the first time. Please rank the following six considerations in order of importance.

Item	Total score	Overall rank
Cost	2,365	1
Environmentally friendly	2,102	2
Performance	2,067	3
Design/aesthetics	1,836	4
Status/social symbol	1,130	5
Other attribute	571	6

The Sustainability "Sprint"

One core driver of the evolution from awareness to intelligence is the wealth of resources being plowed into the sector, advancing our understanding of the environmental problem. Never before has more labor and capital been invested in fields like alternative energy, clean tech, carbon emissions, and deforestation.

To start with, investors are clearly bullish on the sector. Of the $17.7 billion of venture capital invested in 2009, energy investments represent $2.3 billion, or approximately 13 percent.[5]

With the new investment dollars come enticing job opportunities for talented graduates. Around 80 percent of the students we surveyed agreed or strongly agreed with the statement, "Alternative energy and environmental sustainability offer meaningful career paths for people in my generation (see figure 4-2)."

Business schools are launching Sustainability Centers to meet the increased student demand, and indeed, creating entire degrees (such as the Certificate in Green Supply Chain Management at the University of San Francisco).[6] A slew of recently launched sustainability rankings have kept

FIGURE 4-2

Most MBAs view energy and environmental careers as meaningful

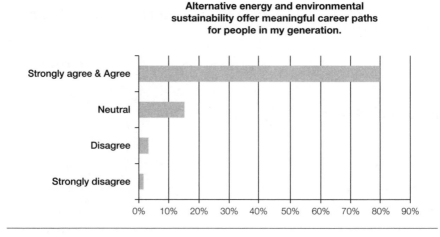

the spotlight on the environmental policies of blue-chip companies.[7] Finally, pop culture has also played an important role in furthering our understanding—Al Gore's Oscar-winning documentary *An Inconvenient Truth* and subsequent lectures on climate change brought about mass awareness of the problem in 2006.

It must be mentioned that many of these indicators are short-term measures that do not account for the long-term viability of resources devoted to the sector. As we step up our search for sustainable solutions, many market observers have warned of a "green bubble," where so-called green investors are bidding up shares of companies involved with alternative energy and environmentally friendly products and services, and scooping up initial public offerings of promising "clean-tech" ventures. Only around 30 percent of those we surveyed agreed or strongly agreed with the statement, "The green and alternative energy sectors are in a bubble." However, if they are indeed in a bubble, this could jeopardize the long-term success of these initiatives just as the dot-com crash in 2001 sent entrepreneurs and investors scrambling and set back Internet innovation.

A New Competitive Dimension

What does this mean for the young leaders looking to shape a sustainable future? Winners of the sustainability sprint will seamlessly fold environmental performance into the core economics of their organizations. In other words, their strategies—on how to attract the best employees, shorten supply chains, and sell more products—will explicitly consider the financial impacts of going green. This will lead to profound shifts in demand over the next two decades.

First, consumers will demand cheaper, more efficient products and services that are environmentally sustainable and delivered by no/low-impact supply chains. Hence, the new definition of "value" incorporates time, cost, quality, *and* sustainability. The best and brightest will reorganize their organizations' manufacturing process to deliver on all four dimensions.

Second, almost *all* job seekers will be more cognizant of a company's sustainability ranking, and will consider it alongside traditional factors such as salary, working hours, and location. Successful companies will emphasize their ranking in their job descriptions and recruiting campaigns.

Finally, students will seek to educate themselves on environmental issues and sustainable practices as preparation for the world at large. Universities must respond by both providing specialized degrees and integrating content into existing fields of study, including, of course, business.

The following stories highlight some of the new ways our generation is thinking about and addressing sustainability issues. They are not intended to be a comprehensive "playbook," but rather to provide flickers of inspiration on how to move beyond mere environmental awareness and compliance toward more long-term, self-sustaining solutions that make sound economic sense.

A Sustainable Career

ANNIE FISHMAN graduated from Yale University with a BA in environmental studies and political science. She came to Harvard Business School after working in the nonprofit sector. After graduating from HBS, she held a number of brand management positions and is currently senior marketing manager for Amyris Biotechnologies. She's the current vice president of the HBS Green Business Alumni Association and a passionate believer in achieving the impossible.

Rural Farms and Urban Blight

Born and raised in New England, I have always felt a connection to the natural world. From picking apples in local orchards to raking leaves to building snowmen in my front yard and flying kites among the sand dunes of Cape Cod, my childhood was colored by the unique environments of each season.

I spent the first half of my junior year of high school at the Mountain School, an academic program that affords students the opportunity to live and work on an organic farm in rural Vermont. Through integrated and interdisciplinary coursework as well as daily farm chores and outdoor environmental education, the Mountain School helped students discover their own relationship with an evolving natural system. Using the farm, pastures, and forests of the three-hundred-acre campus, we gained an understanding of the ecological and cultural forces that have shaped New England, and how these impacts have played out on a global scale.

For the remainder of high school and throughout college, I further pursued environmental studies, but I quickly began to identify a major tension between preserving the quality of our environment and leveraging our available natural resources to drive economic growth. At the

School for Field Studies Center for Sustainable Development in Atenas, Costa Rica, I explored eco-tourism, sustainable agriculture, and natural resource management as mechanisms for balancing the region's growing economic needs with its precious biodiversity.

Back in New Haven, however, I encountered a harsher reality. Children in the neighborhoods surrounding Yale were suffering from some of the highest asthma rates in the state, due to poor air quality resulting from high levels of particulate matter emitted by the power plants and bus depots abutting their homes. Upon graduating from Yale, I felt a deep sense of responsibility to leverage my education for social good. Like many of my peers of this generation, I was—and still am— motivated by impact; I have a bias toward action. Frustrated by the alarming health implications of fueling urban America, I spent my early career working for the Centers for Disease Control and Prevention on asthma prevention in Roxbury, Boston's poorest zip code.

I applied to Harvard Business School because I sought a toolkit of business and leadership skills that would enable me to turn my passion for social and environmental justice into meaningful action. I believed that if I could speak the language of business, I could effect change in the very organizations that were responsible for the poor air quality impacting the children of New Haven and Roxbury. Rather than addressing the symptoms, I sought to impact the root cause.

At HBS, it quickly became clear to me that I was not the only one with this career strategy. As a first-year MBA student, I created a Corporate Social Responsibility Interest Group—an offshoot of the existing Social Enterprise Club—and met classmates who had previously been everything from investment bankers to pharmaceutical chemists and army officers. We all shared a common vision: business could create not only economic but also social value.

Later that year, the 2006 debut of Al Gore's *An Inconvenient Truth* brought heightened attention and a sense of urgency to the tensions between economic growth and environmental preservation that many in my generation had recognized for years. The film brought to an estimated audience of 5 million people the consequences that we would face if we continued with business as usual. For me, those consequences were unacceptable; we need to change course. This directional shift, however, would require behavior change of massive proportions—by corporations and, most importantly, by consumers. Thus, I decided to become an expert in behavior change. In other words, a marketer.

Establishing Roots, Setting Trajectories

Although my decision to join the Clorox Company as an associate marketing manager baffled some friends and family members, I was determined to learn marketing and brand management from a firm known for building some of the most iconic brands in the world. The role was an exercise in patience; despite articulating an interest in working on a brand with a "green" positioning, I was staffed on Tilex and Clorox bathroom cleaners, some of the most chemical-laden brands in the company's portfolio.

Searching for opportunities to become more connected to my daily work, I reached out to the Clorox Eco Office, the company's fledgling environmental sustainability team who had been tasked with developing strategy and tactics to reduce the firm's environmental footprint. Apparently I wasn't the first to make such an inquiry, and along with several colleagues I was tapped to lead the Eco Network, an employee engagement initiative in support of the Eco Office's strategic goals. The two hundred-plus employees who signed up for the Eco Network shared a common interest: how could we be "intrapreneurs" within our organization to drive more sustainable business operations? More than anything, being a part of the Eco Network gave us a sense of ownership in the company's future, and provided us opportunities for cross-functional and cross-brand collaboration.

While the Eco Network gave me opportunity for influence, it didn't provide the sense of impact that I needed to feel fulfilled. I found myself far more engaged in our team's business unit sustainability audits than I did in developing a launch plan for a Tilex line extension; however,

I loved the marketing function. I felt that I could have the most impact in a role where I could lend my MBA and marketing expertise to the commercialization of a product or service that would drive environmental sustainability not only in one corporation, but in many. So I prepared for my first post-MBA career transition: from the marketing of consumer products to the marketing of renewable energy.

My experience at Clorox taught me that human behavior is hard to change. If it was this difficult to get people to change brands of bathroom cleaner, what could possibly get them to change their electricity consumption, their driving behavior, or the length of their showers? I learned that "sustainable" substitutes are most compelling when they require minimal effort and deliver some incremental benefit. Clorox's GreenWorks brand achieved initial market success because it promised cleaning efficacy equivalent to market leaders, but delivered the additional benefit of biodegradability. As I prepared to transition to work full-time on sustainable products and services, I looked for opportunities to leverage my marketing skills to educate customers, and in doing so, remove barriers to behavior change.

Moving to Clean Technology

This search brought me to Solyndra, a manufacturer of photovoltaic (solar) panels for the low-slope commercial and industrial rooftop market. Inspired by the opportunity to leverage the world's 11 billion square feet of low-slope rooftop to serve as a source of clean, renewable energy, I was also motivated by the manufacturing jobs that we were creating right here in California. A well-funded venture-backed company, Solyndra was the first recipient of the Department of Energy's loan guarantee program, which was financing the construction of its expanding Bay Area–based manufacturing facilities. As marketing manager, I developed strategies and tactics to grow awareness of the Solyndra value proposition by both channel and downstream customers.

As I came onboard at Solyndra, I quickly discovered that the impact of my work reached far beyond reducing greenhouse gas emissions. The dawning of the era of sustainability had also coincided with an economic crisis that had devastated the industries in which many of my peers were building their livelihoods. In February of 2009, my partner Scott was laid off from his role as senior associate director in GE Capital's Commercial Real Estate Division. GE Capital virtually shut down its San Francisco–based real estate operations, as did many of its competitors. Having built his career to that point in commercial real estate finance, Scott suddenly found himself in a job market that no longer valued his qualifications.

Fellow members of my HBS class of 2007 were finding themselves in similar situations. On a visit to New York City later that year, Scott and I met up with five HBS classmates and their partners for brunch one Sunday morning. Of the six of us, two had been laid off from their jobs in finance and one had left his firm following a recent acquisition. Like Scott, these friends had suddenly gone from climbing the corporate ladder to having no ladder at all. As my friends sat in this West Village café sharing stories, one thing became frighteningly clear: they could not find new jobs by simply returning to the industries from which they had been shed. There were no jobs left. They would need to change industries—or create new ones.

A Reset Opportunity for Careers

At the nexus of these two generational challenges—economic meltdown and global warming—lies a compelling solution: clean technology. I used to wonder: what if we could combine the ability of business to meet consumer needs with our underutilized human capital, and harness this power to create products and services that sustain rather than deplete our earth's resources? The clean technology industry is doing just that. I now lead marketing for Amyris, a renewable products firm whose laboratories are burgeoning with chemists and biologists developing alternatives to petroleum for use in chemicals, plastics, cosmetics, and fuels.

The intellectual capital of the semiconductor industry is finding work once again building solar modules. Building tradesmen—from roofers to electricians to carpenters—are adapting their skills to provide sustainability-related services. Scott is currently retooling his skill set and quickly becoming an expert in both commercial and residential rooftop solar financing. And all of these renewable energy alternatives require capital to fund their development and financial solutions to sustain their growth.

Creating renewable sources of energy ensures not only a healthier planet, but also a healthier economy. While we can certainly adjust our behavior to reduce consumption, we also have the opportunity to design and develop more environmentally sustainable substitutes. The possibilities for innovation are seemingly endless, as we can—and must—develop solutions that serve the needs of the society we've built for ourselves, while maintaining future generations' ability to meet their needs as well.

From Safety Nets to Trampolines

VALERIE BOCKSTETTE graduated from Brown University with a degree in economics and international relations. After three years as an investment banker, she came to Harvard Business School and discovered her passion for social impact. She is currently a director at FSG, a nonprofit consulting firm specializing in shared value strategies.

In the spring of 2005, I participated in the annual "Portrait Project," a tradition for graduating students at Harvard Business School. Each year, students are invited to answer a simple but profound question, taken from a poem written by Pulitzer Prize–winning author Mary Oliver: "What is it that you plan to do with your one wild and precious life?"

My seemingly odd answer was:

I plan to build trampolines. Remember jumping on one as a kid— the more you jumped, the more support you got—and like magic— you rose higher and higher, as though you could bounce forever? I grew up on such a trampoline. No, my family wasn't in the circus.

When I wrote this essay more than five years ago, I wholeheartedly planned to dedicate my professional career to building trampolines by creating innovative charter schools that unlock the potential of all children. But things sometimes don't turn out the way you intend—I am now a strategy consultant. At my five-year HBS reunion I reflected on my Portrait Project essay and my career ambitions at the time and briefly lamented not becoming an education reformer.

However, it dawned on me that even in my current role advising major corporations, I get to lay the groundwork for trampolines every day. And potentially as important, I have the privilege of being at the forefront of the campaign against the corporate world's prevailing safety-net mentality. This essay explores the future of sustainability by juxtaposing the concept of trampolines with the concept of safety nets. The former is a mechanism for reaching new heights; the latter is a mechanism for protecting against downside.

The Big Sustainability Debate: Trampolines Versus Safety Nets

After graduating from HBS, I participated in the Leadership Fellows Program, which places HBS graduates in leadership positions with selected nonprofits. My one-year fellowship at a small consulting social enterprise in Boston quickly turned into two years, during which I had the privilege of providing advice to dozens of nonprofits in the Boston area. However, it became very clear to me that while nonprofits working on the ground can do a world of good, the sum of their efforts is not going to be enough to tackle the pressing issues facing our planet. The answer lies in convincing the private sector to shed the notion that sustainability efforts are about safety nets, rather than trampolines, for change.

You're probably asking yourself: what is a safety-net mentality in the corporate sector—and what does this have to do with sustainability? A safety-net mentality means viewing sustainability—being "green," corporate social responsibility (CSR), and all the other terms that fit in this category—as activities that help companies avoid risk, mitigate harm to corporate reputation, respond to stakeholder activism, and garner a positive press headline. This inauthentic way of thinking, which sadly still prevails in too many boardrooms, is fundamentally flawed.

What, then, is a trampoline mentality? A trampoline mentality means that companies understand and embrace the concept of creating shared value—the idea pioneered by Michael Porter and FSG, the firm I have been working for since my fellowship ended in 2007—which states that companies can create environmental and social value alongside, and not in opposition to, shareholder value. Companies can be trampolines for sound environmental practices, social progress, and profits. The idea of a triple bottom line approach is not new, of course, but the key difference is that companies that truly embrace shared value are pursuing a goal that is more about proactive value creation and less about the reactive mitigation of potential value destruction. What does this mean in practice?

A safety-net approach means doing the bare minimum, and for the wrong reasons. Companies that view sustainability as a necessary evil of appeasing loud activists, or as a "tick the box" effort to fill out a perceived necessary reporting framework, or as simply reducing their footprint may be missing out on huge opportunities for value creation. Just ask GE, which with its pioneering "ecomagination" efforts was able to generate billions in incremental revenue and raise awareness for the importance of environmental efficiency among its whole client base.[8]

Or Walmart. Reducing its own environmental footprint was not ambitious enough for this giant retailer. Walmart realized that the clout of its purchasing power among suppliers could be leveraged to catapult them to change.[9] Walmart announced in 2010 that it expected its suppliers to take responsibility for minimizing their footprints by reducing packaging, changing production, or even altering product formulation. The Walmart Sustainability Index asked a hundred thousand suppliers to evaluate their own sustainability and analyze their product's life cycles so that Walmart could ultimately provide its customers with transparent information on the environmental impact of its product offerings.[10]

Indeed, both Walmart and GE were driven to these bold moves because they knew it would ultimately bolster their bottom line, not because they wanted to altruistically save the planet. But that is precisely the point. A "saving the planet" mentality might have led them to a cautious safety-net approach, making a few basic adjustments to optimize their use of resources today. However, by instead becoming trampolines for change, these two companies had much more impact on the planet.

So where does this leave me on my journey to build trampolines? At my current job at FSG I get to work with large corporations on a daily basis, and I see it as my passion and purpose to convince them to adopt a trampoline approach to their engagement with society. Along with my teammates I get to inspire companies to look beyond the bare minimum requirements and seek out opportunities to expand the business by turning societal challenges, such as scarce resources, into new products or services, or more productive value chains.

I've gotten to work with companies in the IT industry that have developed new tailored products to help their customers manage and reduce their footprints; I've worked with agricultural input companies that have created ways to help smallholder farmers improve their productivity, all the while making more efficient use of natural resources; I've worked with companies in the pharmaceutical industry that have reshaped whole distribution networks to create new jobs and thereby strengthen the overall communities in which they operate.

As Michael Porter recently said about this new way of corporate thinking:

> I think what's happening now is really a redefinition of the boundaries of capitalism. A redefinition of what productive, effective, operating practices look like in corporations. A redefinition of how one thinks about designing products and getting those products to the market; with a much broader perspective of the impact and effect of a whole variety of social issues, let's take the environment. We used to think that dealing with environmental compliance issues was expensive; it inflicted cost on the firm. The more we've learned over the last several decades the more we've understood that, actually, good environmental performance is also good productivity performance; it reflects greater use of resources. I see this Creating Shared Value as kind of the next stage of evolution in the sophistication of the capitalist model.[11]

In other words, shared value means not only reimagining the individual leadership of companies; it also means reimagining the very nature of capitalism. It describes exactly the type of system I was hoping to find after business school, and I feel lucky that I get to help shape this system every day through my work.

What Trampolines Mean to You

This way of thinking about sustainability is not new news to the current crop of young MBA students looking for inspiring careers. As an alumni mentor at both my undergraduate and graduate alma maters, I get e-mails almost every week from students or recent graduates looking for careers that put passion and purpose ahead of big salaries. An executive at one of the largest companies in the United States recently told me that the firm's Web page that gets the most hits from people after its careers page is its corporate citizenship page, which discusses the company's environmental and social commitments. I believe this should make companies excited—and very nervous.

It is widely known that prospective employees are no longer satisfied with working for companies that pay lip service to sustainability. They are no longer satisfied with companies that issue a 150-plus-page sustainability report with glossy pictures and raw data on reducing their carbon footprint. Today's young employees can see right through that. Companies that embed sustainability into the fabric of their business strategy and attempt to be trampolines for dramatic and lasting progress are much more attractive to the next generation of talent than companies that view sustainability as a safety net that is removed from their day-to-day activities.

Even investors are starting to ask more and more questions about how a company's long-term business strategy is tied to its sustainability strategy. Bloomberg chairman Peter Grauer said in the summer of 2010 that "the firm believes environmental, social and governance (ESG) will become fundamental to equity market analysis" as he unveiled plans for how Bloomberg would embed ESG data into its platform.[12]

What does all of this mean in practice for you? Ask yourself whether your current or any prospective company has a trampoline or a safety-net mentality toward its environmental engagement. If it is the latter, it is not alone. A 2010 report by Accenture and the UN Global Compact found that 93 percent of Global Compact CEOs see sustainability as important to their future success.[13] However, strengthening brand, trust, and reputation was found to be the strongest motivator for taking action on sustainability issues, identified by 72 percent of CEOs. This sounds more like a safety-net reaction than proactive trampoline building. Further, the study found that while 88 percent of CEOs agreed that sustainability should be embedded throughout the supply chain, only 54 percent were actually doing so. You may not be alone now, but you could be in the future. Eighty percent of CEOs in the same study believe that a "new era in which sustainability is fully integrated across their global business footprint" is only fifteen years away.

This means that CEOs, managers, and the next generation of MBAs—in other words, you—have time to get ahead of this curve and put companies proactively on a path of long-term, sustainable value creation. This path could unfold in several ways:

Start with the minimum: Ensure a sustainable footprint. No matter what kind of company you are working for, it is sourcing or selling products that touch our ecosystem. Of course, in the case of Starbucks, it is easy to see that being proactive means enabling sound environmental practices of coffee farmers. But even if you're not working at Starbucks, you can act. Ask your company to audit its supply chain to find all of its touch points with our earth's natural resources, and find places to turn waste and harmful practices into bottom-line savings. If that's too much, start small: procure your company's cafeteria food from a caterer who sources locally.

Think bigger: Develop new products or services that are green. Every company can create its version of the Prius. For HP, for example, this meant developing printers that virtually eliminate warm-up time, cutting a printer's energy use by up to 50 percent—helping avoid 1.3 million tonnes of CO_2 emissions in 2009, equivalent to removing more than 240,000 cars from the road for one year.[14] For SAP, for example, this meant developing a software suite to help customers manage their own environmental footprint. Think about your company's products and services: there is a Prius—an offering that is delightful and energy saving—just waiting to be discovered. Why not organize a brainstorm to ask, "What societal and ecological challenges can our company turn into business opportunities?"

Think bolder: Invest in your "green" competitive context. Finally, on a more long-term basis, think about what will be required in twenty years to keep your company sustainable, and urge that these investments be made now. For Mars, for example, this currently means investing in the cocoa farming sector in the Ivory Coast to ensure a high-quality supply chain for the next generation.[15] For vineyards, this means investing in drip irrigation systems. For companies that source raw materials in Africa, this might mean investing in processing facilities there, rather than shipping product elsewhere for the next step of the value chain. For companies wanting to switch to renewable energies, this might mean partnering with several local peers and even competitors to ensure that the community has the grids in place to connect to renewable energy sources.

You can play an active role in putting your company on the path of the shared-value evolution. Wouldn't you be happier if you could come to work every day knowing you could jump on a trampoline? I know I am.

The Value of Community Partnerships in Addressing Climate Change

CHARLEY CUMMINGS remains vice president of Clean Power Now. After graduating from Brown University in 2006 with a degree in public policy, he spent three years as a management consultant. His other experience includes designing the corporate social responsibility strategy of an organic soup company and working for a member of the House of Commons in the British Parliament. He graduated from Harvard Business School in May 2011. He is a passionate believer in clean technology and renewable energy.

At first there were roughly a dozen of us, including a retired engineer from GE, a ferry boat captain, a former member of the Royal Air Force, a motorcycle enthusiast, the president of another local nonprofit, an Episcopal priest . . . and me, the college student. The only thing we seemed to have in common is that we were all residents of Cape Cod, the nation's vacationland.

What brought us together each Tuesday night in 2003 was an entrepreneur's proposal to build the nation's first offshore wind farm, right in our backyard in Nantucket Sound. Cape Wind, as the project was called, promised to provide clean, pollution-free, renewable energy to three-quarters of Cape and Islands (Nantucket and Martha's Vineyard) residents, offsetting the equivalent of a million tons of carbon dioxide emissions per year.[16]

The project mattered to me personally because it was a big idea. I believe energy and climate change are the global challenge of our generation, and yet I struggle to believe that doing the little things on my own—exchanging incandescent lightbulbs, for example—make much of a difference at all, given the enormity of the problem.

Despite a lot of rhetoric, the extent of the problem has become markedly clear over the past few years. The scientific mechanism behind climate change is little disputed. It is now unambiguous that human activities are changing the concentration of greenhouse gases in the earth's atmosphere and have been doing so since the Industrial Revolution. As our carbon dioxide emissions have increased from roughly 1.5 billion tons per year in 1950 to 6 billion tons today, carbon dioxide concentrations in the atmosphere have increased from 300 parts per million (ppm) in 1950 to 390 ppm today.[17] The debate in climate change thus now surrounds not whether but by how much and at what rate global temperature will increase as a result.

The Massachusetts Institute of Technology Center for Global Climate Change Science has produced some of the most widely cited climate models, which predict fairly severe threats to our livelihood if we do not enact policy changes. From an economic perspective, however, the interesting part of the model is the "long tail" of the probability curve. The model suggests a 9 percent probability of a very severe increase of 12° to 15°F by 2100. According to the U.K.'s *Stern Review*, this corresponds to an estimated drop in world GDP of 20 percent or more, more than $12 trillion.[18] A probability-weighted net present value analysis—and note this is without any bleeding-heart rhetoric—tells any MBA that despite a low probability, the catastrophic costs overwhelm the NPV, compelling one to purchase insurance of some kind.

Cape Wind—and the nascent offshore wind industry it will spurn—provides a piece of this insurance. Unfortunately, just a few months following the initial project proposal, some 60 percent of Cape and Islands residents believed the cost of putting 130 utility-scale wind turbines in Nantucket Sound outweighed the project's benefits.[19] The millions of dollars invested by a well-funded opposition group had paid off. People now believed the turbines would hurt tourism, damage property values, kill fish and birds, destroy our horizon, and enrich a private developer through numerous subsidies and tax incentives, all while increasing electric rates. "Not in my backyard," replied many residents.

Early on, traditional environmental groups were nowhere to be found. We believed this was perhaps because these groups—trained in the LBJ-era of regulation and reform politics—were too used to fighting the regulatory battles of the past. Too used to saying "no" instead of "yes."

Enter our motley crew in late 2003. We were not particularly enlightened; we were really a bunch of residents simply interested in hearing the truth. We invited representatives from the developer to our meetings, asked questions of the federal and state regulators, and did our own secondary research. The retired engineers in our group modeled the visual impact of the project, finding that if you stood on the beach and held out your arm, the turbines would appear as a quarter of an inch on the horizon (perhaps half of your thumbnail).

As a result, we came to the conclusion that most of the oppositions' objections to the project were fabricated, serving as an increasingly transparent veil over their underlying desire to simply not have an eyesore on the horizon. We also believed that the public benefits far outweighed the potential negative impacts of the project.

So we went about our work, distributing black-and-white fact sheets (often with upwards of ten pages of analysis) that made the case to support the project. The opposition group would then publish a full-page color ad in the newspaper with a sketch of the project's footprint exaggerated by ten times and the developer himself depicted as Godzilla, trampling over Cape Cod and stuffing money into his pockets.

Despite our early failures in public relations, we did begin doing things that were somewhat radical in the nonprofit sector. Although we never received financial support of any kind from Cape Wind Associates, we saw ourselves as the sole connecting point between citizens, the developer, and the regulatory agencies. We were unabashed about developing a close relationship with private industry.

Further, while the opposition's argument always included "this guy is going to make a lot of money on this project," our response was that indeed we hoped that he would, so as to encourage more entrants into the offshore renewable industry. This was a foreign concept for many environmental groups: in their view, the profit motive was part of the problem, not the solution. Indeed, this has long been true—the profit motive has been the inducement for many companies to destroy the environment, from the pursuit of natural resources to the production of finished goods. In our mind, however, this was the answer to the problem—if we could show that an entrepreneur could profit from an activity that contributed to the common good, the profit motive was actually something we needed to embrace.

Our meetings grew from six people to twenty-five before it became unwieldy to meet as a group. In late 2003, we formed a 501c(3) organization, voted on a permanent board of directors, and began raising money to hire an executive director full time. We would call ourselves Clean Power Now.

Our membership grew to 4,000 in 2004, doubled to 8,000 in 2006, and now stands at 15,000. With generous support from and collaborations with organizations with a similar view of social change, most notably the Civil Society Institute, we were able to amass the resources to mobilize thousands of citizens to speak at public hearings and empower citizens to educate their neighbors about the merits of renewable energy—and Cape Wind in particular.

In 2010, we felt as though we had achieved success. Our executive director had appeared on Jon Stewart's *The Daily Show* and on the pages of the *Los Angeles Times.* An astonishing 86 percent of Massachusetts residents (74 percent of Cape and Islands residents) now supported the project.[20] And, in the spring of 2010, the secretary of the interior, Ken Salazar, gave the project a final stamp of approval.

The first offshore wind farm in the country would soon be built.

Despite almost ten years and dozens of public hearings later, the Cape Wind project has not yet cleared all of the necessary regulatory hurdles. Steel is not yet in the ground. And it is just a single project, with an average production of 170 megawatts. By comparison, many fossil fuel–fired power plants generate upwards of 2,000 megawatts, enough to power the homes of millions of people. The path toward a sustainable energy future is indeed going to be a long one.

For me, the lesson was clear—the energy and environmental challenges of the twenty-first century would ultimately be solved by small communities of individuals, albeit not in the ways one might anticipate. A real difference won't be achieved just by changing our lightbulbs. Instead, we can make a substantial impact by working together to help pursue sources of energy consistent with our vision for our future.

For young corporate executives finding their way in the energy industry, the lesson in the Cape Wind and Clean Power Now story is that there is tremendous value in identifying, fostering, and assisting groups of supportive local citizens in the course of project development. These groups can build and sustain an autonomous "third voice" in the debate, independent of existing interest groups. This can be vital to achieving public support for a project and, in turn, gaining the approval of a regulatory body charged with determining whether or not a particular project is ultimately in the public interest.

How to do this can be tricky. A well-financed but disingenuous PR campaign is not equivalent to systematically identifying champions of your cause and empowering them with information—not just about the particulars of a project, but about the company's broader mission. However, going so far as to directly fund a group of local advocates would likely compromise this group's integrity and dilute their effectiveness.

Although Clean Power Now was always kept at an arm's length financially from the developer, we benefited from the company's willingness to engage with us, attend our meetings, and provide us with information— in some cases even information they might have been unwilling to release publicly. Energy developers have known for decades that failure to engage a community can sink a project. Conversely, proactively facilitating the development of independent groups of citizens and partnering with these groups—and other existing community organizations—can yield meaningful results, as the struggle over Cape Wind reveals.

Indeed, because all energy projects have a footprint—and renewable technologies tend to have more visible ones—these types of partnerships are the only means to achieving measurable progress toward a sustainable energy future. The private sector can in fact solve the most intractable challenge of the twenty-first century, but it will require a sustained commitment from the energy industry to community partnerships and a concomitant level of engagement from local citizens. Given the environmental and economic benefits that will accrue to both parties, we should be optimistic that a developer—along with a few interested citizens—can change a long-standing industry paradigm in an effort to pursue big solutions to a big problem.

INTERVIEW WITH . . .

Carter Roberts

President and CEO of the World Wildlife Fund

> Carter Roberts reflects on leading sustainability initiatives, weighs in on the green bubble debate, and gives advice to young leaders looking to build sustainability into their careers.

Reflecting on your experience leading teams at Gillette and Procter & Gamble, how should leaders think about pioneering sustainability initiatives within their corporations?

From our operational perspective there are three things a leader needs to provide to move this change through their organization: vision, empowerment, and incentives.

First, vision. Signals from the very top of an organization do wonders for inspiring and motivating teams, and also ensuring that these initiatives survive and flourish during budget debates and business challenges. I've rarely seen a sustainability program succeed without clear direction from the top.

Second, empowerment. The only way to become sustainable is to make changes in the way companies design, source, distribute, and market their products. Giving employees the space to innovate is fundamental.

Finally, incentives. The best companies build sustainability measures into the performance evaluation and compensation of leaders throughout their operations.

From a strategic perspective, I'd encourage any leader to think deeply about the purpose of their business. Divest those parts that don't fit and grow those that embody the sustainability paradigm.

**With companies focusing more than ever on sustainable initiatives
and recently minted graduates seeking careers in the field, do you
see sustainability as a short-lived fad?**

Those companies that embrace the concepts of sustainability and integrate them into their businesses are the ones that will survive and thrive in the decades to come. Those who do not will find themselves obsolete, with little access to natural resources, trying to compete in a world that has changed around them.

The imperatives to move in this direction are not going to change anytime soon. We are growing from 6.5 to 9 billion people; their needs will need to be met in the context of a finite planet. Something has to give.

If we want natural resources to support our needs, we'll need to create new means of delivering food, shelter, and energy while using less land, water, and energy. Those individuals and those businesses that figure this out will have a comparative advantage as things get tight. And things will get tight.

**Both early-stage and growth-stage investors are plowing more capital
than ever into clean tech and energy investments. Are we in the
middle of a "green bubble"? Why or why not?**

We are investing more money than ever in launching new forms of energy, a good thing given the imperative to move beyond fossil fuels and address the enormous risk that climate change presents to our economy, national security, and our planet.

While many investments were made in anticipation of a much-needed price signal on carbon, which never materialized this summer, other countries and even states are moving forward, particularly China, by investing in these technologies and creating related regulatory or planning frameworks. For these reasons, I don't see a bubble per se in this market, more like the emergence of a new market sector, in which I fear the U.S. will become a laggard.

Beyond climate change, however, there is another great horseman of the apocalypse, which is natural resource scarcity, particularly water, and the drying up of our supply chains. Leading companies are beginning to invest more and more into inventing means of production that use less land, less water, and less energy. All of these hold great promise for some of our biggest businesses.

What is the best way to "teach" fundamental principles of sustainability to businesspeople? How do you hope universities and business schools will start to integrate these principles into their curricula?

I look back at my own experience and recognize that HBS would have been the perfect place to begin thinking about these concepts. Twenty years ago we were mostly concerned with the environment in the context of pesky regulations one needed to navigate. Now, most successful businesses reach all the way around the world; they see these great social issues in all their work and know that solving these issues is not only the right thing to do but also a source of comparative advantage.

I don't think you can teach sustainability in some kind of standalone course. Sustainability delivers more to the bottom line by stripping out costs, by securing longer-term contracts, markets, and sources of raw materials, by navigating risks, and by building comparative advantage in emerging markets. There's little reason for consigning these issues to a specialty elective course; they really ought to be integrated into courses on strategic planning, manufacturing, finance, marketing, international relations, and managing in a regulatory environment.

Sustainability principles are all about "how to think," not "what to think." They're about changing the lens through which you evaluate resource allocation, product development, systems management, and, of course, success. They're about seeing things differently. That's what we need to be teaching the MBA students today.

You built a career in the private sector, then switched to the nonprofit side, working at the Nature Conservancy and now as head of WWF. Should young people start in the private sector first, then switch later? How should they think about building their careers in sustainability, clean tech, energy, and related areas? Has this changed over the past twenty years?

It doesn't matter where you begin your career. What matters most is developing the ability to connect the dots between sectors. The rarest and most valuable commodity in our work is those individuals who can bridge government, business, civil society, and academia in solving the biggest problems facing our society.

Twenty years ago, most people went to work in one sector and remained in that sector for the majority of their careers. Now, it is much more prevalent to see executives from business moving to the nonprofit sector and vice versa. For example, today at WWF, we have former executives from Procter & Gamble, McKinsey, Watson-Wyatt, Nike, Chiquita, IFC, Home Depot, and Microsoft on our leadership team. These people bring a different perspective to our "business" and how we develop strategies to achieve our mission.

On the flip side, businesses like Walmart, Kraft, Coca-Cola, and so on are bringing in key staff with public sector or nonprofit sector experience to provide a broader perspective on their business. In both cases, it's about learning from each other and recognizing that we are never too old to learn.

My role models for this are people like John Sawhill, Chad Holliday, Roger Sant, and Larry Linden—people who were famously successful in business, but who also played important roles in government and with NGOs like WWF, and who know how to craft solutions that bridge all these sectors.

Inevitably, the world's most successful business leaders begin to think about their legacy. Besides delivering shareholder value and building wealth, they begin to think about what they are leaving behind, and their role in solving the greatest social issues of our day—whether that's poverty reduction, education, climate stabilization, or ensuring that we don't lose places like the Amazon or the world's great coral reefs. My advice is don't wait too long to think about those issues—build them into every phase of your career and find the company that lets you make that happen.

I'll never forget talking with Neville Isdell and Hank Paulson about this issue—and listening to them agree on an unexpected virtue of taking Coke and Goldman Sachs in the direction of sustainability, which is that it enabled them to attract and keep the best and brightest, since those individuals want more out of their careers than just money.

Some skeptics believe in the inevitable stalemate between being green and being financially competitive. How do you think about breaking this trade-off?

The ultimate reason to pursue sustainability is that it makes money. Short-term you'll see some trade-offs, but over the long term, you cannot escape the challenges of resource scarcity and climate change. Those companies that address these issues will have first-mover advantage in cost reductions through efficiency, in more secure supply chains around the world, and in devising technology and process solutions that will be in demand around the world.

Two years ago I came back to my HBS reunion and attended this standing-room-only lecture by Howard Stevenson called "Make Your Own Luck." Professor Stevenson's main message was that you could make your own luck by building businesses around inevitable trends in the world. When Professor Stevenson polled the hundreds of grads crowding Burden Hall, the top four trends mentioned included China, climate change, and resource scarcity—an intertwined set of issues that revolve around sustainability or meeting the needs of humanity without destroying the planet.

How has the notion of sustainable leadership changed over the past twenty years?

First, there weren't many "sustainable leaders" twenty years ago. Maybe Ray Anderson from Interface, Paul Hawken from Smith and Hawken, Ben Cohen from Ben & Jerry's. They were the "outliers"; lone voices on these issues. Today, the role of the sustainability leader has been transformed from a "nice to do" to fundamental to the future success of the business. It is recognized as a professional field, and the "smart ones" are in demand by major corporations around the globe.

The twentieth-century notion of sustainability was for a company to have its foundation put some minimal funds into a feel-good project to attain some kind of green halo.

The twenty-first-century approach to sustainability is more fundamental. If you just look at the long-term trends—more people, more consumption, finite planet—you realize sustainability has to be mainstreamed. It's about defining the basic nature of your business. Just look at DuPont, which now expresses its vision to be "the world's most dynamic science company, creating sustainable solutions essential to a better, safer, and healthier life for people everywhere."

Have there been any environmental initiatives started by young people that have captivated you?

I am always captivated by the creativity of young people. I look at my two sons and daughter and they surprise me every day with their view of the world. I taught a class at my oldest son's school last year and afterwards the science teacher came up to me and said, "After twenty years teaching this course, this is the first time that my kids are having nightmares about the future of the planet. What should I do?" I told him that we have to give them the tools to do something about it and encourage them to invent and take chances wherever they are.

Just last week I met a young fisherman named Anli who is pioneering the creation of community marine reserves off the coast of Mozambique. After seeing their coastlines stripped by foreign fishing fleets from Spain to China, Anli and his community are taking matters into their own hands by establishing marine protected areas that are patrolled by fishermen, and then enforced by the new government's navy. Five years later, they are now catching more fish and bigger fish as a result. The community invited me and the head of CARE to join them last week in laying the first buoys to set the boundaries of the newest fishing reserve—a stunning place that links coral reefs to mangroves to sea grass beds and a place of great productivity for fish. I got chills down my spine thinking of the power of giving local communities the tools and the authority to chart their own future.

CHAPTER 5

Technology

Competing by Connecting

What used to be cigarette breaks could turn into "social media breaks"
as long as there is a clear signal and IT isn't looking.

—David Armano, Senior Vice President, Edelman Digital

Consider how desktop computing defined the 1980s. The first personal computer, the MITS Altair 8080, shipped in 1975 and sold a few thousand units with very little fanfare. By 1980, the number of personal computers had grown to just under one million.[1] But it was between 1980 and 1990 that the personal computer reached ubiquity, with the total number of PCs shipped hitting 100 million by the end of the decade.[2]

In the early 1990s, this ubiquity paved the way for a global system of interconnected computer networks using a standard protocol suite (the Internet). The Internet carried a seemingly endless array of information, with the World Wide Web and electronic mail redefining how people searched for information and communicated with each other. The growth of the World Wide Web, in particular, was exponential until the dot-com crash of 2000, when tech stocks plummeted but quickly rebounded a little over a year later.

The New Technologies: Web 2.0 and Mobile

When Mark Zuckerberg began coding thefacebook.com in his Harvard dorm room in 2004, little did he know that he was ushering a whole new revolution—Web 2.0. With new social media tools, such as Facebook, promoting openness, connectedness, and user-centered design, people could easily share the things that mattered most to them. Countless virtual communities have since been formed, creating new opportunities for cause-driven collaboration. And companies have found a ready-made marketing channel bursting with engaged fans. From its humble beginnings, Facebook grew to 750 million members in 2011. Web 2.0 is a defining technology for the next generation.

More recently, a new wave of mobile technology has emerged. Driven by the rapid growth in the number of smartphones in existence, now around 250 million units worldwide, companies large and small are introducing never-before-seen mobile-based products and services.[3] For the first time, customer segmentation and targeting can occur at the demographic, psychographic, *and* real-time geographic level. This is leading to unprecedented new business opportunities. For example, location-based start-up Foursquare recently announced a strategic partnership with grocery chain Whole Foods to offer discounts for those who "check in" to stores.[4] Shopkick, a mobile coupon start-up, delivers coupons to consumers as they pass by stores, driving increased foot traffic.[5] Yelp provides reviews on, and directions to, local businesses.[6] Mobile technology is perhaps the second prominent new technology of the next generation.

A Host of Different Technologies

Although this chapter focuses almost exclusively on Web 2.0 and mobile-based technology, various other technologies, such as biotechnology and artificial intelligence, have also seen dramatic growth in the past five years. That said, the types of technology that tend to define generations and be relevant to numerous organizations are usually either consumer-facing technologies or those that revolutionize business models, like the personal computer and the Internet. So for these reasons (and for purposes of brevity), this chapter focuses on Web 2.0 and mobile technologies and digs deeper into how young leaders are applying these technologies in bold and innovative ways. Our surveyed students agree. When asked to rank the top technologies that will be critical to the functioning of business in the twenty-first century, mobile, social media, and cloud computing turned out in the top three, with a considerable 40.6 percent ranking mobile as number one (see figure 5-1).

The intellectual excitement around both Web 2.0 and mobile technology is that the opportunities they present are just beginning to be explored by organizations large and small. The ways that organizations are using these technologies are fascinating.

Twitter, a microblogging platform, is allowing companies and celebrities to address their fans directly with exclusive announcements. Britney Spears, for example, often "tweets" her impromptu concert locations to her 8 million Twitter fans less than ten minutes before beginning a performance, drawing huge crowds in a short amount of time.[7] Groupon, a company worth over $10 billion and the fastest company to reach $100 million in revenue, harnesses the power of crowds to get group discounts on services offered by local merchants.[8] In a recent deal offered in

FIGURE 5-1

MBAs rate importance of new technologies

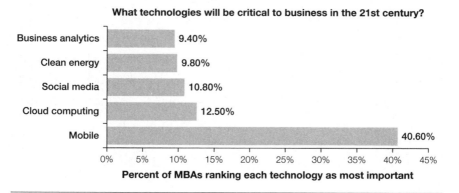

What technologies will be critical to business in the 21st century?

conjunction with Gap stores, Groupon sold 440,000 50 percent off deals in one day, generating over $11 million in revenue.[9]

Foursquare, the geolocation start-up, is allowing people to explore their city by awarding points and rewards for "checking in" to venues, leading to interesting O2O (online-to-offline) business opportunities. For example, Foursquare established a partnership with Starbucks, which awards a free beverage to those who check in most frequently at Starbucks stores.[10]

In this chapter, our contributors describe specific technologies, business models, and applications. The first is social media—the use of Web-based technologies to foster interactive dialogue and sharing. Second, this chapter also looks into two-sided marketplaces, economic platforms with two distinct user groups that benefit from network effects. We also discuss innovative mobile applications, such as location-based services.

Although this is just the beginning of the new-technology phenomenon, experts are already asking questions about the future. Will Facebook be around forever? Which companies will define the mobile space? What does Web 3.0 look like? In this chapter, we resist the temptation to make *ex-ante* predictions about which technologies will end up with dominant market share. In fact, companies investing blindly in new technologies can face enormous write-offs in the future. MySpace is an example, losing over 2 million users per month after reaching a peak of 100 million users in 2006.[11] During this time, MySpace was heralded as the "next big thing" on the Internet, attracting significant attention and resources. Other examples of falls from grace abound. Lycos, for example, was sold for $5.4 billion at the height of the dot-com boom, only to be recently valued at a paltry $36 million.[12] These examples act as a warning for companies to beware of the shiny new thing. Business strategy should dictate which technology is used, not the other way around. And as technology changes quickly, companies need to steadfastly position themselves ahead of the curve.

Building an Online Marketplace

JAMES REINHART is the founding CEO of thredUP, an online kids' clothing swap. He believes in the power of social technology for creating new online communities. Prior to attending the Harvard Business School and the Kennedy School, while working in the Bay Area, he helped develop one of the nation's premier public schools, Pacific Collegiate School—recently named the number seven high school in America by *U.S. News & World Report.* He cofounded Beacon Education Network, a charter management and school turnaround organization, and was a Goldsmith Fellow in Social Enterprise at HBS and a George Fellow at the Center for Public Leadership.

"Here's the fundamental problem: this business breaks real easily around liquidity in the marketplace. Markets are really hard to build. And a market for secondhand children's clothing—I just don't buy it." Eric Paley, the managing director of Founder Collective, one of the nation's hottest new microventure capitalists, was not buying what I was selling. It was mid-October 2009. Eric was not alone. A countless number of advisors, investors, and friends were not convinced there was a billion-dollar online marketplace for gently worn children's clothing. Plus, we stopped swapping long ago. "It's why we invented money!" in the words of one investor.

But what did they know? The Internet was changing. The tools available to business owners on the Web and in mobile applications were rapidly evolving. If 2000 was the year when a room full of guys with a server could build a promising Web application, 2010 was the year a couple of guys with two laptops in Starbucks could do better.

We were those guys. Oliver Lubin, Chris Homer, and I got scrappy—in cafés, bars, and at our kitchen tables. Despite the chorus of investors saying no, and the total, absolute unsexiness of the used kids' clothing market, we scraped together enough seed capital to run the company for about six months (and I use the term *company* generously!). It was just enough money—building a minimum viable product has never been cheaper—to let us launch a prototype and test some assumptions, but it was nowhere near what we were going to need to prove that we were onto something big. In those first few months, it was the words of HBS entrepreneurship professor Joe Lassiter that rang in my ear: "You raise money to buy time for experiments, you buy experiments to produce information, you produce information to make decisions, you make decisions to open or close options . . . You raise enough cash at each stage to get you to that decision point and to deal with its consequences."

November 2009 was the beginning of the "buying experiments stage." Here are four things we learned that might be helpful to entrepreneurs and managers building online marketplaces.

1. Don't *just* build it; nobody will come.

It's all about distribution. Distribution is critical to starting a two-sided marketplace. In two-sided markets where high clearance rates are required—that is, there are enough buyers and sellers to complete transactions in a timely manner—a low clearance rate (illiquid market) is a deal breaker. Would you ever post your available rental on Craigslist if it took ninety days to rent? No. If nobody posted rentals on Craigslist, would you go there looking for rentals? Broken market. If it took three weeks to sell your iPod on eBay would you wait that long? Probably not. If nobody posted iPods on eBay, would you go looking there? Broken market. There is no need to belabor a well-worn path, but we often take for granted two of the best-functioning marketplaces on the Web today: eBay and Craigslist. In today's world, eBay and Craigslist are so part of the Web vernacular that they have become the de facto bar for any emerging marketplace.

But just because they're the dominant online marketplace for second-hand goods doesn't mean they're doing a good job serving all customers.

In fact, many companies have been nibbling at eBay and Craigslist for some time (Etsy—the $300 million handcrafted-goods marketplace—being the most successful example to date).[13] thredUP would take a similar approach: figure out where eBay's one-size-fits-all approach is failing in the secondhand children's clothing market; differentiate and execute. thredUP is very much a classic disruption play. We've sought to change the dimension of competition. It's not about price; it's about convenience. But in a convenience play, market dynamics are even more critical.

2. Build a community (or better yet, plug into an existing one).

Prior to the launch of the seed phase site, we estimated a need for a database of five thousand e-mail addresses of interested parents. There are always people who would not be interested once we launched, so we needed a significant cushion. Like most Web businesses these days, we used social media early on to build a thredUP community—social media is a necessary but not sufficient part of community building because it helps develop the marketplace. We had a teaser page up for collecting information for our "exclusive launch"; we made some funny (and not so funny) videos on YouTube; we built a Twitter following; hosted two blogs; and nurtured a growing Facebook page. This isn't rocket science, but important content distribution and engagement tools were helpful in getting the word out about thredUP and what we were doing.

Where we spent the majority of our energy, however, was at the grassroots level listening to as many mom bloggers in America as we could. There was a community of moms out there talking about clothing swaps and hand-me-downs and sustainable consumption; we just had to plug into it. It's always easier to tap a community than it is to build one. We contacted everyone we could find—starting with the low-hanging fruit of "savings sites," "deal sites," "coupon sites," and "clothing sites." We didn't just tell folks about thredUP either—we engaged thousands of mom bloggers over e-mail and phone to be an integral part of our launch. thredUP's "invite-only" status during the pre-seed phase was a calculated buzz generation tool. Who had the invitation codes to thredUP? Mom bloggers. We offered exclusive access to our private beta site only to "founding members" and their readers. We asked these early adopters for feedback and gave them regular updates regarding launch timing. We made them feel special—and in the context of our community, they *were* special.

What we were ultimately selling prior to launch was belonging—the opportunity to be an early member of a movement. We created an environment where it appeared difficult to be first and where being first actually mattered. Paradoxically, we were selling exclusivity even though we needed the very opposite: lots of people were necessary to make the market work.

3. Find out how your marketplace breaks and confront it head-on.

Given the number of sizes we were offering, we estimated that we needed a thousand boxes of kids' clothing on the site—about fifteen thousand items—that were listed by thredUP members before we could effectively begin trading. Why? Because our hypothesis was that the absolute worst experience would be browsing, looking for a box of new clothes for your child, and not finding anything. If that was your first experience, we thought you might not come back. So we needed real "boxes of clothing" already listed on the site. You must create the impression there is "lots going on"—for example, why do nightclubs keep lines outside even though the place is empty inside? Why do restaurants subsidize early diners and happy hour folks? People respond to action; they want to be where the party is.

Classic two-sided market theory says you need to subsidize one side of the transaction to effectively make markets work. eBay made it free for buyers and they charged sellers (a twist on the old consignment model, where shops took a cut for selling your items). We took the opposite approach. The general operating procedure in the secondhand clothing market was hand-me-downs or donations, so we were competing with a powerful "free" option. Our choice was to subsidize sellers by giving them credits toward future selections by being first in line. We approached folks and said, "Hey, don't just give that great clothing away! We'll give you real money, and let you exchange stuff that doesn't fit your kid for clothes that do." If you were an early founding member of thredUP, we paid you (generously) to use the site. The price? Thirteen dollars per box. And we'd even send you the boxes.

4. Eliminate key friction.

After launch, things were going well, but the one major hurdle we had anticipated, but couldn't quite crack, came back to haunt us. When you registered for thredUP, you were redirected to the U.S. Postal Service website to order the free medium flat-rate boxes. These were the boxes you would use to ship to thredUP. But the Postal Service's site was not easy to navigate, so many members—excited about thredUP—had a difficult time getting the proper boxes to use the service. If marketplace liquidity was driven by the number of new boxes of clothing coming online, we had to make it easy for people to get the boxes they needed, or this would be a huge problem.

A short story to illustrate why you need to keep thinking creatively: we'd been working with the U.S. Postal Service for some time on a distribution strategy for the boxes. We'd hoped that since we were using the Postal Service's most lucrative shipping option (for them), it would be helpful in getting boxes into the hands of our customers. That just wasn't the case. We had to somehow force the Postal Service's hand. So . . . every time a new person registered we'd create a "Turk job" through Amazon's Mechanical Turk service and have someone (usually in the Philippines) order boxes on behalf of the registrant. In just a few days, Turks were ordering thousands of boxes a day. Finally, someone from the Postal Service's distribution center contacted us and said, "Why don't you just send us a file of where you need these boxes sent and we'll take care of it; just please stop having Turks create all these new accounts!" Perfect.

"We're in," Eric Paley said. One of the early skeptics, Paley agreed that thredUP's early results were exciting. He joined Patricia Nakache of Trinity Ventures—who led the round—and two other firms in thredUP Series A financing of $1.4 million.

Just a couple of months after the financing, thredUP members were exchanging more than fifteen thousand articles of kids' clothing a week. This new marketplace, literally built from scratch, was finding its legs.

Online technology continues to shift rapidly, but the fundamentals of building great companies haven't changed all that much. As the next generation of business leaders, it's important to keep a few principles in mind. First, solve a real problem—and solve it well. Think hard about how people hear about what you're doing, because distribution really matters (a word of caution: PR $\neq$ distribution). Especially online, there are communities and enthusiasts for everything. Find these communities and harness their authority online to get others to buy what you're selling. Finally, make sure you've solved the key things that break your business. They are not parts of your planning to avoid—every business breaks on a few dimensions; know yours better than anyone else.

Technology and Social Good

Loans, Relays, and the Power of Community

SHELBY CLARK graduated from Harvard Business School in 2010. Prior to HBS, Shelby received a degree in biomedical engineering from Northwestern University. After serving as a director at Kiva, he started RelayRides, the world's first peer-to-peer car-sharing service backed by Google Ventures, where he now serves as CEO. Shelby is passionate about companies with a cause.

It's a small world. And it's getting smaller. By making it possible to easily make a connection with billions of people around the globe, the Internet has eliminated the notion that a neighbor is someone who lives next door. My career has focused on this principle, and has explored ways to connect people online for the greater benefit of society. I believe the question that could both define and challenge our generation is: how can we leverage online connections to generate offline impact?

As we find new ways to answer that question, the world will become a smaller, and better, place. I've thus far worked toward this goal in two fields—finance and transportation—but countless other opportunities remain.

My quest was inspired while helping to build a young nonprofit start-up called Kiva.org. Kiva connects people in the First World with a few extra bucks to microentrepreneurs in the developing world who need a small loan to start a small business—selling baked goods, say, or running a general store. A decade ago, nobody thought sane people would loan total strangers halfway across the globe hard-earned money on nothing more than a simple promise to repay. Now they do. Technology has empowered people to develop relationships, reputations, and trust with the "strangers" they fund, and Kiva has quickly become one of the

fastest-growing nonprofits in history—on target to raise about
$100 million in loan capital in its fifth year of existence.

I then took what I learned at Kiva and moved on to my next challenge,
tackling the consumption and environmental concerns associated with
cars and traditional car ownership. RelayRides, a company I founded in
2008, is built on those same principles that made Kiva thrive. Say that
one of your neighbors has a car sitting idle, while at the same time you
need a car. It seems like a logical conclusion that you two should be connected, but without technology this would not be possible. RelayRides
provides a simple interface to find the neighbor with the car you need, at
the location and time you need it. RelayRides also integrates in-vehicle
technology, which eliminates the need to exchange keys, making the
transaction convenient. We also provide a bilateral rating system that
keeps both owners and borrowers honest and respectful of the community. While these needs and general concepts have existed for decades, we
could never have built the business without the advent of new technology.

From these past experiences I've noticed that a few of the same
threads create a fabric of new and innovative ways to connect people for
the betterment of society. Specifically, a service should think offline, establish trust, and empower its community.

Think offline. As the Internet has grown, more opportunities have
emerged to connect with others online to establish or improve relationships, or to find and disseminate information. However, there have been
only limited ways to translate online interaction into offline impact. Both
Kiva and RelayRides have leveraged the Web to create new ways to connect offline resources, money, and cars, respectively, when connections
could not have been made previously. Kiva represented the first opportunity for the average consumer to connect directly with a microentrepre-
neur halfway across the world. It allowed the lender to learn about the
borrowers' personal situations and needs, and created a safe and easy
way for the lender to contribute to borrowers' loans.

RelayRides has an even more tangible and visible relationship to the
offline world. It's easy for borrowers to see the thousands of cars sitting

idle in their community. However, there was no way for them to leverage the idle resource. Car owners had no idea that people in their neighborhood would pay them to use their cars when they would otherwise be sitting on the side of the street, and even if they did, they lacked the infrastructure and insurance to make the connection possible.

Establish trust. In a world where strangers used to be anonymous, the Internet has given people an identity. Reputation systems are incredibly powerful tools to establish trust where none previously existed. People must know that they will be held accountable for their actions, and that disrespecting the community will neither be tolerated nor go unnoticed. Kiva prominently displays the repayment rate to a lender considering making a loan. Defaulted loans never disappear from the system, helping to ensure that loans continue to be repaid. To date, Kiva's repayment rate is a staggering 98.9 percent—something the average bank would kill to have.

Similarly, RelayRides has developed a robust peer-to-peer rating system. Before borrowers choose to borrow a car, they can check what others said about it. If a car owner doesn't keep the car clean or well maintained, borrowers will know that, and the car owner will consequently enjoy fewer rentals. In addition, borrowers are held responsible for their actions, and may be banned from the community for returning cars late or dirty. By creating a reliable system that keeps members responsible for their actions, the quality of the service is enhanced, but more importantly, members know they can trust the service and, in turn, the community.

Empower the community. One thing I learned at Kiva and quickly saw at RelayRides is that the community is smarter, more creative, and more effective than any company can be. When a service relies heavily on its members, it must give those members a way to be heard and drive the direction of the service. Kiva did not realize this early on, so its passionate community created Kiva Friends, an independent way to organize and be heard. Kiva Friends is a forum where the entire imaginable gamut of Kiva issues is discussed, from marketing strategies to conversations about quirky loans. Kiva Friends also created a number of useful tools that Kiva didn't provide, such as Kiva Toolbars with links and RSS feeds. It was also a mechanism for lenders to band together to protest when Kiva made a decision the community didn't like.

My favorite story about Kiva Friends tells what happened when someone noticed a loan they felt was inappropriate: seemingly funding an illegal activity. Kiva Friends organized an around-the-clock schedule for members to put the loan in their checkout basket, without actually completing the "purchase" of the loan, thus preventing anyone else from funding the loan. For over twenty-four hours, Kiva Friends passed around responsibility for blocking the loan, taking turns as it subsequently expired from each member's pending checkout basket. The community would not cease until Kiva finally removed the loan.

I learned this principle—the unstoppable power of community—at Kiva, and continue to think of ways we can leverage our RelayRides community to get smarter and provide a better service. Regardless of the amount of research we do, we'll never understand a neighborhood as well as someone who actually lives there. We've developed a RelayRides Ambassador program, which allows someone to self-organize a critical mass of members (four cars and fifty borrowers within a one-mile radius); once that legwork is done we'll come in and set up the service. The RelayRides ambassadors understand their own community, what their needs are, and the best way to spread the word—all things that would waste time and money for RelayRides to figure out on its own. The result is a better service for members, more communities with better tailored coverage, and fewer impediments and unnecessary costs for RelayRides as a business.

While communities have long been a part of some companies, it's clear to me that this connection is the future of business. Cultivating and leveraging communities makes clear sense for the bottom line because it provides better service and coverage at a lower expense. In addition to potentially being profitable, it is good for the community. As our world becomes more fragmented with the myriad diversions and divisions that seem to be splitting people apart, a renewed emphasis on association and commonality is absolutely critical. And it is my thought that by leveraging this latent desire for community, it's not only businesses that can flourish, but also the people they serve.

Mobile Millennials

JASON GURWIN is a serial entrepreneur. After graduating from Wharton with an economics degree, Jason started two successful companies in the media and entertainment space. He graduated from Harvard Business School in May 2011 and now serves as CEO of Pushpins, the mobile coupon company he cofounded while at Harvard. He is passionate about the power of mobile applications to change people's everyday lives.

I was sitting in a wooden outhouse feverishly trying to get a signal before anyone could catch me. It was the summer of 2000. For the sixth consecutive year, I was at sleepaway camp in Casco, Maine. As a geeky overweight fourteen-year-old, spending the summer in the great outdoors was not my top choice. I had been using the Internet since the days of CompuServe and Prodigy, and being away from it for a whole month was a struggle. If you were to ask my bunkmates about that summer, you would probably hear the story of the kid with the "bowel issues." But if you dug a little deeper, you would get a slightly different story of my repeated trips to the bathroom.

Finally, it connected. In poured the world's information. My AOL e-mail, the score of the Yanks game, news of the latest *Survivor* castoff. And this was all from a toilet in the middle of nowhere! This was before any smartphone or even a handset with a text Web browser. It was thanks to my Omnisky external wireless modem tethered to the back of my Palm V PDA.

For months, I had been saving up for the device. From the moment I cashed in my life savings, I was hooked. Today, having the power of the world's information at your fingertips seems trivial, but back then it was remarkable. Despite being among the earliest of adopters, I could never have imagined how disruptive mobile would become.

Originally, mobile phones merely duplicated the desktop online experience. Today, technology built into smartphones capturing location, motion, touch, and video combined with a consistent Internet connection has changed the way we interact with content, people, locations, and even physical objects. From place-shifting live television using SlingPlayer Mobile, microblogging on Twitter, checking in on Foursquare, or interacting with products with my company, Pushpins, these innovations have turned the mobile device into the digital layer on top of the analog world.

Besides a twelve-month lapse in judgment as a management consultant, I am a serial entrepreneur and I always will be. Instead of artwork, my bedroom is covered in whiteboards with mockups and ideas—some good, others ridiculous (anyone want a box of investment banker trading cards?). My first two companies helped solve time-consuming problems for TV networks and movie studios. They brought in more than just beer money, but were not big enough to change the world.

Coming to business school, I wanted to create a company that could revolutionize an industry. So in fall 2009, with three section mates, I started a next-generation mobile coupon company called Pushpins. It was clear to me that the coupon market was ripe for disruption.

In fact, every year 285 billion paper coupons are delivered by brands—the same way it was done over a hundred years ago. While there have been attempts to shift coupons to digital delivery, requiring either at-home printing or text messaging, this has become only a tiny fraction of the overall coupon market. Why? Rather than creating a new type of promotion specifically designed for the mobile platform, companies were trying to create the digital "paper" coupon, without having the same scale as paper distribution.

So we created the "pushpin," a targeted-location-based promotion digitally tagged to the physical barcodes of products in stores. Shoppers can scan the barcodes of their favorite products and redeem rewards or savings directly on their phones. The savings is then automatically credited to the shopper at checkout. With smartphones expected to outpace feature phones by the end of 2011, the technology and distribution necessary for this market to change will be in place.

While building Pushpins, I have come to appreciate how difficult it is to shift a traditional experience to a mobile one. With the potential to digitally interact with millions of people at any moment—how should you do it? By understanding mobile's relevance to your business and by taking advantage of its uniqueness as a platform, you can develop a deeper connection with your customers than ever before.

Ask yourself WWAD: What would Apple do?

Lesson: Design a unique experience for mobile. Leverage mobile technology, but don't abuse it.

A bad mobile strategy is purely duplicating a desktop Web app on mobile. Companies must take advantage of smartphone technology to make the user experience even better than the desktop counterpart.

Apple is the master of this. If you look at any of its applications, like Keynote or iMovie, they are completely reinvented for mobile. For instance, Keynote for iPad heavily relies on multitouch gestures. You can resize a graph with a pinch or edit it with a double tap. In iMovie for iPhone, movies are automatically edited based on themes, instead of manually cut by the user as in the desktop version.

It's about taking advantage of differences not only in software, but also in hardware. With Pushpins, we use the phone's camera as a barcode reader. This makes it easy for users to interact with products in the store. Sega uses motion sensing controllers for games like Super Monkey Ball. Bump allows you to pass your contact information by identifying your proximity to another user's phone. Ocarina uses the microphone to create a digital musical instrument.

When it comes to defining the user experience, focus on utilizing the platform to improve the customer's interaction with the world around them. There is a tendency, especially for the business-minded, to include anything and everything. Because more is obviously better, right? Wrong.

Take Copy and Paste. They are such simple features, but weren't integrated until two years after the release of the original iPhone. Why? Apple needed to redefine it for a touch interface. Design your app with that mentality. How can I simplify the experience for my users? It's not by giving them everything, it's understanding how your value proposition is different on a mobile platform and delivering it using the best features of the smartphone. Don't create the digital "paper" coupon; create a "pushpin."

Mobile is everywhere . . . are you?

> Lesson: Stay consistent to your brand, but be creative in your execution.

It is important to understand what mobile really is. At its core, it is a second screen. It is a dashboard to everyday life that makes every moment an online experience. Mobile allows companies to keep customers engaged whenever, wherever.

For brands, this means you can grab user mindshare at any moment. ESPN Scorecenter sends push alerts of score changes of your favorite teams. Nike+ makes the Nike brand a core component of your running experience. Kraft iFood Assistant gives you recipes with Kraft products when you're preparing a shopping list. As a brand you must maintain the relationship with the consumer on the go.

Mobile also creates the opportunity to gain access to users in places you couldn't before. For example, Pushpins pushes shoppers' savings in-aisle rather than having users clip or print coupons at home. A restaurant review site could provide information on the top dishes to simplify choosing a meal. A sports team could deliver live video of other relevant games to enhance the in-stadium experience. A hotel could allow guests to check out directly on their phone. A TV network could provide real-time chatter to viewers of their show.

Mobile can display all the relevant information that could not be updated in real time in the physical world. Before you were working with a static billboard; now you are working with an interactive display. Take advantage of it.

Is mobile core or supplementary to your business?

Lesson: Focus on the consumer experience. A big brand can drive initial downloads, but a bad consumer experience will prevent repeat usage.

For companies like eBay and Electronic Arts, it is a core component. For others, like Delta Air Lines or Pepsi, it is more supplementary. If it is supplementary, you face the difficult decision of whether to integrate with successful applications or make your own. Pepsi, for example, elected to go the "make" route, creating its own location-based game called Pepsi Loot rather than rewarding people on Foursquare.

While building Pushpins, we grappled with this very issue when talking to numerous large grocery chains. Every conversation involved the same question: why should we support your application instead of creating our own?

It is natural for a brand to want to own the customer experience. However, there is a tension between what companies want and what consumers want. Companies want a fragmented app experience; consumers want a consolidated one. For example, we allow shoppers to use our platform in fifteen hundred stores nationwide. Imagine if instead of a single unified app, we licensed our technology and shoppers had to download a different application for each retailer. Ultimately, if a partner can drive your brand better than you can, let them!

How can you take advantage of your consumer's hardware?

Lesson: Let the consumer make the hardware investment, not you!

Smartphones are powerful pieces of hardware. Given the abundance of smartphone users, companies can often shift the cost of hardware from the business to the consumer. Instead of installing a price checker in-store, allow shoppers to find prices on their phones. Instead of installing paper ticketing machines, send users scannable boarding passes or movie tickets. Instead of having waitstaff, allow users to order food via an app. Instead of having parking meters, have users pay directly on their phone.

Before building expensive technical infrastructure, consider whether you could instead run software on the consumer's hardware. It can provide a huge cost savings and does not deteriorate with age.

Mobile creates a compelling opportunity for everyone from fifteen-year-old app developers to large *Fortune* 500 corporations. Similar to the introduction of the Internet, it has taken time to evolve. When you think back to the launch of the iPhone app store, the app selection was limited at best. When developers finally understood how to take advantage of the hardware, it revolutionized the way people could interact, consume, and create content.

It's nearly impossible to predict where mobile will go in the future with annual hardware overhauls and subsequent software enhancements. However, it certainly will be more social and interactive. Regardless of what the future of mobile entails, it's key to stick to the fundamentals. Delight the consumer. Make the experience unique. Be creative in your execution. Make the experience contextually relevant. Leverage your users' existing hardware. Most important, though, you must understand that mobile is everywhere. It's at your favorite baseball game. It's at your local grocery store. And it's even at that small wooden outhouse in Casco, Maine.

Joe Kennedy

CEO of Pandora

Joe Kennedy shares his key lessons learned across numerous technology companies, provides insights on generational differences he's observed, and talks candidly about learning from mistakes.

What learnings did you take from your previous work experiences and how did they help you at Pandora?

1. **The value of focus:** Spending many years in a very large organization taught me the value of focus. How is it that a small, young company with very limited resources has any chance of beating large established companies with all sorts of resources? Focus. The power of an entire team of people spending all of their time and energy working to achieve just one thing. In early 2005, we rolled out the vision to transform the B2B company then known as Savage Beast Technologies into Pandora, a personalized Internet radio service. One of the engineers asked, "How do we think we can ever beat Yahoo!, MSN, and AOL [the leaders in Internet radio at the time]?" The answer: they have far more resources than we have and they have established market positions . . . but if all of us focus all of our energy on being the best in the world at just this one thing, we can beat them.

2. **Fueling customer enthusiasm:** Saturn taught me the incredible power of unexpectedly good customer service. Just as Saturn owners were amazed to shop for a car and not face haggling over price, I'd like to think that Pandora users are impressed that a free service offers such responsive and friendly listener support. One day back in 2006, a listener sent an e-mail seeking help getting

Pandora to work on his AirPort Express. Within twenty minutes he
had a friendly e-mail back detailing exactly what he needed to
do—instructions that worked out perfectly for him. It's something
that happened thousands of times a month—but he was so impressed that he wrote back and asked if we happened to be looking for any investment. To make a long story short, he ended up
leading a large investment round. While this outcome makes for a
great story, what really matters to us is that our approach to serving our listeners adds fuel to their enthusiasm—enthusiasm that
often leads to word of mouth, further fueling our growth.

3. **Leadership diversity:** Fresh out of business school, I remember the
    irresistible desire to surround myself with others with a similar
    background. It took some time for me to learn that hiring in your
    own image and likeness ultimately means hiring people who share
    your strengths, which can be fun, but also means hiring people
    who share your weaknesses and your blind spots, which is often
    deadly. While it's easy to say and understand, it's hard to bring this
    thought into practice: the best team is one that has widely differ-
    ent talents and experiences yet shares a sense of common purpose
    and mutual respect.

As CEO of a company that encourages the sharing of music between
friends, you must hold social networking close to your heart. What are
the major social networking trends you see in the next five to ten years?

The only prediction one can make after watching the past fifteen years
of Internet development is that society will become more and more
networked. Those who thought they knew exactly how this megatrend
would play out have been proven wrong over and over again—just ask
the people at Friendster and MySpace who thought they had caught
lightning in a bottle . . .

We're seeing the rapid rollout of location-based applications, most
notably Foursquare and, recently, Facebook Places. What is your view

of the evolution of this space? Do you see m-commerce someday overtaking e-commerce?

Mobile connectivity is changing and will continue to change life and society, but we're still in the top of the first inning. Mobile commerce is already growing at a triple-digit annual pace.

As you hire new recruits at Pandora, what do you see as the most profound changes between this generation of young adults and previous generations?

There have been three big changes that I can see.

The first change is the blurring of the line between the "workplace" and the "not-work places" in our lives. Work-life balance used to hinge on the physical, place-based separation of work and not-work. The great challenge and the great opportunity we face today is the ability to work almost any time and any way. The newest adult generation seems to embrace the opportunity side of this, approaching work more flexibly in terms of when and where it takes place.

The second change is the adoption of a view that sees a career as consisting of a series of many different employers. I don't know of any young adults today who look to find a single employer for their entire career—or even have the view that their career will involve only two or three employers. Many employees seem to embrace the opportunity to take responsibility for their own career development, building their skills and experiences throughout their working life.

The third change is the preference to get to work without hopping into a car. Today's young adults have embraced city living to a far greater degree than their parents and grandparents. Mass transit fits this lifestyle—and many choose to not even own a car. Combined with everyone's growing concern about the environment, jobs that re-quire hopping into a car are less attractive than those that can be reached by walking, biking, or mass transit. I was talking with a real estate developer in the San Francisco Bay area who observed that al-most all of the office buildings on the peninsula south of the city are now in the wrong place: close to the Route 101 freeway but away from the mass transit lines that the new generation wants to take to work.

What are the three biggest mistakes you've made in building your companies? How would you do things differently if you had your time over?

The biggest mistake I've made in the time I've been at Pandora was very early on. As we were approaching launch, we prioritized launching a subscription version of the service over an ad-supported, free to the consumer version. It's not just that this decision proved—quickly—to be wrong, it's that, in retrospect, I think we made the decision for the wrong reason. No one on the team had ever been part of an ad-supported company before and I think we were somewhere between ignorant and afraid. The right answer could only have come if we had had a full set of experiences and perspectives in the room—but instead we made the decision that I think we were just more comfortable with. The good news is that we were raising a new investment round and the investor we ultimately picked was a very strong voice in favor of prioritizing the ad-supported free version. He made a solid case and, to our credit, we listened and changed course—and hired a very experienced ad sales executive to be part of the senior leadership team.

At E-LOAN we made one of the classic mistakes that young, cash-flow-negative companies make: raising less money in good times than we could have because we believed that the company would continue to improve, and thus additional money could be raised at a higher valuation at some future point in time. The flaw in our thinking was *not* that company performance would improve—in fact it did; rather, the flaw was the belief that valuation is driven by factors intrinsic to the company rather than extrinsic. Despite the company's significant improvement, the deterioration in investment conditions resulted in a valuation roughly 75 percent less than what the company was able to command in strong market conditions. The harsh reality is that overall investment and economic conditions often affect valuations more than company performance. If a company is cash flow positive, there is much less risk associated with the timing of fund-raising; however, if I ever find myself in a cash-flow-negative company again, I would start by thinking about how much money it needs to go from cash flow negative to cash flow positive *assuming bad economic conditions* (e.g., a recession) and then try to raise *double* whatever amount that calculation shows.

While E-LOAN ultimately turned out to be quite successful, growing from $20 million to more than $150 million in annual revenue (with solid profitability) over the course of my years there, in truth it was quite a struggle. I think the reason it was a struggle is that we fell into a trap that other smart young MBAs might be prone to falling into: assuming that the rational appeal of what we were offering would drive consumers and those helping them (e.g., realtors) to embrace it. In truth, the financial and emotional magnitude of the transactions we were involved with (home purchases) meant that a purely rational approach would leave us blind to some very important emotional considerations. Yes, we could save people thousands—often tens of thousands—of dollars over the course of their mortgage, but consumers took great comfort from having a local mortgage broker whom they could see and touch—and realtors loved having a local person they knew they could light a fire under if and when the need arose. In truth, changing consumer behavior is really hard. It's not just about the rational benefits the change may bring; the cost, particularly the emotional cost, of change can never be underestimated.

CHAPTER 6

Learning

Educating Tomorrow's Leaders

Five years from now, on the web—for free—you'll be able to find the best lectures in the world. It will be better than any single university.

—Bill Gates[1]

By many conventional measures, the next generation is one of the most educated in history, and young businesspeople are certainly looking to educational experiences, within and beyond their everyday jobs, to make them better managers and leaders.

Yet there's a growing feeling among young business leaders that current learning models are not enough. Because of the rapid pace of technological development, increasing globalization, a more uncertain economic outlook, and myriad other reasons that will make future careers look drastically different from those of the previous generation, young leaders are increasingly embracing newer and more diverse ways of learning. After all, they're preparing themselves for jobs that probably haven't been invented yet. There's the somber recognition that the skills built over a lifetime—in universities, internships, and the first job—are no longer enough to prepare them for a more complex and uncertain world. Given this realization, how are young leaders learning to lead? How do they like to learn?

Arguably the two places that have the most impact in helping young business leaders develop the competence and character to succeed, especially in the early years of their careers, are business schools and the world's corporations. This is not to say that other experiences are any less valid. As this chapter highlights, entrepreneurship also offers significantly valuable learning experiences if approached the right way. Nonetheless, business schools and corporations stand out because the large majority of young leaders cut their teeth in these places early in their careers. Both play formative roles in helping young people gain early experiences that enable them to develop a sense of purpose and to exercise their passions in concrete ways. Indeed, in our survey of five hundred current or recent MBAs, work experience in a consulting firm, investment bank, or operating company and a stint in business school rank as the top places where young people feel they learn the most about being a leader.

Business Education: From Profits to Purpose

Graduate business schools don't have a monopoly on developing leaders, nor should they. Yet they are rare among educational institutions for actively emphasizing leadership development in their curricula. The world's business schools profess developing leaders as their central institutional purpose. Harvard Business School, for instance, proclaims that its mission is "to develop leaders who make a difference in the world." The mission of the Stanford Graduate School of Business is "to create ideas that deepen and advance our understanding of management and with those ideas to develop innovative, principled, and insightful leaders who change the world." Founded in 1881, the Wharton School at the University of Pennsylvania was the first collegiate school of business, and was inspired by Joseph Wharton's vision to educate the "pillars of the State, whether in private or in public life."

Business schools possess enormous scale in helping build better leaders, and are gaining in prominence. There are now 12,807 institutions offering business degrees worldwide. Almost 850,000 business degrees were conferred in 2007–2008.[2] In 2007, 150,000 graduate business degrees were awarded in America alone, compared to 5,000 in 1950.[3] This is more than three times the number of law degrees and eight times the number of medical degrees. In India alone, 1,600 schools offer the two-year MBA. And interest in the MBA continues to grow. In 2009, the GMAT exam was taken a record 265,613 times, and Harvard Business School received a record 13,000 applications.[4] Despite the outrage directed at MBA graduates during the global financial crisis that began in 2008, the degree is still seen by most as a ticket to upward mobility. It remains one of the world's most coveted stamps of approval, especially in the developing world, where there is a dearth of qualified managers. These institutions are influential. What are they teaching?

Business schools have traditionally excelled at teaching core knowledge. Witness the plethora of course offerings that cover everything from the basics of finance and marketing to entrepreneurship and private equity. But business schools have recognized that to remain relevant, they have to do a better job of helping graduates develop two other key traits of successful leaders: practical skills and a higher sense of purpose. As this chapter shows, young business leaders themselves clamor for these changes, and as a result, there are a number of implications for graduate business education.

First, business schools are now asserting a greater role in teaching values, character, and higher purpose. When Nitin Nohria became the new dean of Harvard Business School in 2010, he argued that business faced an inflection point because of a "crisis of legitimacy." Nohria explained how business schools must play a stronger role in teaching both "competence" and "character."[5] Today's twenty-somethings grew up believing that they can do well by doing good, and Nohria is right to recognize this shift. Most of all, they believe that leadership can be learned, and that it almost always takes years of self-reflection, discipline, and intense practice.

Second, business schools are doing a better job breaking down the wall between the classroom and the real world. Young leaders are learning by doing, and opportunities to take the MBA experience out of the classroom and to the local community, to industry hubs such as Silicon Valley, or to countries around the world have now become the norm. This is not entirely new. The late C. K. Prahalad, for instance, helped his students at the University of Michigan work on projects with companies around the world. What is different now is how business schools are bringing this activity from the periphery to the core of their curricula. Each year, hundreds of HBS students participate in field-based learning—such as country immersions, company field studies, and individual student field research. Schools are also doing a better job teaching and encouraging entrepreneurship. Today, more than two-thirds of U.S. colleges and universities teach entrepreneurship.[6]

Third, business schools are more focused on interdisciplinary skills, in recognition of the integrative nature of business. As Richard Barker argued in an article in the *Harvard Business Review*, "The skill of integration is the distinguishing feature of a manager and is at the heart of why business education should differ from professional education. The key is to recognize that integration is not taught but learned. It takes place in the minds of students rather than in the content of program modules."[7]

Learning to Lead in the Real World

Beyond business schools, corporate training and development have become a much more crucial ingredient in the professional satisfaction of the next generation of leaders.

Undeniably, the next generation will want to continue learning in the workplace. For most, joining an established management program in a recognized operating company, consulting firm, or investment bank will remain attractive choices after business school. In the MBA class of 2009, 57 percent of HBS graduates joined the consulting or financial services industries, and we don't see this drastically changing in the next few years.[8] Next-generation leaders still value corporate experience as a significant platform for learning.

In our survey, 61 percent agree or strongly agree with the statement, "I find corporate training and education programs crucial to my

FIGURE 6-1

Where MBAs say they learned leadership

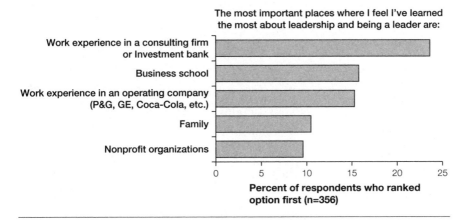

The most important places where I feel I've learned the most about leadership and being a leader are:

Percent of respondents who ranked option first (n=356)

professional development." Indeed, virtually all our contributors found value in the experience of working for an established company with a strong set of mentors. Those who agreed that leadership can be taught ranked work experience in a consulting firm, investment bank, or operating company among the top three most important places where they'd learned leadership (see figure 6-1).

Corporate training is a big business. The largest companies, such as GE and AT&T, spend up to $1 billion annually on training alone.[9] The quality of development programs has a direct impact on employee retention. In a Louis Harris and Associates study, 41 percent of employees who had poor training opportunities planned to leave within the year. In contrast, only 12 percent of those who felt their company provided excellent opportunities planned to leave.[10]

What does this mean for young business leaders and managers responsible for supporting the growth of a strong pipeline of leaders?

An employee's fit and alignment with an organization's purpose have become paramount. We touched on the concept of the "whole person" in an earlier chapter. The next generation of leaders no longer sees a silo that separates professional and personal worlds—for them, work is an expression of individuality and personhood. This has an immense implication for employee selection. This means corporations, nonprofits, and even public sector organizations will have to do a better job of making sure potential employees clearly align with the organization's values, purpose, and culture. For many millennials at the beginning of their career, work is also about being in a place where they can discover a sense of purpose. They're buying into not just a job or a prestigious training program but also a belief system that guides their future choices. Companies such as P&G, McKinsey, and IBM, for instance, are famous for corporate identities and value systems that cut across traditional cultural and national lines.

Young leaders expect to learn as much about themselves as about the job in the early years of their career. As a result, learning has become more experimental, with an emphasis on failing fast early in one's career, and using that set of experiences to iterate one's way to success. It has also become more self-directed, with young leaders trying out a myriad of experiences to test their fitness and competence for the challenge at hand. They understand the importance of mentors—inside and outside work. It's no surprise that in today's start-ups, building a formidable board has become one of the most crucial tasks of an entrepreneur.

The Leadership Boot Camp
Training the Next Generation of Corporate Leaders

KISHAN MADAMALA is a former store team leader at Target. He completed his MBA in 2010 at Harvard Business School, where he was awarded a Rock Entrepreneurial Fellowship. Kishan tells the story of a whole generation who were trained as "good analysts" but were poor leaders, and how this learning gap represents the single biggest opportunity for business schools and corporations.

"This store has so many problems, I have to take a shower after I visit it." And with that comment, my boss, the district manager, handed me the keys to the retail store I was supposed to manage. He wished me luck, shook my hand, and drove off. Here I was, just a few years out of college, responsible for three hundred employees and $55 million in sales. Despite my solid training in store operations, I was not ready for the demanding leadership test ahead of me.

I'm a millennial. My generation grew up in the nineties, during an economic boom. Many of our parents did well for themselves and, in turn, took care of us in every possible way. We don't know sacrifice as well as the generations before us. There were no major wars and no deep recessions during our coming of age. As a result, many of us grew up lacking a certain toughness and resiliency. I believe what you've heard about millennials is largely true—the limited attention span, the need for praise and constant affirmation. We are rarely told what we are doing wrong or how we may have to personally change our behaviors. The overwhelming praise and positive feedback can propel a young person to coast along without undertaking any deep introspection. I was a shining example of this problem.

Good Thinkers, Unprepared Leaders

Our generation is rising to leadership, and we are unprepared. Prior to business school, most MBA students were analysts. Historically, two-thirds of the entering class at top MBA programs have come from finance or consulting. At best, going through one of these analyst training programs is an intellectual exercise. Much like an extension of school, they require participants to gather facts, scope out possibilities, and suggest answers. Accordingly, the type of feedback given to analysts is quite different from the feedback given to executives. In those first few years after college, we were told how to be more diligent and more careful and thoughtful. Reformat this financial model or adjust these PowerPoint slides. Our organizations had a point, though—to develop us into efficient and thoughtful analysts. This form of constructive criticism unfortunately left us with a colossal gap in our leadership skill set. Analysis is just one part of leadership. Executives are given feedback on their style, their communication skills, and their ability to drive alignment and execution through a group of people. If we are to give MBAs and future corporate leaders training in leadership, it is this feedback that we must provide.

Those of us who earned MBAs spent two years in the classroom studying marketing, finance, and strategy, among other core curriculum topics. We even had a sprinkling of leadership and organizational behavior classes. We studied these topics from afar, though. Just as we dissected the strategy of leading global firms, we analyzed the behaviors of leaders, separating out the correct actions from the incorrect ones. This decision analysis was far removed from our personal leadership development. To succeed in these classes, we didn't need to be introspective or reveal anything about who we were. This need for real leadership training is the biggest challenge and opportunity facing business education today.

The "Punk Kid" Learns How to Lead—the Hard Way

In my first job out of college, I was an analyst, and not a particularly good one. I became bored easily. I was evaluated on the small details of my spreadsheets and the style of my note writing on the firm's internal account database. I felt like I was being trained to be a sidekick, not a leader, and I was skeptical of whether being good at the former would really guide me toward becoming the latter. I wanted to learn by doing, so I decided to try my hand at retail. There, I was lucky enough to stumble into a feedback-rich environment.

My store was a turnaround store. Sales were down from the year before. Key departments were critically understaffed and underperforming. Even the building itself was falling apart. Built in the mid-1980s, the store had been updated only once in the last twenty years. On my first day, the main water pipe ruptured. We had to shut down the store restrooms and rent portable toilets for our customers—not the most ideal reflection on new management. Amid all the mess, I walked into that building every day thinking, "If I don't change things here, no one else will." That awesome sense of responsibility was stressful, but it truly gave me purpose—a purpose I had not had in my previous desk job.

My predecessor had been let go for not executing well. He was, however, a favorite among the employees for his overly nice demeanor and understanding temperament. That history made this particular store manager position a difficult one to inherit—anything less than overt friendliness would make me "mean" or "cold" and any push toward execution, precisely what I was brought there to do, would make me "demanding" and "unfair." Was there any way to win?

Within my first month, employees called the corporate whistleblower hotline to accuse me of plotting to fire half the workforce. A department supervisor (an employee two levels below me, reporting to one of my direct reports) yelled in my face in an obscenity-laced tirade, and my HR manager informed me that several employees approached her, asserting

that they would not work for some "twenty-four-year-old punk kid."
Of course, I was twenty-five at the time. If they had only known . . .

All this had a deep personal effect on me. Like many my age, I was
used to following instructions and being liked, appreciated, and rewarded for doing so. Instead, my actions didn't please even half the people they affected. My behaviors were scrutinized under a microscope.
My impatience became offensive. My failure to listen became a failure
to influence. I had to change my behaviors. My job demanded it.

I grew up more in those two years than in any other period in my life.
I started to get a sense for what it took for me to be a leader. That was a
lesson not learned through any seven-point business book or any management case study. Leadership, I learned, is deeply personal. It is not
about your output—your slide deck, your financial model, or your research report. It's not even about your strategy or your vision, so much as
it is about *you*. The real you. Not the Monday morning you, the Sunday
afternoon you. The unrecorded you. The imperfect, vulnerable, yet passionate you.

Retraining the Next Generation of Leaders

Corporate America has been left with a big gap in its talent pipeline. It is
the gap between intellectual analysts and self-aware leaders. It is the
divide between knowledge and execution. Knowing and believing in the
right answer is not enough. The recommendation slide at the end of the
presentation is not enough. As HBS professor Richard Tedlow once said,
"You need more than conviction. You need *the courage* of your convic-
tions." How can the next generation develop the personal qualities, like
courage, necessary to bridge the leadership gap?

There could be a number of approaches, of course. My experiences as
an MBA student and as a field-based manager of a large team have led
me to believe in one particular solution—we should build a leadership
boot camp. Boot camp is of course a colloquial term for military recruit
training. This training is meant to transform civilians into soldiers by

simulating the stress of combat ahead of time. Similarly, I believe business schools and corporations should simulate the stress of real leadership. This approach would fundamentally change the pedagogical bent of business schools, but do so with the student's growth in mind.

Let's take my friend Rafaela as an example. She's starting business school this year after a two-year stint as an entry-level associate at a top consulting firm. Rafaela has a sharp wit and an endearing smile. She has a way of charming and disarming nearly everyone she meets. In short, Rafaela is a star in the making. Still, like the analysts I mentioned earlier, her work was devoted to honing her problem-solving skills. She never received any deep, leadership-oriented feedback. Imagine that Rafaela went through a full semester within the two-year MBA devoted to leadership skill building. It wouldn't be too difficult to pair her and her fellow MBA students with undergraduates interested in business. Rafaela would have the chance to lead a team of five or six undergrads toward a project goal, something she had never been responsible for previously. Each week, there would be an assessment of the team's work, but more importantly, a chance for Rafaela to gain feedback from her direct reports. They would tell her how motivated they felt by her, how honest they thought they could be with her, and specifically which of her behaviors made them work harder and which frustrated them. The business school could also recruit a volunteer team of experienced leaders to act as observers and mentors to Rafaela, providing additional sources of feedback. One such observer, Clint, the manager of a small local chain of coffee shops, would tell her that she needed to follow up better with her employees. Often Rafaela would just assume her directions would be followed, without bothering to check in later to verify progress. Within this feedback-oriented forum, Rafaela could learn to correct that slightly condescending tone she never knew she had. She would gain toughness by battling through discussions with that uncooperative team member. She would learn more about who she was, and who she needed to be, to lead effectively.

To make the program more robust, business schools should operate more businesses. Relatively simple, nontechnical businesses like the campus bookstore, café, or even a car wash could be established with the goal of letting MBA students learn by running them for a semester. Again, feedback could come at the students from all corners—customers, employees, and supervisors. MBAs may think these businesses are beneath them, but leading them might prove crucial to their leadership development.

This type of training, if well done, could change the landscape of MBA recruiting. MBA programs will have produced self-aware, battle-tested leaders. The consulting and financial firms would continue to recruit, of course, but new types of companies would also find this skill set increasingly valuable—the midsize company looking for a new VP, the small business looking for a potential CEO, and the large multinational operating company looking for a line manager. Operating companies might be able to lure MBAs away from consulting and finance because they can bring them in at higher levels and pay them accordingly. The new MBA leadership skill set would justify that upgrade. Imagine if MBAs were balancing offers to be general managers of a hotel, or a distribution center, alongside offers of an associate position in investment banking. In the post-financial-crisis world, a job that offers real leadership opportunity along with in-the-ballpark pay might have a fresh appeal.

Of course, business schools don't have a monopoly on training leaders. Corporate leadership programs must also adapt to keep their talent pipeline robust and ready. Operating companies can create similar leadership boot camps for their strategy and financial analysts, pairing these individuals with those in front-line operations. Procter & Gamble gives its analysts an experience in stores where they stock shelves with the products they handle. Why not do the same in its manufacturing plants, giving these promising leaders a chance to run a small part of the assembly line? Consulting and investment banks can partner with nonprofit organizations to create cross-company training exchanges. Bain & Company offers pro bono consulting services to nonprofits. Why not expand this relationship, allowing consultants to be responsible for managing a food drive or the operations of a homeless shelter?

In this time of economic uncertainty, leadership of multinational firms is part of my generation's calling. Through this recession and reordering of global economic power, our duty to lead differently is becoming increasingly apparent. We still have time to prepare our generation. Leaders need practice and feedback. Business schools and corporate training programs should provide both. Our collective future demands it.

The MBA of Hard Knocks

Why Fast Failure Is the Best Thing for Business Education

PATRICK CHUN is a venture capitalist and technology investor at Bain Capital Ventures. Patrick graduated from Harvard Business School in 2010, where he was copresident of the HBS Student Association, the student body of Harvard Business School. Patrick explains how his greatest learnings at business school did not occur in the classroom or even result from his successes, but rather from his failures, and how business education is at a unique juncture to foster innovation by encouraging experimentation and fast failure.

"Wow, we failed so much." These were the first lines my Student Association (SA) copresident Scott Daubin uttered as we were preparing our final newspaper message to the entire student body. It was ten o'clock on a balmy Monday evening, the copresidents of the next class were taking over in a week, and after working with our successors for four weeks during the transition period, Scott and I were ready for a reflective debrief on our time at the helm of the student body.

We looked back on a year of fun but challenging times. We had been dealt a demanding student body, drastic cuts in sponsorships, and an administration that was itself facing difficult, inward-facing questions about the direction of its educational program. It wasn't all gloom and doom; after all, we had launched several innovative new events, sold over a half a million dollars of SA products to help subsidize student costs, and remained steadfast in our dedication to representing the student voice. But as we reflected on what we had learned during the year, we could not help but think about the great opportunity we had to lead, fail, and learn.

Learning Through Failure

The memories that resonate most loudly with me even now are not the ones that grace my resume or class schedule. Even the great moments with friends and colleagues were memorable highlights of a fun time away from the working world, but concrete takeaways from those experiences are usually lost on me during my daily grind.

Rather, when I think about my two years in business school, I instantly gravitate to the moments of hands-on learning when my hard work did not lead to the intended results, and when we had to change direction to adapt to trying times. These were the times when, after performing the requisite detailed analysis and consensus building, I felt conviction for a specific strategy, yet at the end was clearly wrong. These were the times when I faced a fork in the road, and realized afterward that I had chosen the wrong path. While many of these decisions and leadership opportunities happened on campus and were less risky than equivalent ones in the workplace, they still involved significant risk: financial, reputational, and relationship implications were often on the line.

Along with the classroom discussions and my pre-MBA experiences, I feel like the most insightful learning happened when I was able to implement what I learned, and to learn from both failures and successes. Whether as a student leader facing a financial or strategic dilemma, as a fledging entrepreneur building a minimum viable product to test with users, or even simply as a classmate forging professional relationships with the diverse student base on campus, the opportunities to fail fast and learn have provided me with incredible insights into leadership, strategy, and implementation that would have been incredibly difficult in the more risk-filled corporate setting that I was in before starting my MBA.

I strongly believe that the best way for business schools to create battle-tested leaders and foster innovation is to not only allow students to fail, but to encourage them to fail fast. My own personal experiences at business school are testament to the power of failing, adapting, and learning from those other situations to make lessons stick.

Facing Failure Head-On

When Scott and I were handed the reins of the student body in April near the end of our first year, we were superpsyched. We had several goals in mind, one of which was strategically and financially important: to raise significant sponsorship money to counteract the challenges of the worsening economic situation.

In retrospect, we took ourselves down the path of failure from day one. As we were building our executive team postelection, Scott and I had what started as a simple idea: why not create an executive committee position dedicated to raising sponsorship money? Previously, this fund-raising had been done solely by the copresidents themselves, but based on talking with a bunch of nonprofits, we knew that such a focused role could be successful. Plus, we were already looking to fill a marketing role we knew was desperately needed, and as we rationalized the role to ourselves, we began to see how the responsibilities of both marketing and fund-raising could go hand-in-hand. We cavalierly decided to create this new position and did a search for a new "chief marketing officer" (CMO) position that included both of these hefty responsibilities. After fielding interest from more than fifteen candidates, we were excited to find somebody we thought was perfect for the job. We walked her through the role, gave her direction on our targets, and created a game plan for the summer.

By midsummer, Scott and I were beginning to face the grim realization that we were likely going to miss our fund-raising target. We knew the challenging economy would make this an uphill battle, and that companies that usually supported our events were tightening their purse strings, but we began to see where we had clearly failed to think about elements of our implementation. At the end of the summer, it became clear to both of us that we were in a serious conundrum: without this extra funding, we would likely have to cut spending on student services, which would lead to long debates not only between us but more broadly with our executive committee on what events or services would need to be trimmed and how to deal with any backlash.

Scott and I were facing our first big leadership challenge, and it was something we would have to solve even before second-year classes began. By the time we were back in Boston, we had raised only about 20 percent of our upside funding target. Realizing we had not done enough contingency planning, Scott and I spent three weeks tediously going through every line of our budget to understand where there was fat to be trimmed, focusing first on events or product subsidies that were not broadly enjoyed by the class. We worked with our CMO, starting by admitting our failure to scope the role correctly, and then moving on to creating an emergency plan to do follow-up outreach and figure out creative opportunities for raising money in nontraditional ways. We prepared a communication plan for delivering the budget news to not only the student senate, who had to approve any changes, but also to the entire school, sticking to our promises of financial transparency. We also began work on understanding how this impacted our budget, to ensure we were clear with the auditors and school supervisors who were tasked with ensuring we were responsible fiscal stewards. In the midst of failure, we were learning by doing.

I wish I could say that the fund-raising experience ended on a happy note—unfortunately, we failed to hit our target and had to readjust our budget and realign our executive team with the new realities of the situation we were facing. However, coming out of this experience, and myriad others like it over the course of the school year, Scott and I got a hands-on opportunity to lead, learn, and in many moments, fail. We learned a lot about topics that we were simultaneously covering in our case studies. Regarding leadership, we learned how we had personally failed to empower our CMO and provide her with the right tools and support to succeed with two very different responsibilities. From the recruiting front, we saw how our "brilliant idea" to create a supercharged role that changed too many things at once created a situation where we were stretching one person in too many directions. We also learned about the nitty-gritty realities of budgeting, dealing with a demanding auditor while "reporting to" a large group of type-A personalities who would pick apart anything we brought to them. Much of this we were also covering in cases in the classroom: learnings from our first-year leadership, financial management, and strategy classes would come to mind as I was tackling these real-world problems. But by dealing head-on with failures like this, I and hundreds of other student leaders on campus were given a unique opportunity to take what we learned in class, apply it, and iterate.

Failing at Business School

Ironically enough, however, the personal success that business school candidates have achieved prior to coming to campus may be part and parcel of the challenge management education is now facing. Looking at the backgrounds that populate any top business school campus, you tend to see a strikingly similar profile: young leaders with strong academic performance at a reputable university, rigorous job experience requiring strong analytical and strategic thinking skills, and an amazing breadth of activities and interests. What's really ironic about the picture, however, is the one truly deep learning experience that's missing from the equation: failure. Many students build a fantastic resume to get into an MBA program, and then get their MBA to secure their spot in a fantastic company. Risk taking is usually not in the resume, and some may even say the DNA, of many of these candidates.

"If concepts from books are easy, what's hard?" asks Seth Godin, the best-selling business author and entrepreneur. His two-word response: "doing it."[11] In 2009, Seth began blogging about an innovative free alternative MBA program he had developed and was testing with a small group of aspiring entrepreneurs. After running the experiment for six months, Seth (himself an MBA) described some of his learnings from the program, and in not too subtle terms, shared his insight that "knowledge was easy to transmit" and that the academic aspect of the learning was "not particularly essential." For young leaders who come from great academic and work backgrounds and are accepted to top business schools, it is usually not the analytical toolkit that is missing. Rather, it's the actual "doing." Seth even describes exactly what the word *doing* could mean: "Picking up the phone, making the plan, signing the deal. Pushing 'publish.' Announcing. Shipping."

I would love to see the curricula of major business schools reshaped to highlight the self-driven experience, with a focus on not only how to drive toward success, but also how to recognize and quickly bounce back from failure. I feel that my greatest learnings from business school came not from the classroom, but from my varied experience as a leader, entrepreneur, and colleague. As student body president, I had the opportunity to test my leadership mettle with a class of 1,800 demanding peers. As an entrepreneur, I had the opportunity to write a business plan for, launch, and then shutter a small recruiting venture business. As a research analyst, I had the chance to coauthor a full-fledged business case and try to implement buy-in on the case with several parties on campus.

Business schools have a unique opportunity to shift their worldview and see themselves more as an immersive two-year social network platform, fostering a web of multidirectional interactions between students, classroom learning, professors, and alumni. By combining student leadership opportunities, support for entrepreneurial activity, and school-led structured group work that provides real business exposure, MBA programs can give students an opportunity to lead, fail, and learn in a less risky environment.

Henry Ford, a frequent protagonist in cases I read in business school, is famous for saying, "Failure is simply an opportunity to begin again, this time more intelligently." At a time when the core tools for knowledge and learning are more readily available, and at a lower cost than ever, business schools can create differentiation by helping students move from just "learning by studying" to "learning by doing." The next wave of innovative business education will encourage students to feel less risk in learning by doing, and provide the tools and opportunities similar to what start-up incubators do for human talent, helping prepare and grow for life after school.

The New Corporate Classrooms
Training's Tectonic Technological Shift

MICHAEL B. HORN is the cofounder and executive director for education of Innosight Institute, a not-for-profit think tank devoted to
applying the theories of disruptive innovation to problems in the
social sector. He is also coauthor of *Disrupting Class: How Disruptive Innovation Will Change the Way the World Learns* with Clayton
M. Christensen and Curtis W. Johnson. Michael found his passion in
using technology to advance education in America.

I was a senior at Yale on September 11, 2001. Prior to the events that un-
folded that morning, I did not have a plan for what I would do after graduation. But after that day, although I still had considerable uncertainty
over what I would do with my life, I knew that whatever it was, making a
contribution to society would be an important part of it.

This desire led me to work for David Gergen, a former adviser to four
U.S. presidents, as his research assistant after graduation. Here I had the
chance to track and write about public policy, think about the big challenges of our times, and interact with a variety of people making a difference in the world through an array of pathways.

After my time working for Mr. Gergen, I attended the Harvard
Business School and had the good fortune of taking Professor Clayton
M. Christensen's class for second-year students, titled Building and Sus-
taining a Successful Enterprise. The class changed my life. The theories
of innovation that Professor Christensen taught had so much explanatory
power—from business to one's personal life—that they literally reshaped
how I saw the world.

While in the class, I learned that Professor Christensen needed a
coauthor for a book about applying his theories to help address the

struggles of the United States' K–12 public education system. Because education is one of the biggest challenges facing the country, I was excited by the possibility of applying Professor Christensen's theories to something so important. I pursued the opportunity, and Professor Christensen soon signed me up for the project. Little did I know that working toward transforming the country's education system from its present monolithic factory model to a student-centric one would consume my life from that day forward and lead me on my own entrepreneurial journey—cofounding the Innosight Institute, a nonprofit think tank devoted to applying the theories of disruptive innovation to develop solutions to problems in the social sector, with Professor Christensen and another classmate, Jason Hwang.

Education and learning are changing radically. New technologies are shifting the way people consume education. And that shift may very well occur outside of the K–12 education system first. Corporations and organizations are leveraging these advances to disrupt old models of corporate training—and have the potential to improve the learning experiences of their employees and impact the bottom line in tangible and significant ways.

The Rise of Online Learning

Online learning is on the rise, and as a disruptive innovation, it has the potential to transform learning for everyone. Over 4 million K–12 students in the United States take online courses.[12] In 2010, 30 percent of high school students reportedly took at least one online course,[13] and projections show that by 2019, 50 percent of all high school courses will be delivered online.[14] In the fall of 2009, over 5.6 million postsecondary students were taking at least one online course—an increase of 21 percent from the year prior.[15] And for some time now, corporations have been shifting significant portions of their training online.

The implications of these trends for young leaders in their twenties, managers, and businesses are significant.

In the past, we treated education as a monolithic exercise. We often taught in lecture format, and because of the numbers of students in a given class or training session, we had to teach everyone the same thing on the same day in the same way at the same pace. This would be fine if we all had the same learning needs, the same background knowledge, the same experiences, and the same learning pace.

But that isn't the case at all. Some master a topic quickly and grow bored by the repeated explanations in a class; others master the same topic more slowly and find the teacher or trainer is moving too fast. And when we move on to another topic or subject, the opposite could be true.

Companies have long acknowledged that their employees differ from each other in meaningful ways. Just witness the widespread use of the Myers-Briggs test within many organizations and its impact on how people manage.

But if corporations recognize individual differences and if those differences extend to people's learning needs, why do firms so often fall into the traditional monolithic training patterns like mass lectures and one-size-fits-all training sessions? And why have we endured it?

Until recently, the answer has been that this was really the only viable and economical way to teach and train large numbers of people. It wasn't just corporations that did this; schools embraced a factory model of monolithic education in the early 1900s when they began mass education because it was the only feasible way. Corporations could escape this model periodically because they had the means to employ tutors, coaches, or mentors to work one-on-one with employees; but for the most part, monolithic education has been the norm.

The New Long Tail in Corporate Learning

This is beginning to change. Technology has ushered in an era of "mass customization" in the arts and manufacturing. Many of us now take it for granted that there are companies that will design products and services for the "long tail"—and indeed many of us demand that they do.

Increasingly, technology, in the form of computer-based or online learning, has the potential to do the same in education. And the current tech-savvy generation of corporate employees is likely to accept nothing less.

Online learning is inherently modular—and therefore it has the potential to customize learning and training for differing individual needs. Because time is naturally variable in online learning, I can learn at the pace that makes sense for me. If I understand a concept, I can move past it. If I don't, I can review it until I do. I can follow different content paths to understanding the concept if need be. I'm not held back or passed over in the online "classroom" because I don't have to move at lockstep speed with everyone else in the training.

Furthermore, with online learning, managers can allow people to learn at the times that make sense for them. They don't have to interrupt a work stream because a training session is at a given time and thereby ruin productivity. In essence, online learning can enable learning at any time, any place, any path, and any pace.

Corporate Learning in an Age of Disruption

Increasingly, corporations around the world are utilizing this emerging disruption—and far more quickly than have traditional education institutions. In 2006, for example, a whopping 40 percent of all professional development for corporations occurred online. This disruption has enabled corporations not only to do their training more economically in many cases, but also, if implemented effectively, to achieve far better results than they have before.

This emergent model has at least three implications for managers.

In online learning, rather than look for whether an employee has put in her hours for a given training course, a manager can instead focus on the outcomes: did the employee master the new information she needed to learn? Although end-of-training assessments have always been an option, with online learning, managers can loosen the time requirements and just focus on whether a student masters each concept in the course as she progresses.

The evolving innovations in online learning also create new hiring and training options for managers. For example, Western Governors University, an online university started by nineteen governors, offers an intriguing value proposition.[16] Seeing the high incidence of retraining in U.S. corporations, it approached employers to learn what competencies new hires ideally needed. Understanding that set of competencies, Western Governors then asked, "How would we know if someone mastered those competencies?"—and designed appropriate assessments to do just that. It then found the best online curriculum to train people to master those assessments. Rather than have students progress by the arbitrary time units of the semester or the credit hour, which results in highly variable learning outcomes, Western Governors offers competency-based degrees, so that a student earns credit or a degree only when she has successfully mastered the required concepts.

Historically, managers have considered college degrees in making their hiring decisions, but this is highly imperfect, as a college degree is not proof of a prospective employee's knowledge or competency. College diplomas are only a proxy for competency. With the possibility of competency-based degrees in the emerging online universities, however, managers in the future should begin to demand that universities certify the practical competencies of their graduates so that they can have full confidence in what their hires will be able to do. This will likely result in an evolving set of online degrees that focuses on specific business niches that are much more useful to hiring managers.

In addition, several thousand corporations now have their own corporate universities, up from four hundred in 1990. And universities such as Bellevue, which serves students worldwide through its online programs and is the largest private university in Nebraska, are partnering with corporations.[17] Corporations today spend more than $16 billion on employee tuition assistance programs; 87 percent of U.S. corporations offer this perk. But most of these dollars are not spent in strategic ways that both advance the company's business objectives and help employees.[18]

Bellevue partners with corporations to solve this problem not only by allowing employees to earn degrees from an accredited university, but also by providing specific and targeted training that furthers a corporation's key business objectives, as they've done with partners such as the Home Depot and Verizon.

Bellevue measures the return on investment of training programs like these to make sure that the investment is paying off for the corporation as well as the employee—a practice that smart managers should adopt. For example, U.S. Bank found that improving specific modules of a course designed to train branch managers resulted in a triple-digit ROI that increased both demand deposit activity and consumer loan activity.

Finally, in the future, customization of corporate learning will only get easier and more affordable. Although today third parties create much of the content, increasingly there will be opportunities for corporations to create what we call a "facilitated network," in which employees create content and others consume it, a trend that will revolutionize learning.

Disruption is often a two-stage process. In the first stage, an innovator makes a product much more affordable and simpler to *use* than what exists currently. But *making* the product is still complicated and expensive. This is what has happened in online learning to this point. In the second stage of disruption, additional technological change makes it simple and inexpensive to *build and upgrade* the products.

Is it far-fetched to think that employees not trained in teaching could effectively create usable content for learning? Not at all. One of the most exciting findings in education is that people often learn better when they teach than when they listen. To visualize how this might work, think beyond the creation of blogs and wikis to an even richer use of Web 2.0 technologies. Platforms that enable nonprogrammers to build remarkably sophisticated software for specific purposes are becoming increasingly common in software markets.

There are already signs that this is happening. Sun Microsystems, for example, launched its Social Learning eXchange (SLX) in 2008 to move its training to a "Learning 2.0" model. SLX utilizes an informal and collaborative approach to learning with user-created content at its core—or, as

Karie Willyerd, Sun's chief learning officer said, it is where "YouTube meets iTunes." A study compared the use of SLX to traditional instructor-led training and unearthed some stunning results. First, its use was widespread. It enabled "near instantaneous deployment of critical training titles versus the time required for course development." Second, the cost of developing this content was significantly lower. As a result, the ROI of SLX was a whopping 7,505 percent. In other words, for every dollar invested in SLX, it reduced the need to invest in Web-based training by $75. The content created, while shorter, remained of high quality.[19]

The Future: Not Settling for Anything Less

The revolution that has occurred in every facet of society continues to drive the discussion around social learning and the implications for leading organizations. The generation entering the work force today and over the next many years is likely to want on-demand training built for their individual needs—and won't be willing to settle for anything less, as they'll see it as a bureaucratic waste of time. Having grown up in just this kind of world, there is no reason they will check those experiences at the door of any business, especially as the technology continues to evolve to better enable learning and eliminate our historical one-size-fits-all approach. We've just brushed the tip of the iceberg, and the results could be staggering—not just for learning in the workplace, but also for addressing some of our society's more pressing problems more broadly. This is what motivates me every day to continue to push for innovation and transformation in our education system.

Tackling Financial Illiteracy

ALEXA LEIGH MARIE VON TOBEL is the founder of LearnVest, Inc., and serves as its chief executive officer and director. She received an AB in psychology with honors, with a citation in romance languages and literature at Harvard College. Alexa feels passionate about making personal finance education fun and accessible to everyone. She believes that for the next generation of students, mastering financial literacy will be just as important as learning to read or write.

College graduation—a major milestone, a celebration of accomplishment, a time of excitement and anticipation. However, for most college seniors, the end of college comes with an average of $4,138 in credit card debt.[20]

I graduated college in 2006 and headed straight to a job at Morgan Stanley, where I would work as a trader in the New York Global Proprietary Credit Group.

A few weeks before my graduation, I was sitting around a table with friends, lingering over a Sunday brunch. We were discussing our post-college lives, complete with new careers and new cities. It was over the course of this casual conversation that I had a realization: though I was headed for a career on Wall Street, I had no grasp on my personal finances. Sure, I had a checking account, a savings account, and even a Roth IRA that my parents helped me set up as a teenager. But I could not *really* explain the difference between a Roth and a traditional IRA. Nor did I have any idea what my credit score was or how to check it. How did I get through two decades of education, culminating in one of the top universities in the country, without ever learning these basic skills?

Financial Literacy: A Snapshot

Upon graduation, I felt like I had no foundation of knowledge for managing my money, and the truth is that I was not alone. Indeed, financial education is one of the major challenges for our generation. We are not yet financially savvy. Past educational methods—namely, relying on our families for advice—are clearly not working. How else can we explain the fact that only one in three teens knows how to read a bank statement, balance a checkbook, and pay bills?

As these teens grow older, their finances only get more and more complicated. A shocking statistic from the American Bankruptcy Institute shows that college students represent 19 percent of all those who filed for bankruptcy.[21] And 25 percent of young adults rate their financial situation as "poor."[22] Another survey shows that money is the *number one* thing young people worry about.[23]

How do the overall problems that this generation faces translate to financial concerns? This generation is growing up in a new economic environment, and as a result, saving money is "in." The growing number of personal finance sites and their focus on budgeting speak to this immense market need.

So while the job market and economic climate might seem bleak, there is some good news: I believe that we are a generation who desires change. Just as I would have loved to learn how to manage my money before graduating from Harvard, so do 84 percent of college students indicate a wish for financial education.

This massive problem of financial illiteracy is not easy to fix. The truth is that finances by nature are complicated, and they only grow increasingly so. (Take the subprime mortgage crisis, for example.) Our knowledge needs to grow along with changes in the financial world, but we have a lot of catching up to do. If we can fix this widespread problem of money concerns and instead help young adults feel savvy about their personal finances, they can turn their attention to other things. Why not transform money from a stressor that inhibits young adults to a manageable arena that allows them to follow their passions?

Whether we like it or not, money greatly impacts our lives. To make your greatest happiness a reality, you'll need the power of understanding your finances. Ignoring them is simply not an option.

The LearnVest Story

During my time at Morgan Stanley, I decided to explore my interest in financial literacy. I undertook the (major) side project of researching what financial tools were already out there. I found a significant gap between dry books and expensive financial planners. Neither of these two options was particularly desirable, and I simply could not find a resource that spoke directly to me.

After working at Morgan Stanley for a few years, I enrolled in Harvard Business School. In my first semester at HBS, I learned invaluable information about how to run a company, from various leadership styles to operations management. Ultimately, I realized that as an entrepreneur, there is nothing more important than doing, so I put my HBS degree on hold and dedicated myself fully to building a personal finance company of my own, LearnVest—a name comprised of the words *learn*, *earn*, and *invest*.

Many might think that taking a leave of absence from HBS is a crazy thing to do in any economy, and most would agree that it was particularly crazy in the heart of the greatest recession America had seen in decades. But the collapse of Wall Street seemed like a sign that financial education was necessary now more than ever.

The most useful advice I heard was to truly know your audience. What would be the best way for a twenty-something to tackle his finances? More specifically, what would be the best way for a twenty-something *woman* to do so? In my research, not only had I discovered a lack of resources for my generation, but there were also no resources that spoke to me as a woman—barring glittery pink books advising against excessive shoe purchases. We defined the LearnVest audience as women ages eighteen to fifty, with a focus on young women in their first years out of college and in the real world.

Statistics clearly demonstrate that women have been underserved by financial services companies and are particularly lacking in financial education and literacy. Although the average female income has soared 63 percent over the past thirty years and women control approximately 60 percent of the wealth in the United States, women are nearly *twice* as likely as men to retire in poverty.[24] This inequality in the world of money has serious implications, as 70 percent of women say they are carrying so much debt that it makes them unhappy, and 90 percent of women feel insecure when it comes to their personal finances.[25]

With this audience of young women in mind, we leveraged technology to share personal finances with as many users as possible. We created our website, www.learnvest.com, where users take a brief diagnostic test that generates a personalized action plan. By providing relevant content and walking users through financial milestones step-by-step, we hope to make finances uncomplicated and even fun. We cover everything from how to open a credit card to how having a baby affects your finances, alongside useful tools and calculators.

Running a start-up is a challenging journey, but we seem to have hit a nerve. I'm proud to say that in just one year, LearnVest has helped over one million people make a better financial decision.

Lessons and the Way Forward

Although financial literacy is a major issue for our generation, it is one we should be willing to correct. A study showed that it is not a lack of time that prevents women from becoming more involved in their finances. Rather, it is a lack of knowledge.[26] Finding the proper tone and medium to share that knowledge can be a significant challenge, but there are many ways to address financial literacy.

The first is the straightforward route of infusing financial literacy into our education system. We need to teach students that understanding the basics of personal finance is just as critical as learning how to read and write. Personal finance classes should be a graduation requirement at all high schools, and these classes should focus on real-life examples to fully convey the importance of money in the real world. High school is a great time to share this information, as the transition to college is a time of independence—and often of financial independence.

Personal finance should be included in many levels of education. Though business schools address the world of high finance, it is critical to equip future business leaders with a deep understanding of personal finance as well.

There is also a major opportunity for large *Fortune* 500 companies to provide financial education to their employees. Companies can include personal finance in training programs for new hires, helping them understand their paycheck and 401(k) before diving into a career. Given the numerous free personal finance resources out there, companies have many options for forming partnerships and rebranding these resources to share with employees in a powerful way that benefits both sides.

The topic of financial literacy is something that the government has taken steps to improve, but it simply cannot move fast enough to help the great number of people currently in need of education. Every little bit helps, though, and this seems to be a growing concern for policy makers. The Social Security Administration, for example, has awarded the Rand Corporation, a Washington, D.C., think tank, a grant to research, evaluate, and improve LearnVest. Steps like these on the side of the government can add the needed momentum to bring this challenge to center stage.

Although "financial education" sounds like a daunting subject, I am confident that we can achieve it. If we can help prevent personal finance from being a source of concern, anxiety, and confusion, then it is certainly a worthwhile pursuit. If anything good has come out of the broader financial situation that our generation has encountered—watching Wall Street crumble right in front of us—it is this call to action around financial literacy.

The Education of a Millennial Leader

JONATHAN DOOCHIN is the founder of the Leadership Institute at Harvard College and chairman of the Board of Overseers. He also serves as the CEO of Leverett Energy, a firm focused on financing and developing energy efficiency and renewable energy. He has spent time as a management consultant at McKinsey & Company and is a serial entrepreneur. Jon explores three themes that guide the future of leadership development.

Leadership Can Be Taught

When I was eight, an academic tutor told my parents I probably wouldn't learn to read or spell, and I likely would not attend college. My scores on the Tennessee Assessment Test, the state's SATs for third graders, were in the lowest percentile, and my reading and spelling were at best that of a first grader. But my teachers and parents refused to see my struggle as fate and taught me to see my potential. From them, I learned not to give up on myself or others even when reality seems hopeless. They spent countless hours with me—one-on-one—working through my dyslexia. And that experience, from an early age, taught me the importance of re-flection and optimism, the impact of mentorship, and the potential of thinking like an entrepreneur. I gradually learned to become what I per-ceived to be a leader—always acknowledging my imperfections but never giving up; playing to my strengths, while learning from my weaknesses; and never allowing those weaknesses to define me. Moreover, my experi-ence built in me a conviction that leadership, like any other subject, can be taught.

Believing that we can use structured curricula and experiential exer-cises to teach leadership to people of any age, I cofounded the Leader-ship Institute at Harvard College (LIHC) during my senior year. LIHC is now a hub for learning how to lead at Harvard—and a place where next-generation leaders on campus take seriously their responsibilities not only to each other and to their communities, but to the idea that they can and should learn to lead. Run by college students, supported by graduate student mentors, and overseen by recent graduates and professors, LIHC is founded on the idea that leadership development is a trial-and-error process that causes individuals to reexamine their perspective of the world, pursue objectivity by placing themselves in others' shoes, and develop a vocabulary of underlying theories that define their personal leadership style. It's one model for what I think is a growing and useful trend—leadership education.

Teaching Leadership

Despite the often prevailing opinion that leadership is highly contextual and individualized, I believe there are a few major themes that distinguish the future of leadership development. My passion is building leaders, and I believe both young leaders and the organizations that seek to cultivate them could benefit from employing these themes. Three of these themes—holistic self, the leader as architect, and collective mentorship—have broad applicability and have been foundational to our success at LIHC, in companies I have operated, and in my family life.

Discovering the Holistic Self

All of us are constantly undergoing a journey of self-discovery, awareness, and change. This process may ebb and flow throughout a person's life, but to accelerate leadership development and organizational growth, it is critical to cultivate and encourage that personal journey. This focus on individual reflection, fulfillment, and holistic development is the most significant component of creating a motivating and rewarding environment. Moreover, to be the strongest leaders, we must first work to understand ourselves—our biases as well as our strengths—because only then do we become at home with ourselves, more objective in our decisions, and more able to see the world from the point of view of those we impact. Only then can we leverage our strengths to make the greatest difference.

At LIHC, we engage this process primarily through Leadership Development Groups (LDGs). LDGs, part of a curriculum created by Bill George, work by dividing large groups of individuals into smaller groups that foster self-discovery through reflection and social interaction. Few people fully understand their own personal life stories, the times they have failed and how they picked themselves up, what they truly want to do, or what brings them happiness. Bound by strict mutually agreed upon confidentiality, these LDGs help members uncover their life stories, allowing them to see and understand themselves in a way that they rarely have in the past. This is because in our busy professional and social lives, we rarely have the time to step back and reflect. We are unaware of many things that define us—my growing up with dyslexia, for example—yet these powerful insights into our formative experiences can give us strength and direction. Instances where we failed, events that changed who we are no matter how silly or small to others, are experiences from which we can draw immense strength by realizing that if we found ways to fight through past failures, we can undoubtedly make it through future crises. Conversely, understanding what creates our happiness can help us find meaning and satisfaction in our daily lives. Doing this for individuals within an organization aligns the goals of the organization with its staff, while improving the productivity and effectiveness of employees. The opportunities for reflection are broad, and help participants in LDGs better understand their "authentic" selves.

The more self-aware individuals become, the more they'll understand whether they align with an organization. Poor performers typically aren't deficient because of any inherent deficit, but rather because they don't fit their job or company. Often, this misalignment isn't discovered until both individual and employer have become dissatisfied, colleagues have felt the effects of the lack of motivation, and productivity has suffered across the team. The development of more reflective organizations can drive individual fulfillment and collaborative gain, particularly with a young generation that's more comfortable with personal reflection in a professional context. And this kind of narrative-driven self-discovery can help a young person become more thoughtful, confident, and focused as he or she strives for leadership.

Structuring Success

In the past, entrepreneurship was the domain of a select few. Today, with information and social networks at our fingertips, a generation of leaders is evolving with entrepreneurship in their DNA. But our tendency toward entrepreneurship must be focused, structured, and refined to develop meaningfully.

While working at McKinsey & Company and the U.S. Department of Energy, as well as building a handful of companies from the ground up, it has become clear to me that leaders must learn to structure organizations and tasks effectively to create sustainable organizations. By "structure," I mean stepping back and seeing the big picture, breaking problems into manageable parts, planning their resolution in detailed succession, designing the necessary norms and principles, and matching the skills and capabilities of those in the organization to the problem itself. Such structure doesn't emerge just from a charismatic leader. With a skill set in structuring organizations and teams, very quiet individuals can drive sustainable success. If you ask people what they need within an organization, they may often say "a break" or "less work." However, these people are often simply suffering from a lack of structure and direction and a misalignment of their talents and the work they're doing. To be a good leader, one must be a good listener—discerning needs versus wants, observing flaws in systems, and acting to leave a sustainable structure that remains independent of the leader.

Young leaders must work to develop this structure. When I started my first business, dropping out of Harvard College after freshman year to start a high-end car brokerage business, it was a grab-bag process of innovation—where do I get cars, how do I transfer large sums of money, where do I learn what a Ferrari actually is? Though this model worked, its potential was limited by a staff of one and an organization that was not optimized, not scalable, and not sustainable in my absence. As I brought on six staff members without fully developing the necessary structure, I was forced to realize that a leader who doesn't step back and put in place the right norms and structures—even down to creating a personal daily routine that sets aside and protects time to structure work as well as personal needs—will unquestionably constantly struggle to build an effective and sustainable enterprise. The amount of time, talent, and effort consumed in restructuring situations where young leaders have failed to plan is not only a detriment to productivity, but an insurmountable drain on limited resources that may cause an all-star organization or project to fail.

The first concept every student at LIHC is taught after they learn the organization's mission and vision is a Gantt chart timeline. We could call it structured leadership. Each student is responsible for her own timeline and budget projections, laying out what activities she will lead over the next semester. If she wants others to work with her, she has to convince them to join. Students are asked to present, at every level of the organization, a timeline and budget showing what they would like to accomplish, their goals for impact, and their detailed plans for achieving them. Each timeline is approved and then made public within the organization. This forces each student to lead his own piece of a project— even if that student is a team of one—and creates accountability while encouraging him to take ownership of the process from start to finish.

Developing Collective Mentorship

A collective mentorship model is one in which each individual in the organization is encouraged to build a personal board of advisors, have a mentor and mentee, and cultivate strong professional peer networks.

The collective mentorship model does not assume that only individuals of a certain age, experience, or status have the answers. Rather, it harnesses a collective and connected approach by believing that people can learn just as much from peers as from superiors. Social networks—often peer to peer—that provide collective mentorship can play a much more significant role in both personal and professional problem solving. Trusted mentors help leaders take the crucial first step: acknowledging the existence of the problem and talking about it openly.

I've been blessed with a number of dedicated mentors in my life—from parents and teachers who helped me overcome the limits of dyslexia to those who counsel me on my businesses today. Breaking down walls of "professionalism," I've tried to present those mentors with an honest picture of me—my thoughts, experiences, struggles, and motivations. And they've helped me fight through difficult times and grow as a person. I, in turn, have experienced some of my most satisfying moments working as a peer mentor with others and helping them succeed.

Through a personal board of advisors, LIHC members have different people they can consult to develop ideas, clarify moral standards, and thoughtfully pursue personal and professional development. These types of networks not only act to strengthen individuals by giving them support, but also encourage self-understanding and reflection. Moreover, they allow LIHC members to think about a personal problem in a dynamic way, in the same way they've been using the Internet and social connectivity in tackling business problems.

It's an arrangement that can be fulfilling to both sides. Having a mentee often teaches the mentor as much as the mentee, as it requires mentors to think critically about issues they may also face, encourages them to act as an example, and hones their leadership skills.

Learning to Lead

Each of us has the capacity to lead. Each of us, likely, has also shied away from leadership at times. We've been told we simply don't have what it takes—the intelligence, the charisma, the genetics—and, too often, we've listened. Increasingly, however, there is more awareness among young people that all of the mysterious qualities that once defined "leadership" are not inherent, but eminently teachable. And a generation defined by increasing interconnectedness and diversity understands better than previous generations that although there are universal principles of leadership, the model for leadership is not one-size-fits-all, but should be individualized as we play to our own strengths and personalities.

INTERVIEW WITH . . .

Rich Lyons

Dean of the Haas School of Business, University of California–Berkeley

Rich Lyons is the Bank of America dean of the Haas School of Business, UC Berkeley. Prior to becoming dean in July 2008, he served as the chief learning officer at Goldman Sachs in New York, a position he held since 2006. As chief learning officer, Rich was responsible for leadership development among the firm's managing directors.

How do you think MBA students' attitudes and motivations toward the degree and, more broadly, toward business education have changed in the past twenty years? How do you see them changing in the next twenty years?

A question like this, of course, involves generalizations, so I'll start with that caveat. Nevertheless, I think there are trends that everybody is seeing. I think that MBAs seem to be more purpose-driven in the way they think about their careers. This might be a generational thing, so it could be true of students in lots of different fields. They are less willing to compartmentalize their professional and personal lives. They want a professional life that's more aligned with their personal or private values. And they're willing to give up more to maintain that alignment.

A second characteristic is that students seem to be even more interested than before in both in- and out-of classroom learning and development. They're expecting to draw insights and meaning directly from experience while they're in the program. They're thinking about the curriculum in the total curriculum sense, by which I mean a set of experiences that we might associate with a degree or with a program.

I think an additional trend is the recognition that despite not having a completely flat or borderless world, careers need to take someone across geographies. It's become a must that students think more broadly about geographies in their career. Of course, some students were thinking that way twenty years ago and many businesses were very global twenty years ago. But now it's hard to even find an MBA student who isn't thinking that way or an MBA program that doesn't recognize that it needs to address that need. And I would expect this to continue for the next twenty years. I see no reason why the global economic environment will reverse this trend.

How are MBA programs responding to these trends and where do they need to respond differently?

I think they need to address it on many different fronts, so there isn't any one answer to that question.

One very simple front is that having only 10 or 20 percent international students in an MBA program is way too little. I think rubbing elbows with people from different cultures and different geographies is an absolutely fundamental starting point. I think the relative development of non-U.S. business schools and the demand they're attracting is representative of this.

There are many other areas that are important as well. One of course, has to do with curriculum. To what degree are international global issues discussed in the core classes and in elective classes? Every business school now has an experiential learning or action-learning curriculum within the larger curriculum. And the question is how many international opportunities are within the experiential learning curriculum because there's nothing like going to a place and actually working there, even if for a short period of time.

I don't think it's necessary for a business school to have a remote presence everywhere. My own view here may differ from some other people's, but I actually think that "place" is still an important part of many business schools. The set of experiences that arise out of the ecosystem within which a business school operates is crucial. And to completely distribute that ecosystem, online or in a separate campus, may take some of the essential elements away.

We talked about changes at the business school level. But what do you think are the most important things that today's MBA students need to learn?

Every business school is going to answer this a little differently. And I think that's fine, because there is no one way to think about this.

Setting a direction for an organization often means starting with the future and working backward. So the way I easily talk about this is I say, "Look, my kids are ten and seven, and my wife and I think about our kids differently than how our parents looked at us." This notion that certain commercial paths are no longer viable or sustainable is, in many ways, defining of our time. Our parents had a worldview that we had an inexhaustible world, an inexhaustible set of opportunities. Today when you a look at the model of society and modern economies—things like health care expenditure or energy use or the economics of aging, or access to safe water around the world, or carbon, or public education. This list goes on and on. Many of those areas in the last twenty to thirty years cannot sustainably be extrapolated in a linear way. So that's a huge opportunity.

I'm not going to be around in 2080 but my kids are, so these unsustainable paths need to get bent between now and 2080. I think the business sector will play the lead role in bending the paths, and getting the right public policy and the right nonprofit elements to this larger picture are also going to be essential. So how do we make sure we have the right human capital in the system to bend those pathways?

To get more tangible, what's the competency model? At Haas, we want to tether our vision around sustainability because it feels like a defining feature of our time. It is a sufficiently long cycle that we can think about human capital in ten-, twenty-, thirty-year horizons. And then we ask, what is the task of an innovative leader—what does she or he do?

There are ten items on our capabilities list. Everything on this list needs to meet two criteria. One, recruiters have to say, "That's what I'm looking for. That's what I interviewed for." Two, everything on this list has to be grounded in the social sciences. If our faculty heard some of the items on the list and said, "That's right out of the top ten best-seller lists in that new faddish book," then they would spit the idea out. And they should spit it out. So we needed to make sure we could deliver a list of capabilities with some intellectual heft and some foundation.

I won't go through all ten but let me give you some examples. Here's one: problem framing.

Business leaders and CEOs say to me, "Rich, we will always be problem solvers, that's a given. We will always need problem solvers. But you know what I am not getting enough of? I don't have enough people who are willing to lift their heads up from a transactional mode and seek more deeply upstream in the problem finding and problem framing stages. I don't have people who feel comfortable disengaging for two hours and writing down one, two, or three sentences that define exactly what the problem is. And if they can't do that, then they are going to be wasting a lot of time trying to address the wrong problems."

The second one is experimentation. We had a talk by Google here at Berkeley Haas recently about innovating at scale. Google has thirty thousand employees now, and the question is, how do you keep innovating at a large organization? If I had to summarize that whole talk in a single sentence or question, it would be this: what would your business look like if the cost of experimentation went to zero? How might we do distribution, or how might we do brand management, or how might we do an organizational restructuring? That will require people to ask not how competent do I feel in this decision, but rather, what data would I like to have to make it, and what experiments can I design to get those data?

What do you think are the big changes that firms will need to adopt in the way they teach or conduct learning within their firms, particularly as they bring on board more next-generation leaders?

I think one thing implicit in your question that I agree with is that part of the deal in attracting talent and winning the "talent war" is providing a road map of professional development that people can see, that they understand, and that they want. This is absolutely fundamental.

Let me just take the examples that I gave: problem framing and experimentation. Why are there so few problem-framing skills? If business leaders are saying they want it, why don't they just develop it? Why isn't it happening? I think that's a very important question.

And I think that question helps to answer your question. My best answer is in a lot of these organizations, the norms and values, the culture, for want of better words, don't consciously and deliberately recognize and compensate people for doing the problem framing and for doing the hard thinking. CEOs and business leaders can say, "I need people who can disengage and can think hard and spend a few hours on a few sentences," but in reality we keep such a transaction-oriented rewards system. I think the firm needs to ask, "And why do we have too little of this? And how deeply into ourselves do we have to look in order to change the context so we can get more of it?" And some of those are actually going to require changes in things like culture, norms, and values.

On a more philosophical level, can leadership and ethics be taught? How do you think business schools and corporations should be teaching these?

It's a fundamental question. First of all, can leadership be taught? I have to ask the question, to whom? Because we have to recognize that particularly at the top business schools, we are seeing a remarkable slice of human capital. This is a group of people who are in the top percentile of leadership potential. We select for that. And can we develop their leadership capacity when we're working in that segment? Absolutely, because their potential is so large. The crucible that we can fill is so big. I think the question "Can business schools teach leadership?" is very different from the question "Can leadership be taught in some very abstract sense to a representative person?" I believe business schools can teach leadership.

Some people say, "You can't teach ethics, Rich, these people are all adults. That had to happen when they were five, seven, or twelve. It's way too late." A lot of people put that view forward.

I think that view is not correct. Here's why. Suppose I'm the CEO of a company, and I say that all of my employees are twenty-seven or older, and I cannot influence when they are going to behave ethically, and I cannot influence their ethical judgment. That would be a terrible thing to say, and it would be a terrible thing to think. What should a CEO say? No CEO should say, "Don't worry about ethical behavior in my firm because every one of my people has taken a thirty-hour ethics training course." Bad answer, right? That's kind of the equivalent of, "Do you have ethics in your core curriculum?" Ethics in the core curriculum is a very good thing, but that in and of itself is a bad answer to the question.

What would a CEO say and how do we think about this in a business school perspective? I think a CEO should say this: "Ethics is in everything we do. It's in the norms and values that guide every judgment call that's made in this firm; it's in our culture. We look for, we hire for it. We drill it into every business process. It's in everything I do." I think that's the right answer. Leadership in many ways is a state of mind. Have we created the culture, an expectation among these students? Leadership is not being the CEO; leadership is influencing outcomes. Leadership is often without formal authority. I think that for a lot of these folks, there are the skills of leadership but there's also the mind-set. It's not about me.

When a lot of people get to that point, they're ready to be followed. I usually put it this way to our students. I say, how many of you have been in an organization where somebody one or two levels above you did something that was in his or her best interest, but not in the best interest of the organization? Did you notice? Did anybody not notice? Will you ever forget it?

Leadership is not made from authority. It's made from trust and followership and the idea that it is really not about you. Once you start to get that, then people will start to want to follow. And you will start to have influence even if you don't have the authority.

That's certainly part of what we try to do, on top of building skills among students. Those are all important skills. But ultimately, I think it's about providing somebody a mind-set so that they can understand why a leadership example is working so beautifully and what worldview is behind it.

Moving Forward

We've presented our work in six themed chapters covering admittedly broad ground—from embracing globalization to competing using the latest technology. Throughout the course of collecting these stories, interviewing senior leaders, and conducting our business school survey, we formed views on how today's young leaders will shape the future of business. We think that over the coming few decades, these leaders will:

- **Successfully combine their interests across sectors, cross-pollinating previously tired industries with new insights.** There is an increasing desire among young leaders to "connect the dots" and successfully combine their diverse interests to create meaningful impact—for example, by bringing for-profit analytical skills to leadership positions in the nonprofit sector, or by applying lessons learned in life to business leadership positions. This will continue and will open new arrays, possibilities, and opportunities in areas that previously lacked innovation.

- **Understand globalization more comprehensively.** Today's young leaders live in a world where understanding and harnessing the effects of globalization is essential to successful business leadership. As a result, they are using experience in other cultures to enhance their capacity for global leadership. As this continues, we'll be able to further our understanding of the forces driving an increasingly interconnected world.

- **Fully embrace diversity.** To establish themselves as future leaders, it is increasingly important that young leaders accumulate diverse leadership experiences today that will better enable them to lead increasingly diverse groups of people—creating more "wholeness" and happiness in the workplace of the future.

- **Sharpen the focus on sustainability.** Today's young leaders are more interested than any in recent memory in creating a more sustainable world—and breaking the trade-off between sustainable products and higher prices. They will learn how to push their organizations toward more sustainable production frontiers without compromising financial outcomes.

- **Live as technology natives.** We observed that effective young leaders are already fluent in the sales and marketing tools of tomorrow— social media and location-based networks, regardless of their current industry or job function. They are self-taught technology experts. As technology reaches ubiquity in both the developed and developing world, young leaders will leverage their understanding as users of technology to improve the performance of their organizations.

- **Learn in new and innovative ways.** In the future, young leaders will harness new tools to learn in ways previous generations couldn't have imagined. Young leaders believe leadership can be taught— and are including in their definition of leadership the character and authenticity to lead with purpose.

- **Assume the mantle of leadership.** Most of the individuals we spoke to view leadership as a responsibility, consistently referring back to obligations to those around them, and speaking and writing in detail about what leadership means. Many seem to view leading others as a "calling" starting, in many cases, at a very young age. As business becomes more tightly integrated with society as a whole, it will be crucial for young leaders to assume their leadership positions with a sense of grace, humility, and serious responsibility.

Though *Passion and Purpose* originated from the ashes of the 2008 global financial crisis, we've been amazed at the level of optimism about the future. But is unbridled passion, without purpose, the best way to conclude this book? We didn't think so. In the same way that we tapped senior industry leaders to have the final word on individual chapters, we asked Nitin Nohria, dean of Harvard Business School, to contribute his thoughts as a capstone for the book. Why Dean Nohria? He is a global figure—hailing from India but working and traveling frequently. He's head of one of the most powerful business institutions in the world. And he drives innovation, successfully changing the status quo in every major leadership position he's held. Most of all, however, he's a quiet, humble, and patient individual. This balance of passion and purpose is what makes him the perfect capstone.

Finally, our project of does not stop where this book ends. In fact, one of the challenges we faced writing about the leaders of tomorrow was the sheer volume of inspiring quotes and stories we encountered at every turn. Although only a fraction of the individuals we met could make the print edition, we couldn't resist profiling a host of others online. In fact, we're started thinking of the website as something even bigger—an enduring dialogue between young leaders and their more senior counterparts that will travel well beyond the covers of this book. As a *Passion and Purpose* reader, we encourage you to join the conversation at www.hbr.org/passion-purpose. We look forward to seeing you there.

Nitin Nohria
Dean of the Harvard Business School

> Dean Nohria discusses the future role of business in society, the
> significance of innovation over the next century, and the impor-
> tance of remaining patient in an increasingly fast-paced world.

**Let's start from the beginning. Why did you choose business as a
profession?**

It goes back to very early childhood experiences I had with my father. I
still remember when I was very young, probably ten, my father was CEO
of a large company. Part of his job was to go out and build plants all over
the countryside. In India at that time, the government often gave incentives for large companies to create plants in underdeveloped parts of the
country. So I remember going with him to these groundbreaking cere-
monies that commemorated a new plant being built on site.

We'd go and there was, literally, absolutely nothing. These were
barren areas, and other than a little tent that had been created for that
particular groundbreaking ceremony, there was nothing. And then
sometimes, seven or eight years later, I went back to these places and
where there had been nothing, there was this bustling township. It
was an amazing transformation. Where there had been no plant, there
was now a series of plants because the original plant had attracted
suppliers and those suppliers had in turn attracted new companies. I
remember meeting people in these places whose lives had been transformed by business. They had gotten jobs. They had been able to send
their own kids to school. They had been able, in some cases, to send
their kids to college—and not only in different places, but to schools
and colleges established in these particular neighborhoods because
business had created enough prosperity to fund them.

So in a very deep, visceral sense, I came to realize that business had this amazing power to transform society and to create prosperity in a number of ways.

When I first went to study chemical engineering in IIT Bombay, my hope was at some point to become an entrepreneur. My first instinct on about business was to create one myself. And so when I graduated from IIT Bombay—even though I was going on to the PhD program at MIT—my initial hope was still to be an entrepreneur. In fact, I had even signed a technology license with an Irish company to go out and create a company when I graduated. But it was at MIT that I discovered that in so many ways, being an academic was like being an entrepreneur—it was just being an intellectual entrepreneur. You could choose a topic of your own, and go out and study it. And in an odd way, by accidentally discovering the field of leadership and organizational behavior, I learned that I could study the things that fascinated me— which were people like my father, and the whole act of leadership and management. That's how I got attracted to the idea of a career in business and then in particular, a career as a business academic.

Much of this book explores how young leaders are impacting the world in new ways. Have you seen changes in the ways students are thinking about business during your time at HBS?

One thing that has been constant is that students come to Harvard Business School, or choose business education as something that they want to do, because they view it as an accelerator for success. That I think has always been true. You accelerated because new options opened up for you. You accelerated because you can go back and rise faster in your organization. We have always attracted ambitious people who want to get ahead in life.

There have always been dreams of how one can exercise leadership to make a difference in the world. And even though that's our stated mission, "to educate leaders who make a difference in the world," I don't think it's just what people write on their application forms to get in. There's a very large number of people who do have dreams about how, through business, they can make a difference in the world. And I think that's been an important part of Harvard Business School and the students whom we've attracted throughout my time here at the school.

I think what has changed over time is different fields have risen and fallen in terms of importance. When I first came to the school, which was in 1988, consulting and investment banking were both still hot. By the late nineties, entrepreneurship had become very hot, particularly during the dot-com boom. At various points in the middle, real estate seems to be something that becomes hot and kind of falls off. So in some ways, the students are always searching for what seems to be the hot sector of the economy, and they pursue that. What's hot changes all the time, so there's a dynamism in what our students go into. If you look further back in the first decades of the school, we were having people who were going into railroads, and then we had people going into consumer packaged goods.

You know, everybody worries, "Will the school only produce people who are in consulting and finance?" But we forget that the world always changes and as the opportunity structure changes, our students go to different things. So just in the last five or seven years, we've begun to see clean tech as one of the fastest-growing paths in terms of where people will go from HBS. Health care has also become one of the fastest new sectors. Social enterprise—which was not even a category when I first came to HBS—is extremely popular. So what I think is striking is the constant dynamism in how people are looking for new things, and I expect that dynamism will continue. You pick people who are ambitious, who have aspirations—a combination of wanting to do well for themselves but also do well for society. And as that intersection evolves, the desires of our students evolve as well.

Part of that dynamism is the set of values that people bring to leadership, and those values have changed throughout the years—most acutely in the past two to three years when some have called into question the very legitimacy of business leaders in society. How have you seen people's or MBAs' attitudes toward leadership change over the years? How might that change moving forward?

I think there have been moments in this period where the lure of short-term gains was so high that our students, like many other people in business, were captivated, then captured by it. During the dot-com boom you could create a company and in eighteen months, you became a multimillionaire, multibillionaire—if there's money to be made, you don't want to be the fool who's sitting on the sideline while others are doing it, right?

What has been true in business through millennia is that any place in which you can make money very quickly isn't long-lived. And I think that's a little bit of the trap, the sort of short-term trap, which occasionally business leaders fall into and something that we've now lived through in recent times as well. It's as if a few people benefited from the positive externalities and many, many people got left paying for the negative externalities of this most recent round of short-term value creation. I think that's what's caused a greater anxiety about the culture of business in recent times.

How do you see people dealing with that moving forward, especially young businesspeople? Do you see a change in the way they view business or in the way they exercise leadership?

It's my hope they do. I was struck by the recent MBA Oath movement. The specifics of the MBA Oath are actually less important than the signal it represented. Here was a group of students who felt it really important to declare that they stood for different values than what were being portrayed as the values of business leaders—that we're all about greed, we're only in it for ourselves, we don't care about society more broadly. So here is a group of people who said, "No, no, no, I didn't join business because those are my values. I joined business because I really believe in the kind of positive role that business has for society. And what I want to stand for as a business leader is a difference in our values."

The world is increasingly interconnected, and these global links will become stronger in the future. What differences do you see among leaders around the world? Is there anything that American business can learn from and better develop in terms of values, or attitudes, norms, for doing business?

I think there are quite different values that animate business in different parts of the world. In Europe, I think that respect for the role of the state is still very high, for the most part. In America, we're enormously suspicious of the role of the state. In parts of Asia, there is great respect for the state, but there are other parts of Asia, like in India, where there's no respect for the state. I think the same is true in Latin America, where in some parts of Latin America the state enjoys respect and in other parts the opposite is true.

One thing that Americans need to recognize is that the relationship you can have with the state doesn't have to be one of permanent hostility—you can actually have a productive relationship with the state as well. While regulation can often overreach, as we have found recently, the complete absence of regulation is equally problematic. So some form of productive regulation might be a useful thing for us to think about.

The other difference that you certainly have in America is that when things go wrong, relative to any other place that I know, Americans are willing to cut their losses and move on. You look at Japan and other places, there's so much anxiety about the costs of confronting the mistake you made because it's going to inevitably lead to social dislocation of some kind. They just postpone taking pain that is necessary to confront the mistakes that they made. Whereas I think one of the great strengths of the American economy, relative to any other economy that I know, is this capacity to say, "Okay, we made some mistakes, but this is going to be costly; we're going to take the costs, we're going to write off the cost quickly." Look at the length of a recession in America. America recovers from recessions faster than most places do because they're willing to take the losses more quickly. But it cuts the other way too. So you can say in some countries, there is more empathy for people who are disadvantaged. Whereas in America, some of that empathy might be missing, but that lack of empathy also creates this capacity to move forward more quickly.

Another issue that I think is very important is that Americans have a self-concept of being much more committed to innovation than any other part of the world. And for the most part, I think that's true. The American capacity for innovation and entrepreneurship is much greater than it is anywhere else. But the rest of the world is catching up very fast. So I think that we in America have to be more conscious of recognizing that the global battlefield is now not just about other countries competing on low-cost wages relative to American entrepreneurship and innovation, but other countries are also going to compete on innovation and entrepreneurship, in addition to just competing on low cost. And this is a very profound shift in terms of the dynamics of global competition that I'm not sure we in America have fully come to terms with.

That's an interesting point about innovation. A lot of people would argue that innovation within organizations often comes from younger people. Do you see qualities in the next generation of business leaders that could help to drive that push for innovation? And if so, how can organizations start to effectively use those next-generation leaders to drive innovation?

This is a whole generation of people who have grown up very resourceful at getting ideas from any place, because they've grown up on the Internet and they've grown up with a view that whatever problem I want to solve, I have access to solving that problem in all kinds of ways. Social networking makes you resourceful in a combination of ways. It's not that you can just get data; you can also actually connect to other interesting people from anywhere in the world. If you think about the core of all innovation, it's actually a creative recombination of ideas and people. So most innovation is not actually inventing something new; instead it's putting together existing things in new ways. This was Schumpeter's great insight. And if you actually study the history of science or you study the history of innovation, it is a very rare thing that is genuinely novel. Most things are creative recombinations. I think that there's a generation of people growing up whose capacity to do that is much greater than it ever used to be before—just because that's the way they inherently think of organizing themselves.

There's a series of very significant challenges that business and society face, that will require this kind of imagination to address. How do you balance energy security with environmental sustainability? How do you leverage the amazing innovations in health care that allow us to all live longer, with the cost that these imply? How will we get 3 billion people on the planet the stuff that the 1 billion already have? If we imagine that the resource intensity of producing a car which these people will one day have is the same as the resource intensity of producing it for the first 1 billion, we're dead. We're not going to be able to make it happen.

There have to be fundamentally different innovative ideas for how we even produce existing stuff for the next 3 billion people who all want it. So you have to make the Tata Nano at $2,000, but we'll have to ask the question, what's the next price point at which a car is going to get made? Or what's the next value proposition for how one thinks about each of these things? Because if we just think that all we're going to do is to recreate the existing value chain of the 1 billion for the other 3 billion, the planet can't sustain it. There are not enough resources in the world to do that. But I'm of the view that this generation of people who are now growing up in schools and colleges will be resourceful enough to do it because they've been educated with a different kind of mind.

What's your word of hope and word of caution for this generation?

The word of hope is that there's so much to do right now. The biggest example is those 3 billion people in the world who haven't yet benefited from the prosperity that business can create. That is an extraordinary opportunity for business leaders. Just think about that: three-quarters of this planet still haven't benefited from what business can help provide. And the one-quarter that have benefited also have their challenges. I think that almost nothing that is of any significance in the world today—environmental sustainability, digital revolution, health care—I can't think of a single problem of any significance that's going to be solved without business playing not just *a role*, but a *leadership role*. So to me, that's the amazing hope that exists for anybody who's entertaining a career in business today.

The caution that I would have is this: don't get too impatient with yourself. There's something about the Facebook generation that because things start and end in three minutes, you might believe that all the answers to all of these questions also have to start and end in three minutes, and that they will all get done in some super-rapid cycle in which everything is getting done. The speeding up of the world doesn't mean that everything in your life can be sped up the same way. Have the capacity to be patient, to be committed to the long term, to be able to devote years of energy into something, as opposed to just minutes. That's going to be an important part of what people need to be prepared for. But if they're prepared for this, the opportunities are endless.

About the Passion and Purpose MBA Student Survey

The idea for the MBA Student Survey emerged as we began to gather the individual stories behind *Passion and Purpose*. We noticed several recurring themes—new endeavors in unfamiliar lands; bringing the "whole person" to work; the convergence of private, public, and nonprofit careers. As business students ourselves, we wanted to measure the prevalence of these trends, and develop empirical evidence that certain values, beliefs, and attitudes on the future of leadership are widespread among MBAs, and not just shared by a few individuals.

We invited MBA students to participate in an online survey between September and October 2010. We polled a total of 510 respondents, a relatively substantial sample, and one that reflects the MBA population in terms of gender and country of origin. Due to time limitations, our survey is heavily skewed toward one school, with 44 percent of respondents coming from Harvard Business School. In addition, we polled only American business schools; thus the survey is not meant to represent attitudes of MBAs around the world. Finally, the sample focuses on current or recent MBAs, with 89 percent of respondents graduating between 2010 and 2012 (see a summary of the respondents in figure A-1).

To us, launching the survey just made sense. First, having quantitative data to complement individual, personal stories helped frame the different themes in a wider context. These stories were made more interesting

Snapshot of survey respondents

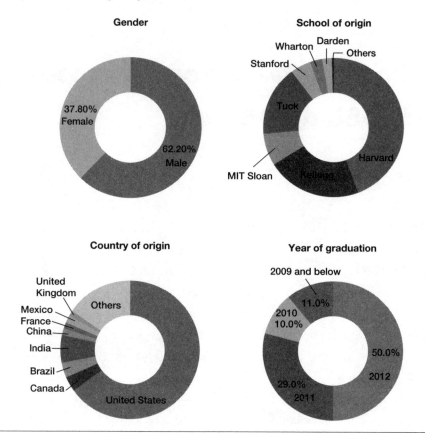

when we uncovered some fascinating facts from the survey, as shown in figure A-2.

The findings in this survey have very interesting implications for young individuals, senior managers, companies, and business schools alike. For example, if young people expect to work in more than four countries throughout their lifetime, how can business schools do a better job of globalizing the MBA experience? How can private sector companies develop young managers who also desire to understand the public and non-profit sectors? How should young people think about their paths to

FIGURE A-2

Fascinating facts from the MBA Student Survey

Intellectual challenge is the most important reason for choosing a job. is significantly more important than compensation or prestige.

4.6 The number of countries respondents intend to work in within 10 years after graduation.

2.4 The number of social networks, on average, our respondents are members.

84% believe that it is essential for business leaders to understand the public and nonprofit sectors.

92% agree that increased workplace diversity can lead to better business outcomes—especially diversity in gender, professional experience, and functional expertise.

80% believe that this generation views leadership differently from previous generations.

leadership when 80 percent of their peers believe that this generation views leadership differently than previous ones? We hope this survey can provide an initial platform for understanding answers to some of these questions.

Second, the MBA Student Survey supplements existing surveys that seek to measure trends and attitudes that set young business leaders apart. These studies inform corporations in their hiring and talent development strategies, and guide colleges and universities around the world in curriculum development. For instance, the IBM Institute for Business Value conducted a global student survey contrasting the views on leadership of current CEOs and senior managers with those of students around the world. Similarly, the Graduate Management Admissions Council, popularly known for administering the GMAT exam, conducts an annual Alumni Perspectives Survey, but mostly focuses on employment, career paths, and salary levels of MBA graduates. More generally, the Pew Research Center conducts research on the values and attitudes of American millennials. The MBA Student Survey is different from these surveys by focusing entirely on current or recent MBAs and their views on the trends discussed in this book. The survey is by no means a representation of the whole picture. We encourage readers to take the time to explore these other reports as they also yield fascinating findings, especially for young people interested in launching a career in business.

Finally, widespread online social networks and do-it-yourself research tools such as SurveyMonkey have made it easy and inexpensive to gather all this information. The technology for generating a relatively substantial data set in an expedient, almost-free manner was an opportunity too good to miss.

An Emerging Leadership Ethos

Perhaps the most interesting part of the survey involved hearing the attitudes of young leaders on the future of leadership. Four out of five current or recent MBAs believe that "this generation views business leadership differently than previous generations." To explore this even further, we asked the open-ended question, "What is the biggest and most imaginative way leadership in the 21st century will evolve?" We then categorized respondents' answers within several of the trends we already saw in this book to get a quantitative measure of its relative importance, as well as provide some excerpts of the responses (see figure A-3 and table A-1).

Young businesspeople interpreted these changing views on leadership in diverse ways. Echoing the convergence of business interests with broader societal and public interests highlighted in the first chapter, a common sentiment that was voiced by many was summed up by one respondent: "Business leaders will be forced to recognize and serve a broader community of stakeholders than in previous generations." Another respondent was more explicit on the role of business and business leaders, firmly believing that "management will no longer be explicitly required to act first and foremost to the financial benefit of shareholders." Another noted the very personal nature of leadership, arguing that it is

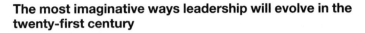

The most imaginative ways leadership will evolve in the twenty-first century

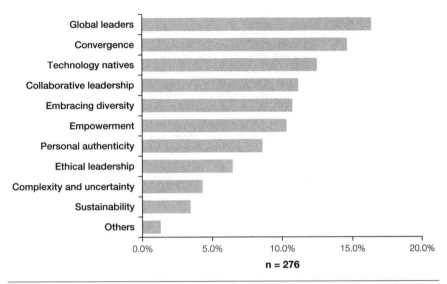

n = 276

"less about climbing a ladder within an established organization. The 21st century is more about defining the ladder through one's actions."

Young leaders are imagining a more global, complex, and fast-paced future. The top three most imaginative ways young leaders envision the future of leadership are clear: the rise of global leaders, the role of convergence in business, and leaders who are also technology natives.

For young leaders, globalization doesn't simply mean getting a plum overseas temporary assignment. With the rise of powerful emerging economies and the relative decline of American dominance, a global career now means moving across countries over extended periods of time, and designing a career path to grapple with that eventuality. After all, young MBAs expect to work in an average of 4.6 countries after business school. This doesn't just refer to jobs in big corporations. As one leader quipped, even start-ups today have learned how to be more global from the beginning.

TABLE A-1

Excerpts from the MBA Student Survey: How future leaders are reimagining leadership

Theme	Direct quotes
Global leaders	"Leaders must know how to operate in a global climate. Simply understanding your local national surroundings will no longer be sufficient."
	"Leadership will require people to learn more about the world around them as businesses, even start-ups, become more international."
	"Leadership will increasingly be attributed to improving the lives of others around the world." "Leaders must be able to adapt their styles to the most powerful developing economies of the 21st century."
	"Leaders need to integrate the development of emerging economies with the growth and development of the for-profit sector."
Convergence	"Management will no longer be explicitly required to act first and foremost for the financial benefit of shareholders."
	"Where people see market leadership in the social enterprise sector to find a free market way to solve our generation's socio-economic problems."
	"Unite social impact and business; expand stakeholder view beyond shareholders; corporations must accept responsibility to community and a more global world."
	"More comprehensive understanding of the ecosystem (not just environmental but political and social) that business operate in. Using that understanding to lessen negative impacts of a business and increase competitive advantage and other positive impacts."
	"Business leaders will be forced to recognize and serve a broader community of stakeholders than in previous generations."
	"It will evolve into having a greater purpose than simple profit sharing or shareholder value creation."
Technology natives	"Being able to utilize social media and networks, virtual and real-world, to broadcast and influence others."
	"Technology will make the flow of information more easy and quick. Leaders will not have the power or the control of information anymore."
Collaborative leadership	"There will be a greater acceptance of and reliance on fluid leadership diffused throughout organizations, rather than leadership being found in defined organizational structures."
	"Drawing upon the collective experience of the masses rather than focusing on the expertise of select individuals."
Embracing diversity	"Team diversity will be ever more important—therefore, leaders must learn to be more effective with their messages and increase the frequency of these messages in order to retain and motivate their best and brightest."

	"There will be a pressing need to understand cross function/industry roles as business and economies are increasingly intertwined."
Empowerment	"Leaders will not be able to be autocratic in the future because news-sharing and opinion-influencing has become so decentralized and democratic. It will be far more important for leaders to be persuasive since they will not be able to control crowds or people by brute force."
	"Leadership will become decentralized, away from the top ranks and into the hands of the doers. The lines between those inside and those outside a corporation will get fuzzier."
	"Leadership emphasis is already shifting from focusing on charismatic superstars who guide the masses, to valuing team leadership to transcend the limitations of any one individual."
Personal authenticity	"Leadership will be less about climbing a ladder within an established organization—the 21st century is more about defining the ladder through one's actions."
	"When they concentrate on developing self-awareness, understand the value of interdependence (rather than independence), and perceive their seminal role in developing human values and social enterprise."
Ethical leadership	"Leaders will be forced to be more transparent about everything from their decision making to their personal lives."
	"True leaders in the 21st century will have to take proactive actions to ensure they are following fundamental ethics rather than just doing what everybody else is doing."

As they move around the world, young leaders are coming to terms with the convergence of the private, public, and nonprofit sectors. They believe that human enterprise and the progress of civilizations require close collaboration of all three. As such, they see themselves as no longer bound simply by the beliefs, attitudes, and practices of any single domain. They need to understand and be comfortable working in all three. The role of business itself will converge with other nonfinancial measures— young people see the objective of corporations expanding beyond shareholder value.

They will do this with the support of diverse teams—firmly believing that diversity in gender, nationality, professional experience, and functional expertise lead to better outcomes. Mobile, social networking, and cloud computing technology will enable leaders to quickly process enormous amounts of data into useful information and extend the boundaries of their organizations to leverage the power of the crowd.

FIGURE A-4

Beliefs and attitudes of young leaders

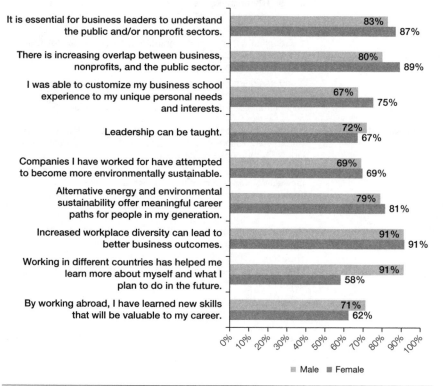

Percent of respondents who agree or strongly agree with the following statements

It is essential for business leaders to understand the public and/or nonprofit sectors.
83% / 87%

There is increasing overlap between business, nonprofits, and the public sector.
80% / 89%

I was able to customize my business school experience to my unique personal needs and interests.
67% / 75%

Leadership can be taught.
72% / 67%

Companies I have worked for have attempted to become more environmentally sustainable.
69% / 69%

Alternative energy and environmental sustainability offer meaningful career paths for people in my generation.
79% / 81%

Increased workplace diversity can lead to better business outcomes.
91% / 91%

Working in different countries has helped me learn more about myself and what I plan to do in the future.
91% / 58%

By working abroad, I have learned new skills that will be valuable to my career.
71% / 62%

Male   Female

Notes

Introduction

1. Pew Research Center, "The Millennials: Confident. Connected. Open to Change," February 24, 2010, http://pewresearch.org/pubs/1501/millennials-new-survey-generational-personality-upbeat-open-new-ideas-technology-bound.

2. IBM Future Leaders Survey.

Chapter 1

1. Jonathan Rauch, "This Is Not Charity," *The Atlantic*, October 2007, http://www.jonathanrauch.com/jrauch_articles/bill_clinton_reinvents_philanthropy/.

2. "Nonprofits' Decade of Growth Outpaces Economy," Urban Institute, 2006, http://www.urban.org/publications/901011.html.

3. Dennis Cauchon, "Federal Pay Ahead of Private Industry," *USA Today*, March 8, 2010, http://www.usatoday.com/news/nation/2010-03-04-federal-pay_N.htm#chart.

4. HBS Social Enterprise Initiative, "History," http://www.hbs.edu/socialenterprise/about/history.html; http://www.socialenterpriseclub.org/home.aspx.

5. http://en.wikipedia.org/wiki/Jessica_Jackley.

6. HBS Career Services, "EC Job Market Update, 2009," http://my.hbs.edu/mbadocs/admin/careers/presentations/ec_job_market_update_09.pdf.

7. Stanford Graduate School of Business, "Joint & Dual Degrees," http://www.gsb.stanford.edu/mba/academics/joint_dual_degrees.html.

8. Tracy Mueller, "Profit with a Purpose," *Texas*, January 14, 2010, http://blogs.mccombs.utexas.edu/magazine/2010/01/14/profit-with-a-purpose/.

9. "Kenya Rivals Agree to Share Power," BBC News, February 28, 2008, http://news.bbc.co.uk/2/hi/africa/7268903.stm.

10. "Awakening Movement in Iraq," World, *New York Times*, October 19, 2010, http://topics.nytimes.com/top/news/international/countries-andterritories/iraq/awakening_movement/index.html.

Chapter 2

1. IBM Institute for Business Value, "Inheriting a Complex World: Future Leaders Envision Sharing the Planet," IBM Global Business Services Executive Report, http://www-935.ibm.com/services/us/ceo/ceostudy2010/futureleaders.html.

2. Eric Beinhocker and Elizabeth Stephenson, "Trend to Watch: Globalization Under Fire," *HBR Now* (blog), July 20, 2009, http://blogs.hbr.org/ hbr/hbr-now/2009/07/trend-to-watch-globalization-u.html.

3. PPI Trade Fact of the Week, "The Number of Transnational Companies Grows by 2,500 a Year," PPI Trade & Global Markets, December 3, 2008, http://www.dlc.org/ndol_ci.cfm?contentid=254841&kaid=108&subid=900003.

4. Renee Dye and Elizabeth Stephenson, "McKinsey Global Survey Results: 5 Forces Reshaping the Global Economy," McKinsey & Company, 2010.

5. IBM, "Inheriting a Complex World."

6. Yojana Sharma, "Changes Looming in Global Student Market," *University World News*, September 13, 2010, http://www.university-worldnews.com/article.php?story=20100918074621118.

7. "Indian Firms' Foreign Purchases: Gone Shopping," *The Economist*, May 28, 2009.

8. Eric Beinhocker, Ian Davis, and Lenny Mendonca, "The Ten Trends You Have to Watch," *Harvard Business Review*, July–August 2009.

9. IESE Business School, International Center for Work and Family, http://www.iese.edu/es/files/ICWF%20-%20Art%C3%ADculo%20Family%20Business%20Dominate_tcm5-3230.pdf.

10. "Education," Peace Corps information page, http://www.peacecorps.gov/index.cfm?shell=learn.whatvol.edu_youth.

11. For a quick read on "One Cow Per Poor Family," see the Rwandan Ministry of Agriculture's Web page at: http://www.minagri.gov.rw/index.

php?option=com_content&view=article&id=207%3Agirinka-program& catid=66%3Agirinka&Itemid=43& lang=en.

12. The Rwandan government's agriculture transformation plan is called "PSTA II: Strategic Plan for the Transformation of Agriculture." It is available at http://www.primature.gov.rw/index2.php?option=com_ docman& task=doc_view&gid=903&Itemid=95.

13. For more on the history of what happened at the Hotel des Diplomates (now the Kigali Serena), see Chris McGreal, "Veneer of Normality," *The Guardian*, February 19, 2008, http://www.guardian.co.uk/world/ 2008/ feb/19/rwanda.

Chapter 3

1. Harvard Business School, "Statistics," http://www.hbs.edu/about/ statistics/mba.html.

2. Harvard Business School, "Perspectives: MBA Class Profile," http://www.hbs.edu/mba/perspectives/class-statistics/.

3. Bloomberg Businessweek, "Full-Time MBA Profiles: Insead," June 9, 2011, http://www.businessweek.com/bschools/rankings/full_time_mba_ profiles/insead.html.

4. Accenture, "Optimistic Outlook," January 19, 2010, http://newsroom. accenture.com/news/despite+obstacles+millennial+women+over- whelmingly+positive+about+career+prospects+accenture+research+fin ds.htm.

5. Celine Roque, "Mix Up the Workweek by Setting Your Own '20-Percent Time,'" *Web Worker Daily*, March 12, 2010, http://webworker- daily.com/2010/03/12/mix-up-the-workweek-by-setting-your-own-20-per cent-time/.

6. Paula Burkes Erickson, "Firms Offer Flexible Hours to Keep Employees Happy," April 13, 2007, *ScrippsNews*, http://www.scrippsnews. com/node/21201.

7. Chuck Salter, "Calling JetBlue," *Fast Company*, May 1, 2004, http://www.fastcompany.com/magazine/82/jetblue_agents.html.

8. Justin Rohrlich, "Religious CEOs: Tyson Foods' John Tyson," Minyanville Media, May 19, 2010, http://www.minyanville.com/

special-features/articles/john-tyson-christian-church-chaplain-methodist/5/19/ 2010/id/28276.

9. Human Rights Campaign, "Domestic Partner Benefits," http:// www.hrc.org/issues/domestic_partner_benefits.htm.

10. Elizabeth Gudrais, "Family or Fortune," *Harvard Magazine*, January–February 2010.

11. Ibid.

12. Herminia Ibarra, Nancy M. Carter, and Christine Silva, "Why Men Still Get More Promotions Than Women," *Harvard Business Review*, September 2010.

13. Nancy M. Carter and Christine Silva, "Women in Management: Delusions of Progress," *Harvard Business Review*, March 2010.

14. M. Argyle, "Do Happy Workers Work Harder? The Effect of Job Satisfaction on Job Performance," in *How Harmful Is Happiness? Consequences of Enjoying Life or Not*, ed. Ruut Veenhoven (Netherlands: Universitaire Pers Rotterdam, 1989); and M. Argyle, *The Psychology of Happiness*, 2nd ed. (London: Routledge, 2001).

15. T. M. Amabile, S. G. Barsade, J. S. Mueller, and B. M. Staw, "Affect and Creativity at Work," *Administrative Science Quarterly* 50 (2005): 367–403.

16. Deloitte, "Redesigning the Workplace," http://www.deloitte.com/view/en_US/us/About/Womens-Initiative/Redesigning-the-Workplace/index.htm.

17. Jennifer Ludden, "The End of 9-to-5: When Work Time Is Anytime," National Public Radio, March 16, 2010, http://www.npr.org/templates/story/story.php?storyId=124705801.

18. Robin Lloyd, "Best Benefit of Exercise? Happiness," Live Science on FoxNews.com, May 30, 2006, http://www.foxnews.com/story/0,2933, 197466,00.html.

19. Deloitte, "Health and Fitness," http://careers.deloitte.com/united-states/students/csc_general.aspx?CountryContentID=16417.

20. "Deloitte Prague Cup 2008," http://www.flixya.com/video/1316961/Deloitte_Prague_Cup_2008; Bain & Company, "Outside the Office," http://www.joinbain.com/life-at-bain/beyond-the-desk/outside-the-office.asp.

21. ROTC has been around for decades, a nationwide college scholarship program that pays for school in return for a few years of military service. Besides helping hundreds of thousands of Americans pay for college over the years, it has also ensured that a wide cross-section of young Americans serve as officers in our nation's volunteer military. Harvard kicked ROTC off campus at the height of its protests of the Vietnam War, and did not allow it back until 2011 when Congress repealed the "don't ask, don't tell" policy that had been Harvard's stated reason for keeping ROTC off-campus until that time.

Chapter 4

1. See http://www.un.org/documents/ga/res/42/ares42-187.htm.

2. Deloitte, "Generation Y Going for 'Greener' Cars," http://www.deloitte.com/view/en_AU/au/services/deloitte-private/thoughtleadership/c56520a25cba6210VgnVCM200000bb42f00aRCRD.htm.

3. Ibid.

4. Johnson Controls, *Generation Y and the Workplace Annual Report 2010*, http://www.scribd.com/doc/36668143/Oxygenz-Report-2010.

5. OECD, http://www.oecd.org/dataoecd/29/14/45188043.pdf.

6. Matt Symonds, "At Business School, Sustainability Takes Center Stage," Bloomberg Businessweek, September 24, 2009, http://www.businessweek.com/bschools/content/sep2009/bs20090924_229220.htm.

7. "Sustainability Rankings for ICT Industry Put Vodafone, Nokia on Top," GreenBiz.com, February 26, 2010, http://www.greenbiz.com/news/ 2010/02/26/sustainability-rankings-ict-industry-put-vodafone-nokia-hp-top.

8. "GE: Ecomagination Revenue to Hit $17 Billion in 2008," *Environmental Leader*, October 22, 2008, http://www.environmentalleader.com/2008/10/22/ge-ecomagination-revenue-to-hit-17-billion-in-2008/.

9. Kelly Smith, "Walmart Expects Its Suppliers to Reduce Greenhouse Gas Emissions," *Green Power Blog*, March 21, 2010, http://www.ecoelectrons.com/green-power-blog/bid/36727/Walmart-Expects-Its-Suppliers-to-Reduce-Greenhouse-Gas-Emissions.html.

10. Walmart corporate website, "Sustainability Index," http://walmart-stores.com/Sustainability/9292.aspx.

11. Nestlé's Second Annual Creating Shared Value Forum, May 27, 2010 (transcript available at http://www.nestle.com/Resource.axd?Id=1C7FD9CF-16F5-4846-BAE3-978BABFA2C39).

12. Daniel Brooksbank, "Bloomberg Chief Outlines ESG Data Strategy," *Responsible-Investor.com*, June 24, 2010, http://www.responsible-investor.com.

13. Accenture, *A New Era of Sustainability, UN Global Compact–Accenture CEO Study 2010*, http://www.unglobalcompact.org/docs/news_events/8.1/UNGC_Accenture_CEO_Study_2010.pdf.

14. *2009 HP Global Citizenship Report*, http://www.hp.com/hpinfo/globalcitizenship/pdf/fy09_fullreport.pdf.

15. Jerry Lewis, "Mars Wants Sustainable Cocoa Certification to Include Productivity," April 23, 2010, http://www.huffingtonpost.com/jerry-lewis/mars-wants-sustainable-co_b_549874.html.

16. Cape Wind, Inc., "Cape Wind Will Reduce Over a Million Tons of Greenhouse Gas Emissions Per Year," August 27, 2002, http://www.capewind.org/news11.htm.

17. National Oceanic and Atmospheric Administration (NOAA), "Trends in Atmospheric Carbon Dioxide," http://www.esrl.noaa.gov/gmd/ccgg/trends/#mlo_growth.

18. Nicholas Stern, *The Economics of Climate Change: The Stern Review* (London: HM Treasury, 2007).

19. John Leaning, "Dueling Wind Farm Polls Encourage Skepticism," *Cape Cod Times*, November 12, 2002.

20. "Support for Cape Wind Rises Ahead of Hearings Next Week," *Cape Cod Today*, March 6, 2008.

Chapter 5

1. Jeremy Reimer, "Total Share: 30 Years of Personal Computer Market Share Figures," http://arstechnica.com/old/content/2005/12/total-share.ars/4.

2. Ibid.

3. Thomas Kang, "Global Smartphone Sales Forecast by Operating System: 2002 to 2015," Strategy Analytics, October 14, 2010,

http://www.strategyanalytics.com/default.aspx?mod=reportabstractviewe
r&a0=5818.

4. Nick Saint, "Whole Foods Is Pushing Its Foursquare Promotion
Hard," Business Insider, August 27, 2010, http://www.businessinsider.
com/wholefoods-is-pushing-its-foursquare-promotion-hard-2010-8.

5. http://shopkick.com/.

6. Ibid.

7. http://twitter.com/#!/BRITNEYSPEARS.

8. Christopher Steiner, "Meet the Fastest Growing Company Ever,"
Forbes.com, August 12, 2010, http://www.forbes.com/forbes/2010/0830/
entrepreneurs-groupon-facebook-twitter-next-web-phenom.html.

9. Wailin Wong, "Gap's Groupon Pulls in $11 Million," *Chicago Tribune*, August 20, 2010, http://articles.chicagotribune.com/2010-08-
20/business/sc-biz-0821-groupon-20100820_1_gender-and-zip-code-chi
cago-startup-coupon-site.

10. Jennifer Van Grove, "Mayors of Starbucks Now Get Discounts
Nationwide with Foursquare," Mashable, May 17, 2010, http://mashable.
com/2010/05/17/starbucks-foursquare-mayor-specials/.

11. "Site Profile for MySpace.com," Compete, http://siteanalytics.
compete.com/myspace.com/; Emma Barnett, "Facebook Hits 500m: Social Media by Numbers," *The Telegraph*, July 21, 2010, http://www.
telegraph.co.uk/technology/facebook/7903071/Facebook-hits-500m-so-
cial-media-by-numbers.html.

12. Robin Wauters, "Lycos Is Still Around—Sold by Daum to Ybrant
in $36 Million Deal," TechCrunch, August 16, 2010, http://techcrunch.
com/2010/08/16/lycos-ybrant/.

13. Faith Merino, "Etsy Raises $20M for Some $300M Valuation,"
VatorNews, August 27, 2010, http://vator.tv/news/2010-08-27-etsy-
raises-20m-for-some-300m-valuation.

Chapter 6

1. M. G. Siegler, "Bill Gates: In Five Years the Best Education Will
Come from the Web," TechCrunch, August 6, 2010, http://techcrunch.
com/2010/08/06/bill-gates-education/.

2. Association to Advance Collegiate Schools of Business, *2010 Business School Data Trends*.

3. Rakesh Khurana, *From Higher Aims to Hired Hands: The Social Transformation of American Business Schools and the Unfulfilled Promise of Management as a Profession* (Princeton, NJ: Princeton University Press, 2009).

4. Graduate Management Admission Council, "Profile of GMAT Candidates," http://www.gmac.com/gmac/ResearchandTrends/GMATStats/ProfileofCandidates.htm.

5. Harvard Business School, "Perspectives: MBA Class Profile," http://www.hbs.edu/mba/perspectives/class-statistics/.

6. "A Post-Crisis Case Study: The New Dean of Harvard Business School Promises 'Radical Innovation,'" in *Schumpeter* (blog), *The Economist*, July 29, 2010, http://www.economist.com/node/16691433.

7. Richard Barker, "No, Management Is Not a Profession," *Harvard Business Review*, July–August 2010.

8. Harvard Business School, "Statistics," http://www.hbs.edu/about/statistics/mba.html.

9. Lou Dubois, "How to Implement a Continuing Education Program," Inc.com, August 18, 2010. http://www.inc.com/guides/2010/08/how-to-implement-a-continuing-education-program.html.

10. Harris Interactive, Harris Vault archive, http://www.harrisinteractive. com/Insights/HarrisVault.aspx.

11. Seth Godin, Learning from the MBA Program, 06/04/2009, http://sethgodin.typepad.com/seths_blog/2009/06/learning-from-the-mba-program.html.

12. Sam S. Adkins, "The U.S. PreK-12 Market for Self-Paced eLearning Products and Services: 2010–2015 Forecast and Analysis," Ambient Insight Targeted Report, January 2011.

13. "The New 3 E's of Education: Enabled, Engaged, Empowered; How Today's Students Are Leveraging Emerging Technologies for Learning," Speak Up 2010 National Findings, Project Tomorrow 2011, April

2011, http://www.tomorrow.org/speakup/pdfs/SU10_3EofEducation_
Students.pdf.

14. Clayton Christensen, Curtis W. Johnson, and Michael B. Horn, *Disrupting Class: How Disruptive Innovation Will Change the Way the World Learns* (New York: McGraw Hill, 2008).

15. I. Elaine Allen and Jeff Seaman, "Class Differences: Online Education in the United States, 2010," Babson Survey Research Group and the Sloan Consortium, November 2010.

16. George Lorenzo, "Online Degrees Make the Grade: Employer Acceptance Now Common," commissioned by Western Governors University, July 2008, http://www.wgu.edu/about_WGU/george_lorenzo.pdf.

17. "The Future Is Now," *BizEd*, May–June 2008, http://www.aacsb. edu/publications/archives/mayjun08/24-35_bized_mj08.pdf.

18. Human Capital Lab, Bellevue University, "*Talent Management* Showcases Human Capital Lab and Bersin & Associates Tuition Assistance Research," October 19, 2009, http://www.humancapitallab.org/news.php?id =29.

19. Human Capital Lab, Bellevue University, "Sun Learning Services *Sun Learning eXchange (SLX)*," June 30, 2010, http://www. humancapitallab.org/article.php?id=221.

20. Kathy Chu, "Average College Credit Card Debt Rises with Fees, Tuition," *USA Today*, April 12, 2009, http://www.usatoday.com/money/perfi/credit/2009-04-12-college-credit-card-debt_N.htm.

21. Dave Ramsey, *The Total Money Makeover: A Proven Plan for Financial Fitness*.

22. "Personal Finances: The Final Frontier for Social Media; Results of a National Survey of Young Adults," conducted for AARP, October 2009, http://www.lifetuner.org/press/Personal_Finance__Final_Frontier_for_Social_Media.pdf.

23. Ibid.

24. On average female income, see Suze Orman, *Women and Money: Owning the Power to Control Your Destiny* (NY: Spiegel & Grau, 2007); on

women's control of wealth, see "Women: The Fragile Financial Super-power," http:// knowledge.allianz.com/en/globalissues/demographic_change/gender_diversity/women_money_us.html.

25. On debt levels, see Liz Perle, *Money, A Memoir*; on financial inse-curity, see "Woman Fear Retirement More Than Men—For Good Rea-son," ConsumerAffairs.com, July 23, 2008, http://www.consumeraffairs.com/news04/2008/07/retirement_women.html.

Acknowledgments

Writing *Passion and Purpose* has been a humbling and heartening experience. By design, it has been a collaborative effort—three authors, dozens of contributors, hundreds of survey respondents, and a bevy of editors and supporters. We are deeply grateful to all of those who have worked so hard to make *Passion and Purpose* a reality. Any virtues in this book are a credit to those who have helped us.

A special thanks is due to Peter Olson. From the beginning, Peter was our guide, our mentor, and a constant source of creativity and encouragement. Drawing on his wealth of experience in the publishing business, Peter coached us through every step of the proposal writing process. Without him, this book would not have been written.

We're similarly indebted to the classmates, friends, and professors who provided us with ideas, reviewed our early drafts, helped with survey distribution, and encouraged us to persevere. This list includes Nitin Nohria and professors Clayton Rose, Carl Kester, Tom Eisenmann, James Sebenius, John Macomber, Nic Retsinas, Arthur Segel, Richard Tedlow, Ray Weaver, and Joe Badaracco. We'd also like to thank Jim Aisner and our friends at *The Harbus*—Elana Green, Joanne Knight, and Kay Fukunaga—as well as Joey Castillo, Jerome Uy, Victor Calanog, William Panlilio, Gerald Yeo, Tyone Almeida, Jonathan Harris, Andrew Hirsekorn, Sunil Pandita, John Peek, Abhijit Dutta, Katharine Bowerman, and Nancy Howley.

We'd also like to thank Daisy Dowling, who shared her experience of going through the proposal writing and manuscript process, and Anne Myra Suarez and Jonathan Chu for their help in transcribing source documents and performing valuable research. We'd also like to express our appreciation to the administration and staff at Harvard Business School for providing us with resources required to complete the manuscript and related research.

Of course, the heart of this book is its pool of talented and passionate contributors—those appearing in these pages and those providing content online and in other forums. Both the emerging and senior leaders have been a genuine inspiration to us, and it was a privilege to work with each of them. We'd also like to thank the participants in the MBA Student Survey—whose views and opinions helped shape our thinking and strengthened our conclusions—and all those at schools around the country who helped us reach this diverse pool of respondents. We're particularly grateful to Professor Bill George. Professor George is a living reminder of "true north" leadership, a brilliant teacher, and a friend and mentor to many. His support has been inspirational.

We could not have written, published, or promoted this book without the talented and tireless team at Harvard Business Press. Melinda Merino and Courtney Cashman were invaluable throughout the manuscript development process, and their passion for bringing out the stories of young leaders was contagious. Similarly, Jen Waring, Stephani Finks, Julie Devoll, Nina Nocciolina, Liz Baldwin, and the rest of the Press team have been instrumental in shaping the final product.

Finally, there are a few acknowledgments we'd like to make individually.

John would like to thank his family—John, Shea, Chris, Dustin, Elliot, Sandy, Josh, Margaret, Karen, and Bryan—for their love and support. And, as always, he is deeply grateful for the contributions and encouragement of his wonderful wife, Jackie.

Oliver would like to thank his parents, Willy and Nanette, for nurturing his entrepreneurial dreams, and his siblings, Joseph, Patrick, and Patricia. He is grateful for Jordana Valencia and her tireless patience and encouragement, and for Jennifer Kelly and Franz Alfonso for their patience as he balanced a start-up with writing the manuscript.

Daniel would like to thank Mel, who was a constant source of inspiration and ideas and who endured his endless enthusiasm for this work. Daniel is forever grateful for his Mum, Dad, and brother Jason and their unconditional love—sent all the way from home.

Index

About the Contributors

Sanyogita Aggarwal leads business development at Dev Bhumi Cold Chain Ltd. in Delhi, India. She received her MBA at Harvard Business School in 2010. San talks about the decision to return to India after studying abroad and the surprising, often counterintuitive, lessons she's learned in bringing global best practices to a traditional family business.

Rye Barcott cofounded Carolina for Kibera in 2001. He graduated from Harvard with an MBA and MPA, is a TED Fellow and a World Economic Forum Young Global Leader, and works at Duke Energy. His first book, *It Happened on the Way to War: A Marine's Path to Peace*, was published by Bloomsbury in April 2011. He is passionate about participatory development.

Valerie Bockstette graduated from Brown University with a degree in economics and international relations. After three years as an investment banker, she came to Harvard Business School and discovered her passion for social impact. She is currently a director at FSG, a nonprofit consulting firm specializing in shared value strategies.

Josh Bronstein has been a human capital consultant since 2005, specializing in talent and change management strategies. Josh holds an MBA from Harvard Business School and a bachelor of science in industrial and labor relations from Cornell University. He is passionate about helping people bring more of themselves to work.

After five years in the consulting practice, **Kimberly Carter** now works as a senior manager in the Leadership Development Group focused on talent development and corporate university launch for Deloitte. Kimberly earned a BS in accounting from Florida A&M University and a minor in

German from Florida State University. She is passionate about education and leadership development.

Patrick Chun is a venture capitalist and technology investor at Bain Capital Ventures. Patrick graduated from Harvard Business School in 2010, where he was copresident of the HBS Student Association, the student body of Harvard Business School. Patrick explains how his greatest learnings at business school did not occur in the classroom or even result from his successes, but rather from his failures, and how business education is at a unique juncture to foster innovation by encouraging experimentation and fast failure.

Shelby Clark graduated from Harvard Business School in 2010. Prior to HBS, Shelby received a degree in biomedical engineering from Northwestern University. After serving as a director at Kiva, he started RelayRides, the world's first peer-to-peer car-sharing service backed by Google Ventures, where he now serves as CEO. Shelby is passionate about companies with a cause.

Charley Cummings remains vice president of Clean Power Now. After graduating from Brown University in 2006 with a degree in public policy, he spent three years as a management consultant. His other experience includes designing the corporate social responsibility strategy of an organic soup company and working for a member of the House of Commons in the British Parliament. He graduated from Harvard Business School in May 2011. He is a passionate believer in clean technology and renewable energy.

Jake Cusack is a former Marine Corps officer who served in Iraq as a sniper platoon commander and intelligence officer from 2005 to 2008. He will graduate with a joint degree from the Harvard Business School and Harvard Kennedy School in 2012, and has written extensively about entrepreneurship and economic growth in Afghanistan. He is passionate about economic development in conflict zones.

After graduating from Wellesley College, **Tasneem Dohadwala** joined an equity sales strategy team at Lehman Brothers. She left to join the Nooril-Iman Foundation, where she executed a program of economic self-sustainment in Myanmar and construction of a medical clinic in Yemen. After graduating HBS in 2009, she cofounded Excelestar Ventures. She reflects on the evolving roles and expectations of women in business.

Jonathan Doochin is the founder of the Leadership Institute at Harvard College and chairman of the Board of Overseers. He also serves as the CEO of Leverett Energy, a firm focused on financing and developing energy efficiency and renewable energy. He has spent time as a management consultant at McKinsey & Company and is a serial entrepreneur. Jon explores three themes that guide the future of leadership development.

Abigail Falik is the founder and CEO of Global Citizen Year and a recognized expert in the fields of education reform, international development, and social innovation. For her work as a leading social entrepreneur, she has received awards from the Draper Richards Foundation, the Mind Trust, and the Harvard Business School. Abigail has made a commitment to using global immersion as a way to equip the next generation of leaders with the empathy and insight needed to overcome twenty-first-century challenges.

Annie Fishman graduated from Yale University with a BA in environmental studies and political science. She came to Harvard Business School after working in the nonprofit sector. After graduating from HBS, she held a number of brand management positions and is currently senior marketing manager for Amyris Biotechnologies. She's the current vice president of the HBS Green Business Alumni Association and a passionate believer in achieving the impossible.

Andrew Goodman graduated from the Harvard Business School in 2010 as a Baker Scholar. Before attending HBS, Andrew cofounded QatarDebate, a civic engagement initiative that aims to develop and support the standard of open discussion and debate among students and young people in Qatar and the broader Arab world. Andrew's story helps young leaders appreciate the importance of cultural intelligence, the right partnerships, and a pipeline of local leaders in building ventures in unfamiliar markets.

Jason Gurwin is a serial entrepreneur. After graduating from Wharton with an economics degree, Jason started two successful companies in the media and entertainment space. He graduated from Harvard Business School in May 2011 and now serves as CEO of Pushpins, the mobile coupon company he cofounded while at Harvard. He is passionate about the power of mobile applications to change people's everyday lives.

Michael B. Horn is the cofounder and executive director for education of Innosight Institute, a not-for-profit think tank devoted to applying the theories of disruptive innovation to problems in the social sector. He is also coauthor of *Disrupting Class: How Dispruptive Innovation Will Change the Way the World Learns* with Clayton M. Christensen and Curtis W. Johnson. Michael found his passion in using technology to advance education in America.

Katie Laidlaw is a consultant in the New York City office of the Boston Consulting Group. Prior to joining BCG, Katie was a senior associate at the Parthenon Group and served as executive director of Inspire, Inc., a nonprofit organization that advises community-based nonprofits. She is passionate about international development and future growth in public-private partnerships.

Kishan Madamala is a former store team leader at Target. He completed his MBA in 2010 at Harvard Business School, where he was awarded a Rock Entrepreneurial Fellowship. Kishan tells the story of a whole generation who were trained as "good analysts" but were poor leaders, and how this learning gap represents the single biggest opportunity for business schools and corporations.

Chris Maloney works as a management consultant on projects for public and private sector clients across Africa, especially in agriculture, health care, and policy. A native of New York, he holds a BA in economics and African/African-American studies from Stanford University, and both an MPA/International Development and an MBA from Harvard University. In reflecting on his experience in Rwanda, Chris realizes how unfamiliar environments abroad can lead one to reevaluate traditional notions of business risk and social return.

Born in Pakistan and raised in Saudi Arabia, **Umaimah Mendhro** was the first woman in her family to leave the country for higher education. She studied human development at Cornell University and completed her MBA from Harvard Business School as a Baker Scholar. Umaimah is currently a senior manager at Microsoft Corporation, where she leads corporate entrepreneurship and incubation efforts. She is also the cofounder of thedreamfly.org, a global initiative that strives to create human connections across communities in conflict around common causes.

Seth Moulton graduated from Harvard College in 2001 and served four tours as a Marine Corps infantry officer in Iraq, two as a platoon commander and two as a special assistant to General David Petraeus. In 2011, he graduated with a joint degree from Harvard Kennedy School and Harvard Business School. He is passionate about service and bringing his experience in the Marines to bear in the private sector.

James Reinhart is the founding CEO of thredUP, an online kids' clothing swap. He believes in the power of social technology for creating new online communities. Prior to attending the Harvard Business School and the Kennedy School, while working in the Bay Area, he helped develop one of the nation's premier public schools, Pacific Collegiate School—recently named the number seven high school in America by *U.S. News & World Report*. He cofounded Beacon Education Network, a charter management and school turnaround organization, and was a Goldsmith Fellow in Social Enterprise at HBS and a George Fellow at the Center for Public Leadership.

Benjamin Schumacher is from Lexington, Kentucky, and studied psychology at Washington University in St. Louis. Ben has worked in management consulting for Deloitte Consulting, McKinsey & Company, and Instituto Exclusivo in La Paz, Bolivia. He holds an MBA from Harvard Business School and finds happiness working with education-oriented nonprofits.

Alexa Leigh Marie von Tobel is the founder of LearnVest, Inc., and serves as its chief executive officer and director. She received an AB in psychology with honors, with a citation in romance languages and literature at Harvard College. Alexa feels passionate about making personal finance education fun and accessible to everyone. She believes that for the next generation of students, mastering financial literacy will be just as important as learning to read or write.

Originally from Lansing, Michigan, **Christina Wallace** now lives in New York City where she is the cofounder of Quincy, an early-stage online women's professional apparel company. She holds a BA in mathematics and theater studies from Emory University and an MBA from Harvard Business School. She has worked as a professional musician, actress, theater director, and arts administrator at organizations including Theater Emory, Georgia Shakespeare, Actors Express, the Schwartz Center for Performing Arts, and the Metropolitan Opera. Contact her through www.christinamwallace.com.

Kelli Wolf Moles worked in investment banking at JPMorgan in New York before graduating from Harvard Business School with the class of 2011. Kelli is founder and CEO of Project Spark, a nonprofit that promotes sustainable philanthropy and organizes volunteer trips. Kelli is passionate about helping businesses give employees greater purpose through public service.

About the Authors

John Coleman holds an MBA with High Distinction from Harvard Business School, where he was a Dean's Award Winner for leadership and service and Class Day speaker. He also holds a MPA from the Harvard Kennedy School, where he was awarded both a George Fellowship and a Zuckerman Fellowship for public leadership.

Raised in Columbus, GA, John attended Berry College as an undergraduate, where he was a U.S. national public speaking champion in 2004. He has experience in both asset management and the nonprofit sector, and his work and education have taken him to places like Europe, Asia, and the Middle East. John published a book on communications in 2009 and has written for numerous publications including *Harvard Business Review* and *Forbes.com*.

After school, John returned to management consulting at McKinsey & Company and lives in Atlanta with his wife, Jackie. He is passionate about his faith, his family, writing, public policy, and leadership development.

Daniel Gulati holds an MBA from Harvard Business School, where he was both a George F. Baker Fellow and an Arthur Rock Entrepreneurial Fellow. He was selected to receive the Robert F. Jasse Distinguished Award in Entrepreneurship & Leadership.

Daniel holds a Bachelor of Commerce with Distinction (Economics and Accounting) from the University of New South Wales, where he served as an Associate Lecturer in Accounting. He has been a Senior Associate at the Boston Consulting Group and worked at Macquarie Bank.

Daniel is currently the Founding CEO of FashionStake, a venture-backed fashion company based in New York City. Prior to FashionStake, Daniel founded and successfully exited two consumer products companies.

Born and raised in the Philippines, **W. Oliver Segovia** holds an MBA with Distinction from Harvard Business School where he was a LeBarron-MacArthur-Ellis Fellow and a board director of the Harbus News Corporation. Oliver graduated with honors from the Ateneo de Manila University, where he was an Asian debating champion and founding editor of a student business journal.

In 2005, Oliver won first prize in the World Bank International Essay Competition for his work on an educational social venture. Growing up in a family of entrepreneurs, Oliver is passionate about emerging markets, innovation, entrepreneurship, and leadership. His work experience spans consumer products, publishing, real estate, and e-commerce. Oliver worked with Procter & Gamble Asia, where he helped launch new products and marketing campaigns in emerging markets.

Oliver has lived in Singapore, Bangkok, and Boston. After business school, he returned to Manila and cofounded a real estate company and an e-commerce start-up.